D0889677

CHANGING IMAGES OF THE WARRIOR HERO IN AMERICA:
A History of Popular Symbolism

CHANGING IMAGES OF THE WARRIOR HERO IN AMERICA:
A History of Popular Symbolism

By
EDWARD TABOR LINENTHAL

Studies in American Religion
Volume Six

The Edwin Mellen Press
New York and Toronto

BR
517
.L57
1982

Library of Congress Cataloging in Publication Data

Linenthal, Edward Tabor, 1947-
    Changing images of the warrior hero in America.

    (Studies in American religion ; v. 6)
    Bibliography: p.
    Includes index.
    1. United States--History, Military--Religious
aspects.   2. Civil religion--United States.
3. Heroes--Religious aspects.   4. War--Religious
aspects.   5. Soldiers--United States.   I. Title.
II. Series.
BR517.L57 1982   306'.27'0973   82-22885
ISBN 0-88946-921-0

Studies in American Religion, ISBN 0-88946-992-X

Copyright © 1982, Edward Tabor Linenthal

All rights reserved. For more information contact:

                The Edwin Mellen Press
                P.O. Box 450
                Lewiston, New York   14092

Grateful acknowledgment is made to quote from Friendly
Fire by Courtlandt Dixon Barnes Bryan, G.P. Putnam's
Sons, New York. © 1976, Courtlandt Dixon Barnes Bryan.

            JESUIT - KRAUSS - McCORMICK - LIBRARY
                1100 EAST 55th STREET
              CHICAGO, ILLINOIS 60615

Printed in the United States of America

For my father, Dr. Arthur J. Linenthal,
who heals in many ways.

ACKNOWLEDGMENTS

With the help of many friends, I have come to appreciate more fully the importance of scholarship as corporate enterprise. Professors Robert Michaelsen, Walter Capps, Richard Hecht, and Lawrence Willson offered both critical and compassionate support during my exciting years at the University of California-Santa Barbara. Professor Nancy Falk, in addition to expert editorial counsel, taught me to separate the wheat from the chaff as I struggled with manuscript revisions. I am also grateful to Professor Robert Chaffin for his generous and insightful editorial comments. Special thanks go to Professor Glenn Johnson, who prepared the index, and to Pat Boettcher, who typed the final manuscript. For my colleagues in the Religion Department at the University of Wisconsin-Oshkosh, I offer thanks for happy and creative years together. Finally, I need and appreciate the loving environment that Ulla, Aaron and Happy provide. They sustain me.

PREFACE

"From time immemorial men have undertaken pilgrimages to places recognized as holy."[1] Among my most vivid boyhood memories are visits to the sites of some of America's most famous and important battles: Lexington and Concord, Bunker Hill, Gettysburg, and more recently, the Little Big Horn. I recall the awe with which I walked over these fields, hoping, as any pilgrim does, to let the power of these special places affect me. I found them mysterious, compelling, in a sense, "holy." This perceived "holiness" of the battlefield, its existence as a place of pilgrimage, reveals the nearly universal human fascination with war and warrior heroes. The power of war experience both attracts and repels us. It introduces a world "wholly other," a world awesome and ego-annihilating in its power and furor. Reflecting upon his own experience of battle, the philosopher J. Glenn Gray has described the human response to war in terms commonly used to evoke religious or mystical experience:

> It becomes clear...that the term "beauty," used
> in any ordinary sense, is not the major appeal
> in such spectacles. Instead, it is the fascin-
> ation that manifestations of power and magnitude
> hold for the human spirit. Some scenes of
> battle...are able to overawe the single indiv-
> idual and hold him in a spell. He is lost in
> their majesty. His ego temporarily deserts him,
> and he is absorbed into what he sees. An aware-
> ness of power that far surpasses his limited
> imagination transports him into a state of mind
> unknown in his everyday experience.[2]

While it is most important to continue investigations
regarding the origins of human aggression, the evolution of
warfare, and the effects of warfare on cultures, we have too
seldom taken into account human perceptions and interpretations of warfare.[3] These perceptions, expressed in a variety of martial symbols, have a powerful effect upon the
manner in which we approach contemporary affairs, for our
interpretations more than "facts" shape our understanding
of the past, our orientation in the present, and our models
for addressing the future. For most people, the facts of
war are less evocative than the stories we tell, the heroes
we venerate, the martial liturgies we celebrate. For instance, addressing the popularity of the television series
"Victory at Sea," Peter Rollins writes:

> Admiral Morison's naval history may ulti-
> mately be correct, but the visual message
> of "Victory at Sea" will continue to affect
> attitudes held by thousands of Americans
> toward the character and utility of war,
> toward the place of the military in our
> society, toward America's mission as a flag
> bearer of freedom.[4]

What kind of stories, then, have we told about war?
The wars of America have often been portrayed as creative
events, mythical events, that bring new life out of chaos.
Warriors are mythical heroes, models of bravery and courage.
They are also saviors, responsible for new life through
blood sacrifice. This martial mythology is a complex of
narratives and rituals that shape our memory of war and
warriors. Novels, films, plays, songs, martial icons, all
the elements of popular culture provide the vibrant symbols
through which we interpret what war is and what war means.

Like so many people, I have been fascinated with the
wars and warriors of America. This book is an attempt to

appreciate the persistent attraction of war and warrior
heroes, and how the changing nature of warfare has made our
traditional manner of interpreting war dangerous. Mircea
Eliade suggests that popular memory thinks "in categories
instead of events, archetypes instead of historical per-
sonages. The historical personage is assimilated to his
mythical model (hero, etc.) while the event is identified
with the category of mythical action."[5] We interpret
current martial crises according to categories and models
inherited from earlier times. Living forward and understanding backward is perilous, because old martial symbols
cannot evoke constructive responses in a nuclear age. In
his study of the American frontier, Richard Slotkin writes:

> Through myths the psychology and world view of
> our cultural ancestors are transmitted to mod-
> ern descendants, in such a way and with such
> power that our perceptions of contemporary
> reality and our ability to function in the
> world are often tragically affected.[6]

War and warriors have traditionally been perceived
through mythological categories. It has been common for
members of historically removed and geographically distant
cultures to symbolize warfare and warrior sacrifice as a
creative, life-giving event. Among the Marind-Anim of New
Guinea, head-hunting brings fertility and good health;
hence, babies are the tangible result of a head-hunt. For
the Jivaro of Eastern Ecuador, killing in battle replenishes
the vitality of an ancestor's soul, necessary for the continued life of the warrior. Among the Yanomamō of southern
Venezuela, warfare, ordained in the myths of origin, is a
means of driving off evil spirits. The Aztecs waged war and
practiced human sacrifice to feed the gods and maintain
cosmic order.[7]

It is not only in unfamiliar cultures that we find evidence that war is sacred activity, for the ancient Israelites also sanctified and ritualized warfare. Johannes Pedersen suggests that for the Israelites, war and peace were seen differently than among us:

> In olden times peace is not itself the opposite
> of war. There are friends and there are enemies;
> Peace consists in complete harmony between
> friends and victory in the war against enemies.
> For in that consists the full development of the
> soul.[8]

War was God's way of making a place for his people. God fought by the Israelites' side in battles whose sanctity was established at the outset by sacrifice and regulated by laws for maintaining the warrior's purity.

The Israelites and their adversaries fought not just as opposing armies, but as a people, each fighting for and with their gods. Each side embodied two distinct spheres of holiness, and sometimes the Israelites' enemies were perceived as so alien and dangerous that their total extinction was required. Pedersen suggests that while demand for extermination increased in post-Exilic times, "the way for it had been prepared by the passionate assertion by the prophets of the peculiar dissimilarity of its God to the gods of other peoples."[9] Among ancient Israelites, war took place within a history where God moved and shaped his people. Part of the Hebraic understanding of history was a belief in the final resolution of the conflicts of history. God would bestow a new Eden upon an elect, a remnant of the faithful people. Severe hardship and judgment, however, would precede the restoration of the original human condition. In such a time, when Jerusalem was profaned by Antiochus IV (Epiphanes), Israelites responded through political revolution and the apocalyptic vision recorded in

Daniel. This portion of Daniel envisions a world oppressed
by demonic evil (often in the form of earthly rulers) whose
power grows until suddenly the righteous overthrow evil and
transform the earth into the kingdom of God. Visions of
the apocalyptic end of history and the eager anticipation
of a messiah passed from Hebraic to Christian sources after
the abortive uprising of Simon bar-Kochba in 131 A.D. and
the complete destruction of Jewish nationality. The most
widely known apocalyptic Christian text is the Book of
Revelation, written during the first century. Using the
Book of Daniel as his model, the author brings the apocalypse into history. Whereas previously the coming of the
Messiah had signaled a radical break in the normal processes
of the world, now all historical events were seen as potentially apocalyptic; thus, the advent of a Messiah could be
an event within the historical process.

Though the idea of a material millennium was condemned
by the Council of Ephesus in 431, and in spite of the fact
that the idea was allegorized by Augustine into an inward
spiritual triumph, the expectation of the earthly paradise
was a major motivating ideology throughout the rest of
western history. At some time, the waiting would be perceived to be almost over, and the drama of the last days
would unfold. Norman Cohn writes of apocalyptic anticipation in the Middle Ages:

> The stupendous drama of the Last Days was not
> a phantasy about some remote and indefinite
> future but a prophecy which was infallible
> and which at almost any moment was felt to be
> on the point of fulfillment.[10]

Therefore, any crisis, any tyrant, any war, was potentially
capable of being read as fulfillment of prophecy. Warfare
could be seen as part of the sacred plan recorded in Revelation. Each conflict could be the decisive event that led

xii   Changing Images of the Warrior Hero in America

to the final destruction of evil, clothed in human form.
These apocalyptic battles were acted out time and again
throughout the Middle Ages. The popular crusades, for example, were battles to wipe out disbelief, for only then
could the millennium come. Cohn writes, "The smiting of
the Moslems and the Jews was to be the first act in that
final battle which--as already in the eschatological phan-
tasies of the Jews and early Christians--was to culminate
in the smiting of the Prince of Evil himself."[11] Any enemy
could easily be transformed into a demon--the agent of
Satan--for the battles against the adversary were not only
human conflicts, but conflicts on which the future of the
world and the coming of the millennium depended. This
"demonizing" has continued into the present age: it includes
powerful images of Germans transformed into Huns, Jews into
Christ-killers, Japanese into rodents, and Vietnamese into
"gooks," a subhuman species of life.

We can appreciate now the persistence of a powerful
symbol of warfare. Just as warfare in other cultures vanquished forces of evil in order to establish order and
fertility, each holy war in our cultural past and in our
national history removed one more demonic obstacle in the
movement toward a new and pure world. Warfare would be the
conflict out of which the millennium would spring. America,
of course, embodied this ancient hope for a new world, where
the millennium could finally be realized. Even in the paradise that was the new world, however, Satan's agents could
be at work, and the wars of the Lord would continue here--
regenerative wars, designed to bring the new world into
being.

If warfare has often been considered a regenerative
event, the warrior is the figure who brings new life, killing, as Robert Jay Lifton writes, "not to destroy life, but
to enlarge, perpetuate, and enhance life."[12] The act of

shedding the blood of one's enemy and the willing sacrifice
of one's own life have often been perceived as acts that
transform the world, acts through which the warrior fulfills
his martial mission of protection and salvation.

As they would any significant vocation, archaic
societies cultivated warrior attributes. Among the Aztecs,
when a male was born, his umbilical cord was buried with a
shield and arrows, and he was told that he had been born to
fight. Boys began their education for a warrior's mission
at the age of six or seven, and eventually had to rise
through several stages of ability. Among the Yanomamō,
young boys grew up engaged in mock battle; as young warriors, they memorized death speeches should they be killed
in battle. Similarly, among the Marind-Anim, sham fights
were popular; it was a warrior's preparation for his vocation. One of the clearest examples of the preparation of
a warrior is to be found among the children of the Samurai,
a ruling elite of professional warriors of tenth and
eleventh century Japan. A young Samurai was given a sword,
symbol of the power of the Samurai, at age seven. At fifteen, boys were initiated into adulthood and, as part of
the rite of passage, were taught the process of *Seppuku*
(disembowelment) or *Hara-Kiri* (belly-slitting). The war
games and war toys so popular in our own culture reveal a
more diffuse and subtle manner of preparation for the vocation of the warrior. For example, Carol Andreas writes of
the 1960s, "Hundreds of thousands of children in the United
States belong to the G.I. Joe Club and re-enact daily the
'adventures' described in the club 'comics.'"[13]

The careful training of the warrior leads to a culmination, just as the instruction of any initiate leads to a
transforming experience. For the warrior, the experience
of battle provides the rite of passage from <u>becoming</u> a
warrior to <u>being</u> a warrior. The phrase "baptism of fire"

carries much truth, for battle is a heightened experience,
one incapable of being adequately described to the uniniti-
ated. It is during battle that the novice-warrior is transformed by "battle ecstasy" or "battle fury." Initiatory
motifs from various cultures suggest that the warrior, like
other sacred figures, becomes "hot," "flooded," Mircea Eliade
says, "by a mysterious, nonhuman, and irresistible force that
his fighting effort and vigor summoned from the depths of his
being."[14] The warriors of the Atoni tribe of Indonesian
Timor experience this sacred force which both empowers and
transforms. These warriors are said to grow hot in battle,
like the fires which prepare the fields for their gardening
practice. Crusading monks of the Middle Ages were said to be
filled with "holy frenzy" when they attacked the infidel; and
Captain John Mason recalled the pleasure with which the Puritans attacked and massacred the Pequot Indians:

> And thus when the Lord turned the Captivity of his
> People, and turned the Wheel upon their Enemies;
> we were like Men in a Dream; then was our Mouth
> filled with Laughter, and our Tongues with Singing;
> thus we may say the Lord hath done great Things for
> us among the Heathen, whereof we are glad. Praise
> the Lord![15]

The age-old experience of battle ecstasy is not limited to
archaic cultures of our own cultural ancestors. J. Glenn
Gray writes of warriors in World War II:

> Men who have lived in the zone of combat long enough
> to be veterans are sometimes possessed by a blind
> fury that makes them capable of anything. Blinded
> by the rage to destroy and supremely careless of
> consequences, they storm against the enemy until
> they are either victorious, dead or utterly exhausted.
> It is as if they are seized by a demon and are no
> longer in control of themselves.

Whether it be a warrior in a state of "heat," as among
the Atoni head-hunters, or a common soldier in World War II
elevated to new heights of ecstasy by virtue of a communal
immortalizing mission, the warrior emerges from battle as a
different person than he had been. Thus, war becomes a
powerful initiatory ordeal from which the novice emerges
transformed into a warrior. Again, Gray observes:

> So often in the war I have felt an utter dis-
> sociation from what had gone before in my life;
> since then I have experienced an absence of
> continuity between those years and what I have
> become...the soldier who has yielded himself
> to the fortunes of war, has sought to kill and
> escape being killed, or who has even lived long
> enough in the disordered landscape of battle is
> no longer what he was. He becomes in some sense
> a fighting man, a Homo Furens.[16]

Revered for the power of his acts and the mystery of
the world he functioned in, the warrior often became a
model, embodying the ideals of a society. The myths and
poetry of the Greeks provided many generations with heroic
models for cultural ideals and standards. Achilles, for
example, became a noble model of the incarnation of *areté*
"a combination of proud and courtly morality and warlike
valor."[17] In Homer's *Iliad*, *areté* signified the obligation
to be brave, to embody the virtues of a warrior. Achilles
aspired to the excellence of the warrior hero. He would gain
areté through acts requiring physical strength. Achilles'
value as a cultural hero does not lie solely in his physical
triumph over Hector, however, but in the conscious decision
to carry out a heroic deed, realizing it will cost him his
life. "Now I shall go," Achilles says, "to overtake that
killer of a dear life, Hektor; then I will accept my own
death, at whatever time Zeus wishes to bring it about, and

the other immortals."[18] Achilles was also known as a figure
of tragic struggle against warrior rage, the rage that leads
warriors to act in excess of their mission.

In Sparta, during the Messenian war, Tyrtaeus rallied
the Spartans to the ancient martial ideals. He saw the
Spartans as direct descendants of the heroes of *The Iliad*
and *The Odyssey*. He modeled action in his present after
Homer's mythical battles. Later figures also traced their
heritage back to these early heroes. Alexander the
Great, before facing Darius in battle, went to Troy and
sacrificed to Athena, then visited the tomb of his ancestor
Achilles. Memories of warriors as cultural heroes have
often provided orientation for martial action, and continue
to do so in our time.[19]

However heroic, the warrior's image may nonetheless be
tainted with ambiguity. The French historian of religions,
Georges Dumézil, has pointed to this ambivalent status of
the warrior in his studies of Indo-European mythology. In
the Ṛg Veda, Indra, the personification of the warrior ideal,
is guilty of several sins, and with each one, loses some of
his martial power. According to Dumézil, the ambivalence
evidenced toward warriors in myth is a reflection of a social
reality. In every society warriors are prone to excess, and
their autonomy of action could not be tolerated outside of
battle. Dumézil comments that a warrior's autonomy was
"weighed with temptations and risks for the one who possesses
it, and is disturbing as well for the social order and the
order of the cosmos."[20]

Warriors violate rules of the social order, including the violation of their own warrior ideals. The sins
of the warrior bring him into inevitable conflict with
other social figures. The warrior "finds comfort...in
being strong absolutely, the strongest of all--a dangerous
superlative for a being who occupies the second rank."[21]

Further, warriors possess by the nature of their given function a vulnerability to excess, "the heightened prowess and
the blind fury--which comes over the warrior and enables him
to perform otherwise impossible feats."[22] This excessive
martial fury and the ambivalence which it engenders is not
limited to Indo-European societies. Achilles is both chivalrous and brutal, and while not viewed ambivalently among
Greek heroes, his sins lead him to his tragic and heroic
(and thus redemptive) decision. Again, we shall see the
persistence of the ambivalent perception of the warrior as
we examine our portrayals of American warrior heroes.

     Like members of other communities, Americans perceive
war through mythical categories. Furthermore, although
American interpretations of war have in some respects added
to or altered traditional patterns of understanding, still
many of those patterns continue to persist. Our martial
myths have portrayed warfare as regenerative, with warriors
represented as saviors who sow seeds of a new life by killing the enemy or sacrificing their own lives. We have
celebrated the initiatory dimensions of war, as it transforms boys into men through its battle ecstasy. Although
we, too, have been ambivalent about warriors because of this
same warriors' ecstasy, we have also singled out the warrior
as a model for society. Despite this ambivalence, the warrior is often a model for his society, embodying bravery,
honor, and social responsibility. It is striking to follow
the life of these images throughout American martial history.
We live in a time when traditional martial imagery has been
radically altered by nuclear warfare and the effects of the
war in Vietnam. Traditional martial images will now function
only murderously, yet our nostalgia for comforting national
symbols of righteousness exercises a powerful pull. I hope
that this book will help us appreciate the power and poverty
of martial symbolism today.

TABLE OF CONTENTS

CHAPTER ONE

THE CHEVALIER IN AMERICA: WASHINGTON, CUSTER, AND PATTON

Americans have often exhibited ambivalent feelings towards warriors. The colonists inherited English distrust of military control, and often perceived each other as natural fighters, more effective fighters, because they did not belong to a military class. This ambivalence is reflected in the rejection of "dangerous" military heroes for high political office (notably George McClellan and Douglas MacArthur) and the continued suspicion of the professional military temper. Yet, despite this ambivalence, Marcus Cunliffe suggests, "America's national origin, and the first expressions of national character were largely military in form."[1] To acknowledge this is not to indict America for being more warlike than any other nation. We have seen that war exists in many forms in various cultures. I have also suggested that in western ideology history is in some sense both "war" and the stage on which cosmic conflict is carried out. This ideology, which transformed most American wars into crusades, was part of our Puritan heritage. William Haller illustrates how English Puritan sermons set the stage for the spiritual battle between Christ and Satan, a battle which takes place in the soul. Life was pictured as a pilgrimage and a battle; the soul was like a soldier in battle. The preacher "was above all the leader of a crusade and holy war," depicting the image of a soldier fighting for Christ.[2]

These images were not lost in the migrations to
America. In William Bradford's *History of Plymouth
Plantation*, life was portrayed as a war with Satan. "It
is well knowne...how ever since the first breaking out of
the light of the Gospell, in our Honourable Nation of
England...what warrs, and oppossisions...Satan hath
raised, maintained, and continued against the Saincts."[3]
In England, as subsequently in America, it was impossible
to keep spiritual warfare an interior conflict. Warfare
against Satan must be carried out wherever the enemy is
found.

A most obvious and early candidate for the role of
demon in America was the Indian, who symbolized the natural,
often depraved condition of wilderness America. Of significance for the war against Satan were the numerous captivity narratives, reporting the experiences of colonists
torn from civilization, tempted and threatened by Satanic
Indians, and often saved from them. Roy Harvey Pearce
says, "The first and greatest of the captivity narratives
are simple, direct religious documents."[4] The captive and
the experience of captivity had symbolic value for the
whole white community. Richard Slotkin writes,

>   American history is seen as a narrative of
>   man's regeneration and purification from sin,
>   through the suffering of an ordeal by cap-
>   tivity; the captivity occurs in the context
>   of a universal race war, in which the strife
>   of Indians and Christians is identified with
>   the warfare between the World and the Soul,
>   the Devil and Christ.[5]

These narratives became a kind of archetypal drama for
the Puritans, molding their attitude toward the world.
Slotkin suggests that the "myth of regeneration through
violence became the structuring metaphor of the American

experience."[6] The Puritans were both alienated from and
attracted to the Indian. On the one hand, the Indian
represented unregenerate man at his worst, placed in
America to keep the colonists from completion of their
task. As Cotton Mather put it, the Indians were "pieces
in Satan's grand design of conquest."[7] On the other hand,
the Indian tempted the Puritan by his natural life-style
so suited to the wilderness and by his apparent openness
in sexual matters. The Indian became the outward sign of
Puritan inward temptation, and had either to be regenerated (a difficult task) or exterminated. Thus, total war,
with the demon changing location and person, is present in
early American experience. The Puritan captive and warrior
fit a paradigm: he inhabited a pastoral country threatened
by terrors of various kinds; his world polarized when he
saw the enemy; his wrath grew from his perceived difference
from his enemy; he felt captive to his enemy in some way;
finally, he ceased to be a victim and became an avenger,
doing the Lord's work. Further, as Richard Drinnon has
shown, the process of holy extermination brought a religious ecstasy for those involved in the harvest.[8]

The symbol of war as a providential act and the
warrior as a legendary and symbolic figure are present not
only in the formative years of colonization, or only on
the frontier, but in the great events that formed the
United States. In the American Revolution, many historians centered their accounts on "the details of battles,
the celebrations of military encounters, the deeds of
warriors and heroes."[9] Before the Civil War, Ruth Miller
Elson has discovered, one-third of school textbooks were
devoted to military events; and for adults, there were
large numbers of books relating the gallantry and patriotism of war.[10] The numerous wars prior to the Civil War
suggest that our mission, whether as model for the

unregenerate world, or as transforming agent of God, has
not often been a peaceful one. War and warriors have been
honored, imitated, and perceived with awe throughout American history. For it is through warriors that the military
is able to accomplish its mission. It is through completion of this mission that the warrior becomes immortal.

There are numerous types of warriors in America, and
within each type there are figures who reflect both the
fascination with war and the process of changing perceptions of war. One type of warrior is the Chevalier, the
"man on horseback," warrior leaders who by their daring
and aggressive acts exemplify the creative power of martial
action. George Washington epitomized the New World
warrior, a perfectly balanced warrior, not susceptible to
the classic sins of the warrior. As "Father," Washington
is the model for most future American warriors. George
Armstrong Custer has provided generations of Americans
with a sacrificial hero, and the battle of the Little Big
Horn has been a powerful martial symbol. George S. Patton
was a modern warrior in the old berserker tradition, highly
conscious of his role as a high priest of battle.

A second warrior type is the Rifleman. He is represented by the Virginians led by Washington in Braddock's
army, the Minutemen, those who fought with Jackson at New
Orleans, the thousands who were called "Johnny Reb" or
"Billy Yank," the doughboys or the G.I.'s. The Rifleman
is the essence of the patriot, the volunteer, "a mixture
of the genial and the brutal, the callous and the senti-
mental, of patriotism and patrioteering, he is the prime
type of a nation which is 'martial but unmilitary.'"[11]

A third type of warrior is the Executioner or
"socialized warrior." The socialized warrior no longer
fulfills the regenerative functions of a warrior hero.
Rather, this type of warrior kills "as if" there were a

larger mission, but in fact technological prowess in
killing is now the real mission.   While there have been
numerous examples of socialized warriors in America, this
figure is personified most powerfully by the symbol of
Lt. Calley.   Emerging from the frustration and division
brought about by the war in Vietnam, the symbol of Calley
struck at the heart of cherished martial values, and
called into question traditional interpretations of warrior
heroes.   The symbol of Calley exemplifies the degeneration
of martial symbolism in America during the Vietnam years.

    There are, obviously, a number of other warrior
figures who would fit well into these categories.   Each
of these figures is fascinating in his   own right, and
in addition, each provides an avenue for us to examine
both the persistence and transformation of American martial
symbols.

Part I

George Washington:

The Man of Founding Martial Power

George Washington was the primary symbol of the new
nation. His virtues and skills reflected the uniqueness
of American culture. As Americans began to reflect on
the emergence of a nation from a colonial past, Washington
was the symbolic center of the nation. Clive Bush writes,
"If internally the gathering Washington cult became a
psychological foundation of legal order, externally it de-
fined the country as a nation state to other nations."[12]
Washington was a founder, "answering the calls of patriots
who required him to summarize the act of leadership which
they had begun themselves."[13] Through his martial actions,
Washington brought the world into recognizable form.
According to one student of the literature about Washington,
he was considered a hero "to the majority of his countrymen
during his lifetime."[14]

Whether Washington appears as the Sunday school figure
so prominent in Parson Weems's account, the fearless Revolutionary leader, or the majestic and remote Father of his
country, it is impossible to separate the historical Washington from the myths about him. "The man is the monument;
the monument is the man."[15] It is in the presentation of
Washington through biography, oratory, art, etc., that he
"lives" in our collective memory. If Cunliffe is correct,
the search for the historical Washington would result in
only a snapshot next to the portraits painted over many

years.   The symbolic Washington is multivalent, and crucial
to the mythic memory of America.

There are many images of Washington present in Amer-
ican memory, yet the most popular image has been that of
General Washington, "the Sword of the Revolution, the
Deliverer of America, the Savior of his country."[16]

Washington's actions as a founder were not only
national acts, but cosmic acts.   During the centennial of
his birth in 1832, Senator Daniel Webster said:

> Washington stands at the commencement of a new
> era, as well as at the head of the New World.
> A century from the birth of Washington has
> changed the world.   The country of Washington
> has been the theatre on which a great part of
> the change has been wrought; and Washington
> himself a principal agent by which it has been
> accomplished.   His age and his country are
> equally full of wonders; and of both he is
> the chief.[17]

The power of the figure of Washington and the power
of his acts reveal a proper mode of being in the world for
Americans.   The creation that Washington brings about
abolishes old historical time.   America is new and pure.
Washington is at the center of this creation.   Concern
that the symbolic power of Washington emanate from the
center is obvious in the saga of the erection of the
Washington Monument.   Henry Clay, speaking in 1816, said:

> An image....A testimonial to this great man,
> Father of his country should exist in every
> part of the Union as a memorial...but of all
> places, it was required in this Capitol, the
> center of the Union, the offspring, the
> creation, of his mind and of his labors.[18]

The acts of Washington gave birth to a country of
wonders, a country which inaugurated a new era and changed
the world. These actions were not merely benign or passive
actions; they were largely the acts of a protector and a
savior, the acts of a warrior bringing a new birth of order
out of chaotic disorder. Washington was the symbolic
center of power of the revolution. Gabriel comments,
"Where Washington established his headquarters, there was
the heart of the Revolution."[19] That this motif was not
just one which emerged after Washington's time is clearly
shown from Robert Treat Paine's song written in 1798 called
"Adams and Liberty." Sung to the tune that Francis Scott
Key used later for the "Star-Spangled Banner," Paine wrote:

Should the tempest of war overshadow our land

Its bolts could ne'er rend freedom's temple asunder;

For, unmoved, at its portal would Washington stand.

And repulse with his breast the assaults of his
        thunder.[20]

Early paintings showed the formative martial power of
Washington. John Trumbull's *Washington Before the Battle
of Trenton* (1792) showed the general as "the focus of the
forces of history and nature."[21] Bush notes that the aide
controlling the horse in the painting "provides an ex-
teriorization of the hero's will in conflict with forces
that threaten to turn anarchic."[22]

Four days after Washington's death in December 1799,
Henry Lee proposed a Congressional resolution which contained these famous lines, "First in war, First in peace,
First in the hearts of his countrymen."[23] These triumphs
are portrayed in an oil painting by Frederick Kemmelmeyer
celebrating Washington as the unanimous choice for President.
Here, the words are "First in war, First in peace, First in
defence of our country." General Washington is in full
dress uniform, surrounded by cannon, cannonballs, and many

flags, while above his picture is a version of the seal
of the United States. This consists of an eagle holding
both arrows and an olive branch.[24] In most portrayals,
it is Washington the soldier, the man on horseback, who
is the prominent image. Catherine Albanese suggests:

> The patriots found in Washington a hero who
> epitomized the military values they embraced.
> From the beginning, the histories and biogra-
> phies painted a vivid portrait of Washington
> the soldier and general, a portrait in fact
> so vivid that it far eclipsed the treatments
> of his political involvements and his Presi-
> dency.[25]

These military values came from classical and English
sources. The founding fathers saw themselves as classical
figures, "analogies of the farmer-republicans who sought
to prevent the establishment of Caesarism."[26] As a classical figure, Washington was the perfect example of the civilian soldier, the "American Cincinnatus," who was a great
military leader, but voluntarily retired to civilian life.
In many funeral orations Washington was compared to biblical and classical figures, always to their disadvantage.
Allusions to Cincinnatus are much like this stanza written
by Philip Freneau in 1783:

> Now hurrying from the busy scene,
> Where thy Potomack's water flow,
> May'st thou enjoy thy rural reign,
> And every earthly blessing know;
> Thus he who Rome's proud legions sway'd,
> Return'd and sought his sylvan shade.[27]

Along with his perceived classical roots, Washington was
an heir of the English military honor code. He was an
officer and a gentleman, and through combat fulfilled his
martial duty.

Biographies of Washington were rare before his death.
An exception was the work of John Bell, a revolutionary
soldier. He wrote a letter to a friend in 1789 in which
he offered a detailed sketch of Washington which was
eventually printed. He stated that Washington was one of
the "greatest military ornaments of the present age, and
that his name will command the veneration of the latest
posterity."[28]

Biographies and biographical sketches began to appear
within a few years after Washington's death, and generally
emphasized his actions in the Revolutionary years. John
Marshall's *Life of George Washington* (1804-1807) emphasized
the war period. Samuel G. Goodrich's biography of 1832
(intended for children) divided up Washington's life in
this manner: twenty pages on his life before the Revolution; one hundred twenty pages on his war years; and
thirty-two pages on the rest of his life. Even the first
biography by a trained historian emphasized the Revolutionary years. Jared Sparks' *The Writings of George Washington*
portrayed Washington as a model for the nation, and half of
the biography was devoted to the war years. James Kirke
Paulding's *A Life of Washington* (1837) spent three-fifths
of its space on Washington in the Revolution.

One of Washington's biographers was J. T. Headley, a
former minister and semi-professional writer who published
his two-volume biography entitled *Washington and His
Generals* in 1847. It remained a best-seller for two decades. Headley's chapter on Washington in the first volume
consists almost entirely of his exploits as a soldier. The
warrior image of Washington portrayed in Headley's book
was an image not only of a heroic warrior, but a warrior
divinely ordained to fulfill a martial mission for his
people. Headley saw in Washington's early exploits the
hand of Providence guiding him toward his martial mission.

> When in imagination I behold this youth of
> twenty-one years of age in his Indian dress,
> his knapsack on his back and his gun in his
> hand stealing through the snow-covered
> forest at midnight, or plunging about in
> the wintry stream in the struggle for life...
> I seem to behold one whom angels guard through
> the desperate training which can alone fit him
> for the stern trials ahead.[29]

The angelic guardian is never more evident than in the
ambush Washington experienced as an officer with Braddock's
troops during the French and Indian War. Headley reports
that Washington had two horses shot from under him, and
four bullets tore his clothes, yet he was not injured.
William Starbuck Mayo wrote in 1851:

> Six times a chief his rifle points
> Against his manly breast,
> With careful and delib'rate sight
> And firm and steady rest.
> Six times at that same noble mark
> His braves aim far and nigh-
> Six times the missing volleys pass
> The hero harmless by.[30]

Several months after this battle, Rev. Samuel Davies
prophesied that just as God had raised Alexander, Caesar,
Homer, etc., he had raised Washington "for some important
service to his country."[31] Similarly, Headley wrote that
a prophet waited in the forest in 1775 after a revelation
from God that he would consecrate a deliverer. Washington
arrives and the prophet says:

> The voice of God has spoken to me, in my
> thoughts by day, in my dreams by night--
> "I will send a DELIVERER to this land of
> the New World, who shall save my people

from physical bondage, even as my Son
saved them from the bondage of spiritual
death."[32]

Epic verse often focused on Washington as a warrior
savior and also on his martial deeds.

For he's the hero firm and brave,
Who all our country's Glory gave,
And once again he shall us save,
Our armies bold commanding.[33]

Bryan concludes, "It is unlikely that any other man in
history, with the possible exception of Napoleon, was so
widely 'orated' upon in his latter years and for more than
a half century after his death as George Washington."[34]

In the Indian ambush that he so narrowly escaped,
Washington is portrayed as exhibiting the ecstasy of the
warrior. "Absorbed in the fate of the army, and intent
only on saving it, he seemed to forget he had a life to
lose."[35] Such recognizable warrior traits and virtues
were present throughout Washington's life. At Valley
Forge he was a model of bravery. A surgeon at Valley
Forge wrote, "When in health and with what cheerfulness
he meets his foes and encounters every hardship--if bare-
foot he labours thro the Mud & Cold with a song in his
mouth extolling War and Washington."[36] His sacrifices
were ordained. As eleven-year-old Emerson wrote in 1814:

In former years when Britain ruled these states
And like a tyrant doom'd our hapless fates
The God of Israel heard our groans and cries
And bade to life a WASHINGTON arise.[37]

Washington the farmer and fighter was also a midwife,
presiding at the birth of freedom for a country under an
eschatological sign. As a protector, he was fighting to
save what had been conceived.

The popularity of Washington as a hero and savior illustrates the appeal of the New World Chevalier in America. He was a civilian-soldier; he did not long for war for its own sake, yet he had the passion and the virtue of the warrior and was captured by his ordained martial mission. Headley wrote of thoughts in his first battle, "'I heard the bullets whistle, and believe me, there is something charming in the sound.' There spoke the bold young warrior, for whom the rattle of musketry and thunder of artillery are the music that his stern soul loves."[38] Yet whatever joy or ecstasy Washington exhibited in battle, Headley makes it clear that he did not fall victim to the traditional sins of the warrior. They were "arrested at once by the stern mandate of his will."[39]

Unlike traditional warrior figures, Washington was the perfectly balanced man. In early biographies he appears as a flawless god who "descended to earth...freed his people from oppression, steered their government for a few years, and then returned to heaven."[40] In speaking of Washington, Thomas Jefferson said he "Scrupulously (obeyed) the Laws through the whole of his career, civil and military, of which the history of the world furnishes no other example."[41] Washington was dignified, command-ing, balancing the wisdom of civilian leadership with the passion and courage of the warrior.

Washington was more than a great man, for Providence had shown him to be a holy man, chosen to bring liberty (salvation) to his children. His task was not without precedent; he followed in a long historical tradition of heroes which extended

    to the first generation of their ancestors in
    the New World, and beyond them to the conflicts
    of their Fathers in the Puritan Revolution, the
    struggles of earlier Anglo-Saxons for the rights

of Englishmen, and the sufferings of ancient
Hebrews in the Exodus which brought them out
of slavery and into freedom.[42]

This warrior hero was <u>first</u> a man of war, and <u>then</u>
a man of peace, for the new world could only emerge out
of conflict. Washington was above all a man of <u>power</u>,
the power of a founder, protector, and savior. His perfectly balanced personality, the unity of emotion and
will, would be recalled by North and South in the war
which lay ahead. The South claimed him as a "freedom-
fighter" of Virginia, who opposed the same kind of alien
oppression that they were facing in the 1850s. The North
looked to him as a symbol of national unity and called
Americans to solidify the Union he brought into being.
For example, Oliver Wendell Holmes reacted to the violence
in "Bloody Kansas" in 1856 with an "Ode to Washington," in
which Washington appears and pleads for national unity,
saying, "Cherish the fraternal spirit; Love your country
first of all!"[43]

Washington's actions, the actions of a warrior,
brought a new world of liberty into being. Thus, the
annual oratory on his birthday and the restoration and
veneration of Mount Vernon became oral ritual and sacred
space, where the power of founding action can revivify
principles for which the founder struggled.[44] Every
warrior figure is, in some sense, a descendant of the
Father-Protector-Savior. As Catherine Albanese puts it,
"He was a veritable warlord of the spirit, the epitome of
the warrior religion of Americans who knew that in their
democratic faith they had donned the helmet of salvation
and were wearing the sword of the spirit."[45]

The symbol of Washington was multivalent. He was a
model of American virtue, martial courage, and revered
for his unifying power as President. He became not only

the cool and perfectly balanced warrior, fighting for the
birth of the new world, but also a model for future warrior-
presidents. Jasper B. Shannon writes, "The presidency was
created to fit the personality of George Washington, a revolutionary hero and the embodiment of the virtues of the
British landed gentry."[46] In the future only certain kinds
of warrior heroes would be acceptable to Americans: those
who exhibited both the martial courage and balanced temp-
erament could hope to overcome the classic ambivalence of
attitudes exhibited toward the warrior. Louis Smith notes:

> The habitual procedure has been for the warrior
> hero who aspired to higher recognition from the
> Republic to shed his uniform and in mufti offer
> himself as a candidate for office...but it is
> well to keep in mind that most of these presi-
> dents had been soldiers simply by the necessities
> of war and had not chosen military life as a
> profession.[47]

Thus, Americans have preferred Eisenhower to MacArthur,
or Grant to McClellan. This does not mean that the memory
of the warrior's creative and salvific acts are forgotten
or dismissed as insignificant; rather, it is a preference
for civilian warriors who allay the fear of traditional
warrior excess, a fear that the model American civilian
warrior (Washington, for example) helped allay.[48]

As a symbolic figure, Washington may be viewed in
numerous guises. In images and memories about Washington,
I have suggested that the images of his martial acts overshadow all others. His military acts are the powerful acts
which bring about the birth of the new nation. The memory
of General Washington served as a model for future American
warriors. The perfectly balanced man, with full control
over classic warrior rage, sired generations of American
warriors, perceived as humane but ferocious, and formed

American notions of what kinds of warriors were fit to
assume the Presidency. For our purposes it is most important to note that Washington was venerated for his actions:
the founding of a nation born in war, the salvation of a
millennial idea, and the formation of traditional char-
acteristics of the American warrior. He, more than any
other figure of the formative period of American history,
is the one who "opens" American national history.

PART II

GEORGE A. CUSTER:

SACRIFICIAL WARRIOR OF THE WEST

There is perhaps no better example of a classic
American Chevalier than George Armstrong Custer. From
the monuments dedicated to him in Michigan and Ohio, the
battlefield named after him at the Little Big Horn, to
his burial place at West Point, Custer and the Last Stand
remain an important part of American mythology. What
many have called "Custer's Luck" brought him through West
Point (1857-1861) and into significant leadership for the
Union during the Civil War. He was a newspaperman's delight, for his habit in battle was to charge the enemy,
regardless of their strength. "His charges," Stephen
Ambrose says, "although by no means always successful,
made him a favorite of the national press and one of the
super-stars of the day."[49] Custer was always at the head
of his men, a natural leader with a genius for the flamboyant.

> He wore a velveteen jacket with five gold loops
> on each sleeve, and a sailor shirt with a very
> large collar....The shirt was dark blue, and
> with it he wore a conspicuous red tie-top boots,
> a soft hat, Confederate, that he had picked up
> on the field, and his hair was long and in curls
> almost to his shoulders.[50]

Custer led a number of dashing attacks during the
war. At Gettysburg he led the 1st Michigan Cavalry

against an important Confederate counterattack. In 1864,
under the eye of General Sheridan, he defeated Jeb Stuart's
famous cavalry, and was promoted to Major General. Finally,
"Custer's Luck" brought him to Appomattox, where his division cut off General Robert E. Lee from his last source
of supplies. Custer personally received the white flag
from Lee's men and also received the small table on which
the peace terms were written, a gift from General Sheridan.[51]

Harper's Weekly carried a picture of Custer on the
cover of its March 19, 1864, edition. Copied from a Matthew
Brady photograph, it showed Custer, saber in the air, leading
his men in battle. This kind of portrayal, a popular one
during the Civil War, especially with one so suited to glamorous portrayal as Custer, made him one of the pantheon of
Northern military heroes. He shared glory in the victorious
mission of the North, which was widely seen as a divine
blessing on America. His men, for example, led the victory
parade of Union troops in Washington on May 23, 1865.
Though Custer did play major roles in crucial battles of the
Civil War, it is doubtful that he would have remained im-
bedded in the public mind any more than Sheridan, Buell, or
a number of other Civil War figures. Yet his Last Stand
immortalized him, for it was his death that made Custer a
symbol of the warrior mission in the West.

There was little glory in fighting Indians in the
latter part of the nineteenth century. The army was often
seen as either brutal or ineffective, and Mrs. Custer's
stories reveal the harsh life of the cavalryman on the
Great Plains. Yet the West as significant place was different, "other" from conventional civilization. The idea
of the frontier is largely the idea of a boundary between
the known and the mysterious. Henry Nash Smith writes
that the West was an "exhilarating region of adventure and
comradeship in the open air. Its heroes bore none of the

orders and bringing on the disaster himself. Yet within
a month, Custer had become a hero, a martyr for cause and
country.[56] The idea of his redeeming sacrifice was pre-
ent from soon after the battle. The first newspaper
account of the battle, appearing in *The Bismarck Tribune*,
was a terse account, yet the paper still thought it important to note that Custer was among the last to fall,
and "The Indian dead were great in number...(they) were
certainly severely punished."[57] In a letter to Mrs.
Custer in 1889, General Sherman wrote that the battle
was the end of the Sioux nation, it was the "Battle of
Civilization." He continues:

> I say that the Indian wars are as much wars
> as conflicts with foreigners or our own
> people...the Regular Army of the United
> States should claim what is true and sus-
> ceptible of demonstration, that it has been
> for an hundred years ever the picket line
> at the front of the great wave of civiliza-
> tion.[58]

Thus, shortly after the battle, Custer was seen as
fighting to the last, giving his life for a high price,
and the belief emerged, as expressed by General Sherman,
that Custer's life was given so that the great wave of
civilization could advance. *The Boston Globe*, on the
fiftieth anniversary of the massacre in 1926 wrote, "As
Custer's widow turns her face toward the setting sun she
sees the field of bloodshed come to flower...she reads
the record of her hero's patriotic service, written in
terms of peace and plenty."[59] The idea of Custer's
sacrificial and redeeming death lived long after the
Globe's comments. Upon dedication of a monument to Custer
at his birthplace in Ohio, C. B. Galbreath said that
Custer was

A soldier on the plains, ever obedient to
his country's call; riding like the warriors
of legend into the red whirlwind of battle
on the banks of the Little Big Horn and
falling--but not in vain. Before sunset of
the following day the mighty hosts of red
warriors were scattered in flight and the
last concerted battle of Indians against
whites in three centuries of warfare was
at an end.[60]

In the same dedication Col. Ralph D. Cole said, "General
George Armstrong Custer had both the courage and power
to challenge and conquer in every crisis; even his death
removed the last barrier to national progress 'as westward the course of civilization has taken its way.'"[61]
In 1957, Eugene McAuliffe wrote, "It was the 'Regular
Army Man' who bore the brunt of the advance of civilization...Let the memory of their brave deeds and gallant
sacrifices be never forgotten."[62] For these and many
others, Custer's Last Stand fit into a scheme of history
in which "history was...a moral drama...the visible manifestation of the cosmic Providential scheme."[63]

Biographies as well as informal remembrances portray
Custer as a sacrificial saint. The earliest and perhaps
most influential biography was written by Frederick Whittaker in 1876, shortly after the Last Stand. In Whittaker's
book, Custer "is born in glory, suffers persecution, and
then dies for the Cause, which in Custer's case is not God
but country."[64] Whittaker was instrumental in popular-
izing Custer for the American people in much the same way
that Weems and Headley had done for Washington. Whittaker
dramatizes the heroism of the sacrifice, suggesting that
the Crow scout, Curly, had a chance to save Custer during
a lull in the battle. "There was no hope of victory if

he stayed, nothing but certain death."[65]   Custer thought
quietly, put his head down and "weighed in that brief
moment of reflection, all the consequences to America of
the lesson of life and the lesson of heroic death, and
he chose death."[66]   Custer, the model of heroic death
for a generation of Americans, is naturally killed by the
bravest warrior, Rain-in-the-Face.

The Last Stand had been transformed into a great
moral victory, "as great a display of heroism as the
world had ever witnessed."[67]   It is through a heroic
stand of a small group against overwhelming odds that
"the majesty of these vanquished is manifested."[68]   There
are also a number of narrative elements which help shape
the majesty of the Custer epic: Custer is often portrayed
as carrying a sword, though the Seventh Cavalry carried no
sabers into battle.   The last of the Seventh died on a
hilltop, and as we have mentioned, Custer was thought to
have been the last to die.   Also, Custer is thought to
have sent a "last call" for help to Reno, who abandoned
him.   Finally, the hero's pride and bravery lead him away
from the temptation to escape, and all are massacred except the "lone survivor."[69]

According to some military historians, the Little
Big Horn was a battle after the fact.   The army knew that
the dwindling buffalo herds would end the Indian's life-
style and force them into a desperate situation.   The
victory over Custer gained little for the Indians.   The
battle, then, was not crucial.   It did not "win the West."
Indian casualties were greatly exaggerated.   The Indians
"melted away," not because of casualties, but because it
was not their practice to fight "campaigns."   The battle
was fought.   It had been won.   The "campaign" was over.
Yet Custer's Last Stand has been transformed into a cosmic
battle.   It was a "'Thermopylae of the Plains' (suggesting

a heroic defense) and...a 'Charge of the Light Brigade'
(suggesting a heroic assault)."[70] Rosenberg suggests
that stories about Custer "bear a striking resemblance
to other heroic legends," such as the Last Stand in the
Chanson de Roland, Saul's death as recorded in First
Samuel, Thermopylae, the battle of Maldon, and the
Alamo.[71]

We tend to shape reality symbolically; thus, Custer's
Last Stand becomes a battle in the "creation" of the West,
and the latest in a long line of heroic Last Stands. The
battle is a hierophany, a manifestation of sacred power.
Through the actions of Custer and his men, the immortalizing mission of the warrior is successful, and the place
of the battle becomes sacred space, a place where the
nature and destiny of a new world are brought into being
by the warrior's action.[72] J. R. Kelly, reflecting on a
trip to the Little Big Horn in 1957, echoes this idea:

> I remained alone at the 'monument,' memories
> flooded my mind....I thought of another bleak
> and barren hill...and of a MAN who stood there
> long, long ago--His garments stripped from his
> body. I thought of an old parable: 'Take the
> shoes from off thy feet--you stand on sacred
> ground.'[73]

As the battle of the Little Big Horn became an immortal Last Stand, Custer the warrior was transformed
into an immortal warrior figure. He was an epiphany of
the ancient warrior who lives on in each generation. He
was called an American Hector or Achilles and likened to
Christ. In 1896, Ella Wheeler Wilcox wrote one of the
many epic poems about Custer. Part of it is quoted in
The Western Hero:

> All valor died not on the plains of Troy
> Awake, my muse awake! Be thine the joy

To sing of deeds as dauntless and as brave
As e'er lent Custer to a warrior's grave.
Sing of that noble soldier, nobler man,
Dear to the heart of each American.
Sound forth his praise from sea to listening sea-
Greece her Achilles claimed, immortal Custer, we.[74]

Custer serves America through his sacred mission the
way Hector served Troy, or Achilles served Greece.   Yet
it is not only his <u>mission</u> which is of importance, for
Custer became like Achilles, a model: the ideal American hero.   Steckmesser has suggested that "the history
of Custer interpretation in dime novels, juvenile biography, and boy's fiction is to some extent a record of
American ideals."[75]   Custer's biographer, Frederick
Whittaker, who wrote over one hundred dime novels, popularized Custer in *The Dashing Dragoon*, written in 1882.
In a sense, these stories were means of "socializing or
initiating boys into the heroic world," for often the
hero of the story was a boy who served as Custer's com-
panion "and...accompanies the great General as a junior
scout...(he) serves as the vehicle for vicarious partici-
pation in the battle."[76]

We should remember the emphasis on military events
in the schoolbooks of the time.   Ruth Miller Elson
writes, "The very books that express the most solemn
strictures against war devote much of their spaces to
glamorous descriptions of it."[77]   Almost every reader of
the time contained many battle scenes, instilling a belief that loyalty to America was the highest form of
loyalty and that heroism cannot be evidenced more than
by giving one's life for America.   Elson depicts the
popularity of sacrificial warriors.   To children of the
nineteenth century, "Benjamin Franklin symbolizes the
American in ordinary circumstances...American war heroes

symbolize the American in extraordinary circumstances."[78]
Quentin Reynolds, a World War II reporter, wrote a biography of Custer in 1951 for the *Landmark* series.   To
read his book is to see warfare as romantic and Custer
as a symbol of the highest American ideals.   Thus, in
addition to perceiving the warrior as a model of American
areté, warfare is the phenomenon through which ideals are
exercised at their highest.

After Elizabeth Custer died in 1933, debunking biographies made their appearance, led by Frederick F. van
de Water's *Glory Hunter* in 1934.   Edward H. O'Neill, in
A History of American Biography, says that van de Water
"seems to have knocked Custer from his pedestal and destroyed the pedestal as well."[79]   It is evident that this
is not true.   Custer and the Last Stand continue to live
in American consciousness.   Don Russell's *Custer's List*
cites 967 known paintings and illustrations of Custer
and the Last Stand.   There have been numerous movies,
television shows, and records.[80]   The most famous painting,
the Anheuser Busch lithograph, has sold more than one
million copies, showing Custer "indelibly associated with
cavalry, with glamour, with *eclat* and heroism."[81]   Custer
has also appeared in a bubble gum card series, in a jig-
saw puzzle, as a cut-out figure in breakfast food cartons,
and has been portrayed in a series of educational posters
distributed to schools entitled "Winning the West."   One
of the posters illustrates Custer's Last Stand.

This fascinating compilation of "trivia" is much
more than that.   These various depictions are messages
to the observer that the mythic picture of Custer as a
warrior and the Last Stand as an epic battle are very
much alive in the everyday "history" of Americans.   In
addition to revealing the persistence of the warrior as
a symbolic figure, a "Custer cult" reveals a nostalgia

for the _kind_ of warrior figure Custer symbolized, and
perhaps, nostalgia for warfare in which heroism and
warrior virtue were possible and necessary in order to
complete the ritual of battle. There is, for example,
a group called "The Little Big Horn Associates," who
publish a quarterly research review and make pilgrimages
to the battlefield. Indeed, since 1877, numerous celebrations have taken place at the Custer Battlefield, and
in the early years of this century, thousands of people
would come to this sacred place to take part in a ritual
that revivified American bravery and heroism. These
rituals celebrated the creative sacrifice of Custer and
his men, and symbolized the "friendship" between Indian
and white, while suggesting the formidable civilizing
power of Anglo-American ideals. The tone and content
of these events remained constant until the centennial
celebration in 1976, when native American voices made
clear that the symbol of Custer and the battle communi-
cated a quite different message. Hence, native Americans
forced others to confront the dark side of the symbol and
the relentless ideology that it symbolized for them. The
symbol of Custer and the battle persist as evocative
martial symbols, but also are interpreted in new ways.[82]

On a symbolic level, the re-creation of a sacred
event, taking place in sacred space, is illustrative of
the important formative events of a history-making people.
For in a real sense, the last stand was perceived as giving
birth to a new American West. Custer, through his heroic
sacrifice (the fulfillment of his warrior mission) allowed
a place to come into being where civilization replaced
wilderness. As a model, Custer epitomized the virtues
necessary to conquer obstacles, and also the ideals for
which each American should strive. The ritual ceremonies
at the Little Big Horn recited a cosmogony; the rebirth

of the American West, the new world founded by Custer and
and his men through their actions at the Last Stand. To
enter (through the battle ceremonies) the sacred time and
space when these "worlds" were formed and ideals were
clear was also to hope to regain the power of the acts
and ideals. The ceremonies made visual what generations
of Americans wanted "refurbished," heroic action and revivified ideals.[83] In addition, the ceremonies point out
a nostalgia for the traditional action of the warrior.
J. R. Kelly writes:

> We have heard the roar of the Army tanks,
> the groaning screaming shriek of the bomb
> diver [sic], the 'swoosh' of the jet plane
> ...but can anyone who has ever heard or
> seen it--forget the bugle's call and the
> Cavalry's response?[84]

The ceremonies held at the Little Big Horn since 1877 have
helped keep Custer "alive." Like medieval savior kings,
Custer as a symbolic warrior is not dead, but has only
changed forms.

Part III

George S. Patton:

The Archaic Warrior in the Twentieth Century

The various forms of the Chevalier were reflected
in the changing forms of war. The use of cavalry gradually receded and became strategically obsolete after the
development of the tank in World War I. Yet though the
forms changed, symbols persisted. The tank, especially
in World War II, was known as "mechanized cavalry," and
crossed sabers as the tank insignia replaced the cavalry
general leading his troops into battle with sabers held
high. The tank commander was in many ways a twentieth-
century version of the cavalry officer of the American
West. General George S. Patton was seen as a "combination of Confederate Generals Nathan Bedford Forrest and
Jeb Stuart and of General Custer."[85] Patton was also
seen as a man of the West, much like Custer. Martin
Blumenson writes, "Two-gun Patton, wearing his .45 Long
Colt Single Action revolver and his .357 Magnum Smith
and Wesson revolver in matching holsters, personified the
image to perfection."[86]

Patton is another powerful example of the classical
instance of the warrior in America. Though a twentieth-
century warrior, versed in the arts of mechanized warfare,
he has often been understood as a warrior lost in his own
time. Vagts believes he was a "nearly archaic personality,"[87] and Blumenson suggests, "The era of warfare
inaugurated by Napoleon came to an end with Patton. He

was the last of the Romantic warriors. He was the final
nineteenth-century figure in military history."[88] Patton's
own aide-de-camp, Charles Codman, writes:

> What seems to have escaped most contemporary
> journalists is the fact that General Patton
> is not a contemporary figure...he brings to
> the art of command in this day and age the
> norms and antique virtues of the classic
> warrior.[89]

Patton has been compared to Custer, Stuart, et al.,
because their tactics were so similar. Patton used armor
the way Stuart used cavalry: exposing flanks, ignoring
frontal assaults, and constantly using the element of
surprise. However, it is not only for his tactical skills
that Patton has been compared to these men. He is perhaps
the warrior who symbolizes "the last heroic gasp in the
proud myth of American invincibility."[90] Patton's dash
brought back images of Custer. His victories could bring
back a whole pantheon of American warriors. He was not
only a warrior, he was, in the language of the twentieth
century, a fighting machine. He was totally dedicated to
war, to victory, to his destiny. He was determined to
lead his men through military initiation and see them
emerge as American warriors. He would help them acquire
the "warrior soul." Though he was a fighting machine, he
was an "archaic" warrior. The warrior virtues of duty,
obedience, and courage were his constant guides. His
wish was to meet Rommel in personal combat, tank to tank.
He was a complete warrior, in his sins as well as in his
virtues.[91] His warrior sins, like those of so many traditional warrior figures, would plague him constantly and
illustrate the ambivalence with which America viewed a
traditional Chevalier in the mid-twentieth century.

As a boy, Patton "lived and played in a world apart from his contemporaries; a world peopled by the great names from history."[92] From early childhood, he wanted to become a general partly because his ancestors were often military men. One of them, Hugh Mercer, was a general in the Revolutionary War. His grandfather, George S. Patton, was a Confederate captain who fought with Stonewall Jackson and Jubal Early and was killed at the battle of Winchester. The power of these martial roots was strong. Once, when under heavy fire in World War I, Patton was lying on his belly when he looked up and saw a vision of his grandfather and his grandfather's brothers. They looked at him and their eyes said, "Georgie, Georgie, you're a disappointment to us lying down there. Just remember lots of Pattons have been killed, but there never was one who was a coward."[93]

It was not only his own family that formed his warrior soul, but also the power of the ancient warriors whom he emulated as a boy. He was aware that the history of war was the history of warriors. In a lecture to tank officers in 1919 he said, "We, as officers of the army, are not only members of the oldest of honorable professions, but are also the modern representatives of the demi-gods and heroes of antiquity."[94] Patton saw himself as more than a modern representative of a past time; he was a reincarnation of the eternal warrior. This is expressed vividly in his poem, "Memories," written in 1917.

And now again I am here for war

Where as Roman and knight I have been.

Again I practice to fight the Hun

And attack him by machine.

Later, in 1944, Patton repeated this theme in a poem, "Through a Glass Darkly."

So as through a glass and darkly
The age long strife I see
Where I fought in many guises,
Many names--but always me.

And I see not in my blindness
What the objects were I wrought
But as God rules o'er our bickerings
It was through His will I fought.

So forever in the future,
Shall I battle as of yore
Dying to be born a fighter,
But to die again once more.[95]

Patton "knew he had been to France before as a Roman
legionnaire, but he also knew that he had been there
later encased in knighthood's armor on his way to the
Crusades."[96] His romantic and ancient notions of warrior
chivalry were alien to warfare in the twentieth century.
He could not understand the loss of gallantry nor the
loss of the desire for personal combat. When he remarked
that after the war he would like to discuss tactics with
Kesselring and von Rundstedt, he was severely criticized.
The modern public and the archaic warrior could not truly
understand one another.

Just as Patton was conscious of the weight of ancestors and of military tradition, he was equally conscious of his own role as a Chevalier. His flamboyance,
his "color," his rough language, his unique style of
dress were all calculated to accomplish a function: the
creation of a warrior model for his men.[97] He earned
the respect of his troops because he appeared to be invincible, he was loyal to his men, and he was a model of
courage. Herbert Essame writes, "No commander in World

War II succeeded more effectively in impressing his own
personality on the officers and men under his command
than Patton....It was even said that he had created Third
Army in his own image."[98]   Codman notes that "an entire
army, from corps commander to rifleman, is galvanized into
action by the dynamism of one man."[99]   Patton's legendary
harsh discipline, strict dress regulations, and vivid
speeches were all designed to make his men efficient
warriors, with Patton as the model.   In the movie biography, George C. Scott as Patton opens the film by addressing his soldiers (the audience) against a backdrop
of a huge American flag.   His speech is a version of
Patton's "fight talk" delivered to his troops before
battle.[100]   In reality, this particular speech delivered
in the movie was given in a little town in France.   John
J. Pullen recalls, "So vividly did his words impress themselves upon me that some eight hours later, that evening,
I was able to write them down with confidence of considerable accuracy."[101]

Patton was accused in both World Wars of being too
reckless for an officer.   He was often at the front, and
often disregarded personal safety if he could be an inspiration to his men.   This, too, was part of his warrior
virtue.   He said that leaders must lead by "bold example."
It was a mistake, he thought, for officers to "save themselves" for their troops.   This kind of officer had forgotten that the "inspiration of an heroic act will carry
men to victory...the blood of heroes like the dragon's
teeth will sprout new leaders to replace his loss."[102]   A
commander must be a "living presence, an all pervading
personality."[103]   There were two areas in which command
presence functioned for Patton: in battle as inspiration
(Patton as a model of warrior virtues) and in training
(Patton as the instructor in the acquisition of the warrior

soul). He made it clear that combat, the art of killing,
is an experience removed from the beginning soldier's
world. In 1921, he gave a lecture entitled "The Cavalryman":

> Civilization has affected us; we abhor personal
> encounter...we have been taught to restrain our
> emotions, to look upon anger as low, until
> many of us have never experienced the God sent
> ecstasy of unbridled wrath.[104]

The military life, a life of demonstrated courage, culmin-
ated in the disciplined ecstasy of "unbridled wrath."
Patton believed that the warrior soul was "that vitalising
spark, intangible, yet as evident as lightning."[105] The
acquisition of this soul was the key to victory for Patton.
That he saw himself as the "high priest" of this military
initiation and was arrogantly sure of his methods is not
surprising, because he produced results in battle. Discipline (mental practice) was a key virtue in Patton's
training. For after acquiring the

> ability to develop on necessity, momentary and
> calculated savagry, [sic] you can keep your
> twentieth century clarity of vision with which
> to calculate the chances of whether or not to
> charge or fight on foot, and having decided on
> the former, the magic word will transform you
> temporarily into a frenzied brute.[106]

To become such a "frenzied brute," Patton demanded discipline which would become habit, discipline so strong
that it was "stronger than the excitement of battle or
the fear of death."[107] Patton believed that leaders must
impart the kind of discipline they had learned at West
Point or be guilty of "murdering" the men they led.[108]
It was only through this kind of training that men could
overcome their fear. Patton believed every man was scared

in battle, but proper training made it possible for him to
ignore the instinct of survival and let the "ecstasy" of
disciplined wrath take over. The culmination of this
training and the completion of a soldier's initiation is
combat. On December 20, 1941, Patton spoke to a division:

> Battle is not a terrifying ordeal to be endured.
> It is a magnificent experience wherein all the
> elements that have made men superior to the
> beasts are present: courage, self-sacrifice,
> loyalty, help to others, devotion to duty.[109]

The sacrifices that military men must make are made,
according to Patton, for the most sacred cause: national
existence. Patton emphasized that the individual owes
service to the country. A warrior must insure the life of
the country. "In doing his utmost, even unto death, the
officer is not conferring a favor, he is privileged to be
able to give that much for his country."[110] Likewise, it
is the highest privilege of citizenship to be able to
fight for one's country. The power of Patton is most evident in his speech and action directed toward turning
civilians into fighting men and making the mission of the
fighting man clear. Patton believed that the warrior role
could be gained, in fact, could be brought to the surface,
because men, "real" men, like to fight. In 1917 Patton
wrote:

> They will disband their armies
> When THIS great strife is won
> And trust again to pacifists
> To guard for them their home.
>
> They will return to futileness
> As quickly as before
> Though truth and history vainly shout
> THERE IS NO END TO WAR.[111]

In 1945, Patton wrote "'Man is War' and we had better
remember that."[112]

The rage of the warrior was the key to victory. "The
fierce frenzy of hate and determination flashing from
bloodshot eyes squinting behind glittering steel is what
wins."[113] Further, Patton made no bones about the brutal
mission of the combat soldier. In a lecture entitled
"Mechanization" delivered in 1934, he said, "In the last
analysis the successful soldier is the courageous fighting
man--the killer."[114] Later, in a message to his troops on
Memorial Day, 1943, Patton declared, "We must remember
that victories are not gained solely by selfless devotion.
To conquer, we must destroy our enemies. We must not only
die gallantly; we must kill devastatingly."[115] In North
Africa, Sicily, and finally in France and Germany, Patton
conveyed the nuts and bolts of military training and
organization, and also conveyed the sacred quality of
battle and the warrior's mission. Much like a high priest
of battle pronouncing a blessing, he quoted to his troops
during the Battle of the Bulge from General Winfield
Scott's remarks at Chapultepec, "Brave soldiers, veterans,
you have been baptized in fire and blood and have come out
steel."[116]

Prior to a battle in North Africa with Rommel's forces,
Patton declared, "It seems my whole life has pointed to this
moment."[117] Conscious of his warrior mission and destiny
from childhood, he maintained faith even in times of personal difficulty: his failure to advance after his first
year at West Point, the post-World War I period, and his
various trials during World War II. Some of this faith
came from his father, who assured him in 1926 that he "would
be in the biggest war in history."[118] Even biological
factors entered into his destiny as a warrior, for great
warriors came from "fortuitous blending of complementary

blood lines at epochs where chance or destiny intervenes
to give scope to their peculiar abilities."[119] Patton believed that as an American, he was a member of the chosen
race, for "Americans, with arms in their hands, are fools
as well as cowards to surrender. If they fight on, they
will conquer."[120] When it came time for a warrior to die,
he was again the romantic warrior, wishing for a "quick and
painless death inflicted by the last bullet of the last
battle."[121]

In addition to ideas of personal destiny, Patton emphasized the national mission to his men. He believed
World War II was fought to defeat and destroy the Nazis and
preserve liberty in the world. Echoing John Winthrop's
sentiments several centuries before, Patton told his men in
Casablanca, "The eyes of the world are watching us; the
heart of America beats for us; God is with us. On our
victory depends the freedom or slavery of the human race.
We shall surely win."[122] The voice that speaks here is the
voice of the protector and savior, and surely Patton fits
the description offered by Frank Cavaioli, "In this war-
torn, fear-ridden century, Americans have come to regard
the professional military leader as a protector of American
civilization."[123]

Likewise, after the war, Patton spoke to his men,
saying, "Now that all or nearly all of you are returning to
civil life, I believe that I should continue to do my best
to instruct you how to save your lives and the lives of
your children."[124] This, however, would be impossible, for
Patton was a romantic warrior who was an anachronism in the
twentieth century. He was an ambivalent figure, as so many
warriors have been. He was prone to excess, was both chivalrous and brutal, and was, although a hero, also often
a dangerous figure in contemporary society.[125]

Curiously, like classic warriors, Patton was guilty
of three sins, which, if they did not strip him of martial
power, gradually reduced him to the innocuous role of a
general in charge of a paper army. His first and most
famous sin was the slapping incidents during World War II.
Patton slapped two soldiers in field hospitals because he
thought them cowards. They had no wounds, and to an
archaic warrior, battle fatigue was not an acceptable injury; it was proof of cowardice. Eisenhower reprimanded
him privately, but several months later, in November, 1943,
Drew Pearson broke the story in America. Suddenly the rage
of the warrior, adored when it was unleashed to kill Germans, became dangerous and excessive. Patton was called a
brute, and even compared with the Nazis. Senator Langer
inquired into possible pro-Vichy ties, and stories circu-
lated about other brutal actions of Patton, notably the
shooting of a donkey on a bridge and the killing of some
army polo ponies.[126] The Senate Military Affairs Committee,
considering his permanent promotion from colonel to major
general, withheld action.

Patton's second sin occurred several months before
the invasion of Europe. He was giving a speech in England
at the opening of a Welcome Club for American soldiers. In
the speech, he apparently stated that the Americans and
English were to rule the world.[127] By leaving out the
Russians, Patton caused an uproar, and his competence and
judgment as a combat leader were questioned because of
this sin. Eisenhower warned him again about his impulsive-
ness and was on the verge of relieving him. However,
General of the Army George Marshall told Eisenhower to make
his decision solely on the basis of the success of Operation
Overlord. Patton's warrior virtues saved him, barely one
month before the invasion.[128]

Patton's third sin took place when he was in charge of

the pacification and de-nazification program for part of
Germany. He longed to go and "kill Japs," for he was not
suited to this kind of work. Blumenson remarks, "Like
many military men, Patton was temperamentally and intel-
lectually little fitted for the task of supervising the
restoration of a bankrupt nation and grappling with political, social, and economic matters of enormous complexity."[129] The warrior rage now exploded in the realm of
the governing power. Patton became strongly anti-Semitic
in his writings and wanted to get the inevitable war with
Russia over while American forces were strong. He was
also slow in removing old Nazis from certain civil posts,
declaring that they were needed for a time to run things,
and that some Nazis were just like Democrats and Republi-
cans at home. The warrior whose mission it was to kill
Germans now was accused of being soft on Nazis, and
Eisenhower relieved him of his command of the Third Army,
thus relieving him of his martial functions.

     Portrayals of Patton during and following the war in
biography, magazines and newspapers display this ambivalence toward the warrior. It was hard to feel comfortable
with a man who said, "I...have been fighting all my life
and hope to continue to do so for the simple reason that I
love fighting."[130] Patton (often called "Old Blood and
Guts") was described as colorful, rough, demanding, complex,
arrogant, unique. None of the descriptions captured either
the man or the warrior. By the time of the Second World
War, Americans felt more comfortable with the "military
manager" who was linked to civilian society rather than the
traditional warrior. The latter appeared in novels of
World War II as a kind of neurotic, like Captain Queeg, or
General Hearn.[131] Novelists wrestled with the officer
"whose apparent fascism was disturbingly counterbalanced by
those qualities of competence and aplomb that draw an

instinctive response from the American mind.[132]   Aichinger
believes that novelists are uneasy with the ruthless capacity of the professional officer, yet also admire him as
a "manager of violence." American novelists, unlike their
British counterparts, hardly ever take the point of view
of the officer. Aichinger concludes, "the nature of the
officer and his function remained enigmas with which the
American novelist struggled unsuccessfully."[133]

     Perhaps in Patton's case, the difficulty of portrayal
was partly rooted in the person as much as his role as an
archaic warrior. Patton was a "romantic embodiment of
several antithetical values."[134] Codman speaks of the
"impossible" contradiction, Patton's aversion to suffering.
Frederick Ayer notes that Patton was torn between a belief
"that battle was romantic and chivalrous and brave, and the
realization that it was dirty, gut-wrenching, and very
dreadful...[this] was part of the inner conflict which tor-
mented him."[135] J. W. Montgomery wrote in *Christianity
Today* that Patton was a tragic hero, a noble warrior with a
tragic flaw. Montgomery believes that he appealed to
Americans because he was in many ways an old nineteenth
century Protestant figure. He was a man who loved success,
believed that Americans were uniquely fitted for success,
and had the ability to spread that success throughout the
world. In a world of constant conflict, we conquered in
the "wilderness of war," supported by a God of Battles who
was our leader.[136] Whether Patton was a tragic figure or
not, he did have a peculiar relationship with the people
of his country. He was both an esteemed protector and
savior, a warrior knowledgeable in the mysteries of war,
and he was also obsolete, for "the age of 'total wars' and
'total victories' for which he was made had already passed;
the age of crisis management had dawned."[137]

     Immensely popular shortly after the war, Patton "came

to symbolize the ruthless strength and will required to vanquish Hitler's evil."[138]   In June, 1945, he returned to the United States on leave and received a hero's welcome. *The New York Times* estimated that one million people welcomed him on his drive from the Bedford Army Base to downtown Boston, and that a million and a half welcomed Patton and Doolittle in Los Angeles.[139]   *The Los Angeles Times* gives a good description of Patton, the warrior returning from battle:

> His lacquered helmet bearing the four stars of
> a full general, the wise old eyes with just
> the hint of a tear in them, the battle jacket
> with its five rows of campaign ribbons and
> decorations, the whipcord cavalry breeches,
> the belt with a four starred revolver grip
> protruding from a holster, the riding crop
> and the burnished cavalry boots.[140]

There was a great celebration honoring Patton and Doolittle in the Coliseum with over one hundred thousand in attendance.   "The Coliseum was transformed with the magic of Hollywood into an arena where Patton's Third Army again spearheaded the thrust toward the Rhine, toward Berlin, toward victory in Europe."[141]   Through this simulated battle, the sacred and regenerative acts of the warrior were re-enacted, and the victory of good over evil witnessed by those who had been at home during the war.   The warrior witnessing the re-creation of his army's deeds said, "It was the nearest thing to a real battle I've ever seen.   And, God help me...I love it."[142]

Patton was injured in a car accident in Germany in December of 1945, and died of the injuries and further complications on December 24.   At his funeral two appropriate hymns were offered, "The Son of God Goes Forth to War," and "The Strife is Over, the Battle Won."   His image

as a protector and liberator persisted in Europe. The
British named a Rhine bridge for him; the French planned
a commemorative highway stretching along his battle route
from Normany to Metz; a street in Nancy, France, was named
after him; and in Luxembourg, commemorative stamps were
issued. In America, a memorial window was dedicated to
him in the Church of Our Savior in San Gabriel, California;
he received a posthumous Medal of Honor; proposals were
made for a Patton national monument; and memorial statues
were dedicated in several states. In 1972, a Patton Museum
was dedicated at Fort Knox. The memory was of the invincible warrior, terrible in battle, yet an honorable fighting
man.[143] Blumenson notes, "The belief in Patton's invincibility continued long after the war was over, even when
the United States became involved in Southeast Asia. If
only we had Patton, they said."[144]

The persistence of the Patton image lasted into
the middle 1970s. We cannot predict how the image will
fare, for as we shall see, the warrior image as savior
model and hero undergoes a radical change during the American involvement in Vietnam. It will not be until well
after our period that the Patton legend will find its
place in American thought. In the early seventies, however, Patton was still causing some controversy, and the
ambivalence appeared again. The movie *Patton*, released in
1970, drew conflicting reviews. Most critics praised
George C. Scott for his powerful portrayal of Patton. Yet
critics believed Patton appeared as either "the last
humanist warrior...in an age increasingly dominated by
warfare-technocrats, computers, and ABMs"[145] or as an
"archetypal military maniac, a Genghis Khan of the Western
front."[146] *Patton* was shown at West Point in 1970 and
"many of the cadets were enamored with the Patton image
and still believed that wars could be heroic conflicts

between men of honor."[147] The release of *Patton* during
the conflict in Vietnam suggests to me a nostalgic desire
to relive the triumphs of warriors who fought in wars
where good and evil were clearly apparent, and good
won.[148] Despite portrayals of his sins in the movie,
the popularity of *Patton* and *MacArthur* indicates the continued importance of the warrior figure for the general
public. For in war as in other symbolic cultural activ-
ities, nostalgia is more than a wistful memory of past
events or people. It is a desire to regain a period when,
in this case, war and the warrior were in a right "relation" with their enemy, when the ritual of battle pro-
ceeded according to clearly recognized classic motifs.

Patton, perhaps more openly than any American officer
of recent time, considered war as a sacred event and the
warrior as a sacred person. He was conscious both of his
role as a model and initiator and of his personal mission.
He was the most recent and possibly the last total warrior
in America.

CHAPTER TWO

THE RIFLEMEN IN AMERICA: PERCEPTIONS OF THE VOLUNTEER SOLDIER FROM LEXINGTON TO VERSAILLES

The European style of warfare in the seventeenth and eighteenth centuries was rigidly structured and limited to conflicts between professional armies. Each side was fully cognizant of the strength and tactics of the opposing side, and the orderly array of colorfully clad armies presented an aesthetically pleasing sight. The warriors were usually members of the nobility; thus, warfare was not only orderly, but carefully limited to members of a certain class.

The early American colonists presented a different picture. From the outset each community consisted of armed colonists and militia companies, necessary both for sustenance and protection. The military function never became associated with a class, nor was military action seen as a conflict of glory and conquest, but, as Washington said in 1775, "A defense of all that is dear and valuable in life."[1] Defensive warfare was the correct action of any honorable patriot. The warrior function was, as Millis puts it, "democratized." Both circumstances and geography led Americans to this alteration and democratization of military function. John Shy suggests:

> The colonies did not have the means to create a
> hard military shell, composed of specialists,
> that could protect the soft center of society,
> composed of the great mass of people, nor
> would such a shell have been effective against
> Indian tactics.[2]

Natural conditions in America produced a new type of
warrior, not merely a colonist who learned measures of
defense, but a type naturally ready to fight, instinctive
warriors born of wilderness America. Writing in 1877,
General John A. Logan, paying homage to the volunteer
soldier, saw him as a type of warrior new on the stage
of world history. Unlike the robot-like character of
European mercenaries who "moved in military grooves as
fixed as the orbit of the earth,"[3] the immortal host of
American volunteers became soldiers from principle and
conviction. "One day he was a civilian quietly following
the plow; upon the next he became a soldier, knowing no
fear and carrying a whole destroying battery in his trusty
rifle."[4] From Bunker Hill to Appomattox, the Volunteer
had protected American destiny with the sacred qualities
and animating power of personal courage, freedom, and
patriotism. The Volunteer was a new type of warrior because of these attributes. Logan declares:

> It is wholly safe to say that in his character
> of defender of right and justice, with no
> feature of the despoiler and oppressor, and
> in his attributes of lofty patriotism, of un-
> selfish, inflexible, and enduring courage; of
> patience under suffering, and of moderation
> under victory, and finally of effectiveness
> in the dread perils, the sudden surprises,
> and the capricious results of battle, he has
> had no faithful counterpart in any age of the
> world.[5]

Colonists looked to a new beginning in the new world,
freed from the contamination of a corrupt Europe. The
taint of classic warrior sins was left behind; each colonist became or could become a "new warrior," driven by God-
given virtues, yet whose mission was that of the

professional warrior: protection, salvation, and ultimate
sacrifice.[6]

Victor Hicken states, "The common denominator of
victory in each American war is the fighting American.
Though he has a nameless face in history, the circumstances of battle have given him a number of aliases."[7]
Whatever he <u>was</u> as a civilian, in warfare "He is a man
being shaped by the powerful discipline of war."[8] Even
the Volunteer, the "instant soldier," may follow what
Campbell calls the adventure of the hero: separation,
initiation, and return. War experience is experience
apart, though the experience no longer belongs to a class
apart.[9] The Volunteer could be mythologized in the public
mind as both the person and event become archetypal and
are identified with mythical action. We shall see the
symbolic nature of these "nameless faces" as perceived
in American public memory.

Part I

The Minutemen:

New World Warriors in America

One of the classical forms of the Volunteer is the
figure of the Minutemen, the "embattled farmers" of Lexington and Concord. Dixon Wecter sees them "In homespun,
with rifle and powder horn, simple, clear-eyed and brave--
the pride of an agrarian civilization."[10] The Minutemen
illustrate an early instance of mass heroism in American
wars.[11] They were the embodiment of the citizen-soldier,
portrayed by Ralph Waldo Emerson as "Poor farmers who came
up that day to defend their native soil [and] acted from
the simplest instincts."[12] They were new warriors fighting
in a new war, a war not only for colonial liberty, but for
the birth of universal freedom which would spring from the
new world. The Minuteman is characterized by Daniel
Chester French's famous statue "with resolute face, one
hand on the plow, the other grasping his flintlock, near
Concord Bridge."[13] Samuel Ripley Bartlett, in *Concord
Fight*, conveyed the sense of power emerging from the land:

> The country is aroused, and every home
> Pours out defenders for the sacred hearth;
> Heroes full-armed start breathing from the sod,
> And pools of blood mark out the homeward path.[14]

The heroes emerging from the land were praised by Henry
Archer, who wrote the "Volunteer Boys" in 1780 locating
the citizen-soldier in the guise of squire, lawyer, old
soldier, and the farmer:

> Here's to the farmer who dares to advance
> To harvest of honor with pleasure;
> Who with a slave the most skilful in France,
> A sword for his country would measure.
> Hence with cold fear,
> Heroes rise here;
> The ploughman is chang'd to the stout volunteer.[15]

The Minuteman is a versatile warrior, who in a "minute" can shed the pastoral life and assume the attributes of a warrior which are instinctive, if they are called into play.[16] All Americans could become warriors should the cause demand it. After the capture of Ticonderoga, Ethan Allen's men sang "The Green Mountaineer":

> We owe no allegiance, we bow to no throne,
> Our ruler is law and the law is our own--
> Our leaders themselves are our fellowmen,
> Who can handle the sword, or the scythe, or
>   the pen...[17]

The Minutemen were not only portrayed as natural soldiers in the poetry of the time, for earliest pictorial representations of Lexington and Concord show the Minutemen in civilian garb, scattered in various postures opposing the straight-lined, rigidly-erect British troops. With the addition of French's statue, Whitehill is accurate in saying, "For better or worse, our visual concept of the events of the nineteenth of April, 1775, are forever shaped by the stumbling efforts of a young Connecticut silversmith-turned engraver."[18]

The symbolic power of these natural soldiers was increased through several views of history that emerged in eighteenth century America. According to Stow Persons, the idea of historical progress emerged from a belief that the divine purpose revealed itself in events, moving the world

toward the millennium. A second view understood history
moving in cycles, societies thus moving from youth to
maturity to old age. America, according to this view,
was a youthful organism approaching maturity. Progress
was the "offspring of a union of the millennial hope with
the moralism of the cyclical view of history."[19] The
Revolution could be seen as a millennial event; the regeneration of the world was at hand, declared Tom Paine
in *Common Sense*. Those who saw history as cyclical rise
and fall perceived the passage of empire westward, to
America. This view of progress provided the warrior with
his mission, the advancement of the millennium and the
momentum for the proper course of empire. So could propa-
gandists of the Revolution stress, and be understood, the
"future glory of America which was the last asylum for
civil and religious liberty on the face of the earth, the
home of the brave and the land of the free."[20]

     That the colonists were God's agents in history was
not an idea new in revolutionary times. In the seventeenth
century, Edward Johnson wrote in *Wonder-Working Providence
of Sions Saviour in New England*:

> You shall with all diligence provide against
> the malignant adversaries of the truth, for
> assure yourselves the time is at hand wherein
> Antichrist will muster up all his forces, and
> make war with the people of God...and see
> that with all diligence you incourage every
> Soldier-like spirit among you, for the Lord
> intends to achieve greater matters by this
> little handfull than the World is aware of.[21]

     From the beginning, colonists fought what Ezra Stiles
would call "Wars of the Lord," and battle revealed the
direct action of God in the land and among the people.
Benjamin Spencer writes:

From the Revolution...one might glimpse
divinity itself; for the American victory
such patriots as Hazard, Belknap, Barrow,
and Dwight perceived the same providential
hand that Edward Johnson and Cotton Mather
in the previous century had seen in
cisatlantic affairs.[22]

War was translated in America from wars of conquest or
the sport of kings to sacred wars of purification, wars
of regeneration, which had universal import.[23] The
Revolution was not merely a war of national liberation,
but of a way of life against a way of death. Often Old
Testament images were employed, England seen treating the
colonies as Egypt and Babylon had treated Israel. The
loss of civil and religious liberty (feared mightily by
the colonists) and the increasingly strident action of
the British were seen as a form of slavery, a chaotic
condition. Philip Freneau expresses this:

If Britain conquers, help us, Heaven to fly!
Lend me your wings, ye ravens of the sky.
If Britain conquers,--we exist no more;
These lands shall redden with their children's gore,
Who turned to slaves, their fruitless toil shall moan--
Toils in these fields that once they called their own!
Haste! to your tents in fetters bring
These slaves that serve their tyrant of a king.
So just, so virtuous, is your cause, I say
Hell must prevail--if Britain wins the day![24]

As liberty calls for liberators, ultimate salvation
depends upon saviors, and the burden of both liberation
and salvation fell upon the warrior. As Zabdiel Adams
said in his sermon at Lexington on April 19, 1783,

It was the will of heaven, and agreeable to
his general plan that the principal part of

America should become separate and independent
of Britain. This separation <u>must</u> be brought
about, like most other events, by the agency
of men.[25]

Likewise, Robert Smith in 1781 declared, "The cause of
America is the cause of Christ."[26] The American Soldier's
Hymn expresses the image of the volunteer as crusader:

'Tis God that girds our armor on
And all our just designs fulfills;
Through him our feet can swiftly run,
And nimbly climb the steepest hills.

....

'Tis God that still supports our right,
His just revenge our foe pursues;
'Tis He that with resistless might,
Fierce nations to his power subdues.

Our universal safeguard He!
From Whom our lasting honors flow;
He made us great, and set us free
From our remorseless bloody foe.[27]

The colonial warrior was a protector and a savior of
a "remnant" community, struggling, as Abraham Keteltas
wrote in 1777, in the "cause of heaven against hell--of
the kind Parent of the universe, against the prince of
darkness, and the destroyer of the human race."[28] In
addition to his role as protector and savior, the colonial
warrior was seen as a kind of world-parent, responsible
for the form, for the birth of the new nation. In the
spring and summer of 1777, when Howe and Burgoyne had
powerful armies ready to split the colonies, a stanza was
added to the song, "The Times":

The times, it seems, are altered quite;
The scales are cracked, the sword is broke,

Right is now wrong, and wrong is right,
And justice is a standing joke.[29]

Echoing the inversion symbolism known in times of war in
traditional societies, this stanza illustrates the feeling
of chaos during the war. The form and birth of the new
world could be accomplished by warriors. James Russell
Lowell's "Ode Read at the One Hundredth Anniversary of
the Fight at Concord Bridge" imagined the feminine figure
of freedom found by the "Fathers," and

That a hundred years ago
Scattered here in blood and tears
Potent seeds wherefrom should grow
Gladness for a hundred years.

Sharing the martial potency of the Father of America, the
actions of the Minutemen give birth to a new form of being
in the world,

Yet the earth heard,
Nor ever hath forgot,
As on from startled throne to throne,
Where superstition sate or conscious wrong,
A shudder ran of some dreadful birth unknown.
Thrice venerable spot!
River more fateful than the Rubicon![30]

Samuel Ripley Bartlett expresses similar feelings,

Here still in Concord sleeps the ancient force;
Here rebels wild, fanatics fierce, we find,
Who war against a tyranny more dread
Than that of old--the thraldom of the mind.
What! The old spirit dead? No, no!--it lives.
Here o'er the stream today first shots are heard,
First blows are struck, for freedom, truth, reform;
And ours the noblest thought, the truest word.
Sons of a race of preachers, hail to thee!
Thy congregation is the world; thy sermons ring

Deep in the inmost souls of all thy flock;
They strike the holiest chord, the truest string.
Hail, home of Rebels! birthplace of Revolt!
By thee is freedom's banner wide unfurled;
Thine the command to march to glory on,
And from thy hand 'the shot heard round the
world.'[31]

That the Minutemen gave birth to a new world at the
battles of Lexington and Concord was noted in 1847 by
Benson Lossing. He said the battles were the "first labor
pains that attended the Birth of a nation, now still in
its infancy, but powerful as a youthful Hercules."[32] As
Catherine Albanese suggests, the actions of the Revolution
molded the patriots from a traditional people into a
charismatic people. The events surrounding them were
bringing into being a new world, and a number of these
primal events and creative people would be considered as
a part of sacred and creative time. The Volunteer warrior
was a crucial element in the creation story of the new
nation.

The valor of the warrior was seen most clearly in the
sacrifice he willingly made for his country. The regenerative death of the Volunteer was celebrated as well as the
glorious death of the Chevalier. In Concord, the Soldier's
Monument was dedicated in 1867 with the following inscription on one side:

Their names shall live. They shall teach those
who come after us lessons of patriotism and
courage. The children of the village shall
spell them out, and learn them by heart. The
young men shall be trained by them in the
shining ways of disinterested virtue; and the
cowardly and selfish shall always feel their
rebuke.[33]

The Minutemen who gained freedom through their sacrifice,
and the Civil War soldiers who preserved it, were models
of common virtue, common courage, and American patriotic
death. That the blood of the patriots was regenerative
was a common theme. Remarks at the Monument's dedication
illustrate this well: "The blood of your people, shed
that day, has proved the nourishment of patriotism and
the blight of treason."[34] America was twice baptized in
regenerative blood, and the site of sacred beginnings was
also a suitable place for a monument to those who were
sacrificed for its preservation during the Civil War. An
ode read at the dedication stated, "Beneath the shadow of
the elm, where ninety years ago old Concord's rustic
heroes met face to face a foreign foe, we come to consecrate this Stone to heroes of today, who perished in a
holy cause as gallantly as they."[35] It was not only in
later memory that regenerative sacrifice was portrayed;
on April 19, 1776, Rev. Jonas Clarke said, "They bleed,
they die, not in their own cause only; but in the cause
of this whole people--in the cause of God, their country
and posterity."[36] Also in 1776, an unknown poet wrote a
series of poems set to the tune of a sailor's song. Part
of the last stanza reads:

> With loyalty, LIBERTY let us entwine,
> Our blood shall for both, flow as free as our wine.
> Let us set an example, what all men should be,
> And a toast give the world, Here's to those [who]
> dare to be free.[37]

Similar in theme is the message of the Captain Parker
Monument in Lexington, dedicated to the first martyrs of
the Revolution:

> Who fell on this field, the first victims to the
> sword of British tyranny and oppression on the
> morning of the ever memorable nineteenth of April

an. dom. 1775. 'The Die Was Cast.' The blood
of these martyr's [sic] in the cause of God and
their country was the Cement of the union of
these states, then colonies, and gave the spring
to the spirit.[38]

The cause of liberty was a cause worthy of heroic
death, and the death of the warrior was made meaningful
by the life his sacrifice gave to the cause. Nathaniel
Niles's poem, "The American Hero," written in 1775, conveyed defiance and courage in the face of war:

> Life for my country and the cause of freedom,
> Is but a cheap price for a worm to part with:
> And if preserved in so great a contest,
> Life is redoubled.[39]

Samuel Ripley Bartlett expresses the belief that

> Each heart agrees to perish, if it must:
> Martyr in such a cause, who cannot feel
> It is a blessed privilege to die.[40]

The theme of regenerative sacrifice is a persistent
one in American life, and we will meet it in each war
period we examine. It spread into the nooks and crannies
of the American mind through the ritual remembrance of the
sacred places and events of the Revolution, through poetry,
sculpture and other artistic forms. The remembrance of
the meaning of Revolutionary sacrifice was found even in
dime novels of the Revolution, popular in the late nineteenth century. Many of them suggested that war was inevitable. A heroine observes that

> In all history...it is recorded that the price
> of liberty is blood and never is this envied
> boon yielded by the grace of rulers--it is
> wrested by the sword, and so fatal is usually
> the struggle that the sweets which freedom gives
> to life are rarely enjoyed by those who win them.[41]

In traditional western painting, the Death of Christ
provided the model for all visual images of sacrifice.
During the Enlightenment, the hero (often a military hero)
replaced Christ as the principal actor in history. Irma
Jaffe discusses form and theme in some heroic representations in the eighteenth century and suggests that "The
theme of self-sacrifice in the cause of patriotism or
truth is stated, like a religious oration, so that the
image assumes the character of ritual re-enactment."[42]
Doolittle's engravings and John Trumbull's paintings,
both contemporary to the creative events and descriptive
of them, keep before us the heroism of the actors in the
conflict. Yet Jaffe suggests that Trumbull's paintings
did not become part of symbolic remembrance until the
American imagination had developed further in the nineteenth century.

For the generation of the Revolution, the myth of the
Revolution and the adventures of symbolic figures were
presented in dramas of the Revolution. Read more than
acted out, these plays helped Americans clarify the ideals
they were fighting for. Several of these pamphlet plays
were illustrative of martial themes and noble warriors,
and though the martyred figures in each are not common
soldiers, but leaders, it is not hard to imagine that the
lesson in warrior virtue and mission preserved by these
officers would apply to any of the volunteers of the
Revolution.

Hugh Henry Brackenridge, teacher, preacher, and Con-
tinental Army chaplain, wrote both *The Death of General
Montgomery* and *The Battle of Bunker's Hill*. *The Death
of General Montgomery*, published in 1777, was originally
written for students at the Academy in Somerset County,
Maryland. Norman Philbrick suggests that it was acted
out at other schools, possibly even at Harvard.[43] A

eulogy of the dead heroes of the Revolution, the action
takes place on December 31, 1775, and January 1, 1776,
on the Plains of Abraham, before Quebec. General Montgomery has a foreboding of death and says to his aide-de-
camp:

> Say not young soldier, that thy life was short,
> In the first bloom, of manhood, swift cut off.
> All things are mortal, but the warrior's fame;
> This lives eternal, in the mouths of men.[44]

Montgomery is fighting on sacred ground, hallowed by
General Wolfe in 1759. After Montgomery's death, Wolfe's
ghost appears and wonders if his sacrifice is futile:

> False council'd king and venal Parliament!
> Have I then fought, and was my life blood shed,
> To raise your power to this ambitious height,
> Disdainful height, of framing laws to bind,
> In cases whatsoever, free born men,
> Of the same lineage, name, and quality.[45]

Wolfe then sees the strife and bloodshed as the will of
God, necessary for the colonists' separation from Britain:

> Yes, from your death shall amply vegetate,
> The ground idea of an empire new...[46]

In another play, *The Fall of British Tyranny*, General
Putnam cries upon learning of the death of Montgomery:

> Who can die a more glorious, a more honourable
> death than in their country's cause--let it
> redouble our ardour, and kindle a noble
> emulation in our breasts--let each American
> be determined to conquer or die in a righteous
> cause.[47]

For those who choose a glorious death,

> Posterity will crown the urn of the patriot who
> consecrates his talents to virtue and freedom;
> his name shall not be forgot; his reputation

shall bloom with unfading verdure, while the
name of the tyrant, like his vile body, shall
moulder into dust. [48]

Dealing with the sacrifice of Dr. Joseph Warren on Bunker
Hill, the unknown author of *The Fall* draws together important motifs:

Eager the patriot meets his desperate foe
With full intent to give the fatal blow;
The cause he fights for animates him high,
His wife, his children and his liberty:
For these he conquers, or more bravely dies,
And yields himself a willing sacrifice. [49]

More than just entertainment, these plays presented
the living myth of the Revolution to Americans; they were
the ritual re-enactment of the history these people had
made, and were still making. The sacrifice and hardships
undergone by these men were not merely typical of traditional warriors, for colonial warriors were New World
warriors. The bravery and virtue of these men had the
powerful effect of traditional warriors, but these soldiers
did not have the sins of the traditional warrior. Their
rage, like that of Washington, was "cool." [50] Thus, we see
the continuity and the transformation of traditional
symbols of war. The warrior continues to be the actor who
gives the land new life by his "harvest" of death (either
his or the enemy's), yet the American warrior is a new
warrior, consciously portrayed as having shed the dangerous and disruptive martial rage of his ancestors.
Brackenridge portrays this in *The Battle of Bunker's Hill*.
In the first scene, General Burgoyne complains to General
Gage that the British being confined in Boston by the
rebels are

A veteran army pent,
In the enclosure of so small a space,

By a disorder'd herd, untaught, unofficer'd.
The British should drive back this rabble
    to Alleghany hills,
    In woody valleys, or on mountain tops,
    To mix with wolves and kindred savages.
Gage answers,
    This mighty paradox, will soon dissolve.
    Hear first, Burgoyne, the valor of these men,
    Fir'd with the zeal, of fiercest liberty,
    Nor fear of death, so terrible to all,
    Can stop their rage.[51]

The holy cause of the American warrior was a vital part
of confidence in victory. As for the ancient Israelites,
moral status as well as physical prowess was crucial. Part
of this unique moral condition was righteous motivation for
battle. Edward Everett echoes this theme in 1835, noting
that homage is paid to those called not by the "ambition
of power, the hope of promotion, nor the temptation of
gain, but a plain, instinctive sense of patriotic duty."[52]
Conversely, the British actions were like those of "sav-
ages." Shortly after the battles of Lexington and Concord,
the *Essex Gazette* reported that

    We have the pleasure to say, that,
    notwithstanding the highest Provocations
    given by the Enemy, not one Instance of
    Cruelty, that we have heard of, was
    committed by our victorious Militia;
    but listening to the merciful dictates
    of the Christian Religion, they "Breathed
    higher Sentiments of Humanity."[53]

Likewise, in a sermon given in 1781, James Powers stated
that American soldiers should treat the enemy dispassion-
ately and "demonstrate the Godliness of their cause by the
goodness of their courage...engaged in a just defensive

war [the soldier] is the Minister of God."[54]   Philip
Freneau stressed the balance and humanity of the soldier
when he wrote:

> While others kindle into martial rage
> Whom fierce ambition urge to engage,
> An iron race, by angry heav'n design'd
> To conquer first, and then enslave mankind;
> Here, chiefs and heroes more humane we see,
> They venture life, that others may be free.[55]

The poets, ministers, and artists of the Revolutionary
period set a pattern of understanding and visualizing
American war experience and the American warrior. Every
cosmogony creates new heroic models, and the impact of
these models evokes a nostalgia for the creative, powerful,
heroic and sacrificial acts of Revolutionary beginnings.
Ralph Waldo Emerson expressed this collective longing in
his "Historical Discourse" at Concord in 1835: "Every
moment carries us farther from the two great epochs of
public principle--the planting, and the revolution of the
colony."[56]

The Minutemen and other heroes were clearly models
for later Americans looking to the creative power of past
events for guidance. On the eve of the Civil War, the
South looked to the Revolution as a model for current
action.[57]   William L. Yancey of Alabama thought that the
South should "produce spirit enough...to call forth a
Lexington, to fight a Bunker's Hill."[58]   Harold Schultz
reports that in addition to the rise of Southern martial
spirit, as evidenced by the growth of rifle clubs and
rifle companies, a group called the Minutemen organized
to march on Washington and prevent Lincoln's inauguration.
These warriors would, like the original Minutemen, protect
their homeland from chaos and form a new republic. Schultz
outlines the temper which helped form this group:

Newspapers and speakers at political meetings
pictured the social horrors of abolition, the
economic loss that would result from Republican
rule...the glorious prospects in store for the
people in a new slaveholding Republic.[59]

Revolutionary tales were popular among the soldiers of
the Civil War, who avidly read Beadle's dime novels and
other similar series of novels.[60] These dime novels were
popular in the mid to late nineteenth century, and even
after their heyday a series began in 1901, entitled "The
Liberty Boys of '76," and continued until 1925. Leithead
calls it

American history in story and picture, the
action centering, as the publisher's blurb
puts it, in a "Brave band of American youths
who were always ready and willing to imperil
their lives for the sake of helping along
the gallant cause of Independence."[61]

The model of the Minuteman and the power of the
formative martial events of the Revolution are adaptable
to any war in our history. The model of the Revolution
in the imaginations of the soldiers of the Civil War
linked them in the struggle "to save the independence
that had been won by their forefathers at Concord, Lexington, Saratoga, and Yorktown."[62] Ernest Peixoto,
visiting battlefields of the Revolution during World War I,
wrote:

Now that a new wave of patriotism has swept
over the land and created a revival of the
"American spirit"...the moment seems peculiarly
propitious to awake anew the story of the deeds
of our ancestors--the men who risked their
lives and staked their all to found our nation
and make its ideals possible.[63]

The New York Tribune found a new spirit of Concord in the
gathering of Concord men to fight in World War I:

> In the broad avenue at the foot of the hill...
> he will see a new Concord company, a new
> gathering of young men, not alone acting as
> a guard of honor...but preparing for the
> service which may yet be asked of them. The
> Spirit of Concord is not merely a glorious
> memory--it is a living fact. Of five gener-
> ations that separate April 1775 from May
> 1898, three have marched. From father to
> son there has been handed down not a tra-
> dition but an example, there has been trans-
> mitted the lesson that life, liberty, and
> the pursuit of happiness, are not easy
> inheritances...but rather that they are
> the fruits of an ancient sacrifice, to
> preserve which there is demanded of Concord
> boys a service, and there may be demanded a
> future sacrifice as well. This is the spirit
> of Concord and it lives.[64]

The pervasiveness of the Minuteman model finds expression not only in times of war. In 1932 and 1933, the
Farmers Holiday Association in the corn belt publicized
farm grievances, blocked highways, dumped milk, and defied
various court orders. A violent sub-group in northwest
Iowa called themselves the "Modern Seventy-Sixers." In
our own time, the modern Minutemen are preparing for the
eschatological battle against the Communists, who have
replaced the British as the enemy. The objectives of the
Minutemen are to "prepare for the day when Americans will
once again fight in the streets for their lives and their
liberty."[65] These modern warriors scoff at bomb shelters
or other forms of refuge, believing that American tradition

calls them to "stand up and fight." Harry Jones, Jr.
reports that at a convention of the Patriotic Party,
Robert DePugh, head of the Minutemen, gave an emotional
address, and soon he had "traveled back to 1776 [sic]
and Captain Parker of the original Minutemen was on stage
telling his men to hold the line, but if there was to be
a fight, let it be here."[66]

As the Minuteman became a model for future American
warriors, the American Revolution became a model for the
perceived course of American wars. John Shy writes that

> The American Revolutionary war...became in the
> national memory and imagination paradigmatic
> of how America saved itself from being like,
> and part of, Europe and Europe's problems.
> The Revolutionary story of defeat (Bunker
> Hill), near collapse (Long Island and New
> Jersey), desperate hope (Trenton, Princeton,
> and Saratoga), endurance (Brandywine, Valley
> Forge, and the loss of the whole deep South),
> and ultimately victory (Yorktown) has the same
> rhythmic structure apparent in both the Seven
> Years' War and the War of 1812. The Revol-
> utionary War repeated and permanently implanted
> in national consciousness the patterned exper-
> ience of the last and greatest colonial war,
> and the War of 1812 reinforced that collective,
> enduring perception of what a major armed
> struggle must--and ought to--look like.[67]

The Revolution stands symbolically as both sacred and
creative event in the continuing mission of America and
gives birth to a new form of freedom, brought forth out of
conflict by the saviors and protectors, the Volunteers,
the Minutemen. Perhaps Ralph Waldo Emerson best expresses
the awe-fullness with which these men are remembered:

You are set apart, and forever, for the
esteem and gratitude of the human race.
To you belongs a better badge than stars
and ribbons. This prospering country is
your ornament; and this expanding nation
is multiplying your praise with millions
of tongues.[68]

The prospering country rose, according to a Fourth
of July speech in 1839, on the arch of the British empire
in the West. W. S. Hammond says:

When the keystone of the arch...was with-
drawn, the entire arch sank, a mass of
shapeless ruins. The land of freedom arose
in its stead. The articles of confederation
was the ark, ordained to bear in safety the
liberties, the hopes and glorious destinies
of an enfranchised race, over the heaving
flood of Revolution. When it landed the
tempest-driven voyagers on the Ararat of
the new-world, and the olive leaf was received from the messenger of peace, it had
fulfilled the great ends for which it was
designed in the economy of the Supreme Ruler
of nations.[69]

Part II

Johnny Reb and Billy Yank:

Redemptive Warriors of Twice-Born America

America had risen new-born, divinely ordained for her
mission of freedom. The promise and potential of the West
revealed a hope for a new Eden, and the fervor of reform
movements would show Americans' willingness to lend a hand
in building the kingdom of God, in ushering in the millennium. Yet, as Ernest Tuveson points out, the optimism of
the new nation was mixed with a sense of apocalyptic drama.
The nation, born of strife, would have to be purified, reborn, before the millennium would be at hand. Thus, the
Civil War was "more than just another war about a moral
issue, even if a great one; it was the crisis of mankind,
even if only one nation was involved."[70] The war would be
one of purification, the defeat of Antichrist and the
powers of evil.

America, in addition to being the regenerative hope
of mankind, was the site of the crucial conflicts of mankind. Gail Hamilton, writing in the *Atlantic Monthly* in
1863, said, "Three hundred years ago a world was unfolded
for the battle-ground." The war would solve not only a
national problem, she says, but

> It is the question of the world that we have
> been set to answer. In the great conflict of
> ages, the long strife between right and wrong,
> between progress and sluggardy, through the
> Providence of God we are placed in the van-
> guard.[71]

The Civil War, like World War I, was seen as the final
battle for freedom. We were motivated in these wars
largely by an apocalyptic view of history.[72]   This view
molded a belief that the "Golden Age must be won in a
struggle supernatural in issue and direction, even if
conducted on the national plane."[73]

The struggle for the Golden Age was a struggle of
principle. An editorial in the *Century Illustrated
Monthly Magazine* of 1889 stated, "Theoretically, wars in
modern times have a moral purpose, and almost always
there is a moral issue involved in every great strife."[74]
Both sides felt that they were fighting a moral war,
qualitatively different from the wars of other nations.
Bell Wiley writes:

> Billy Yank was fighting to subdue a revolt
> against national authority and to free the
> slaves; Johnny Reb was fighting to establish
> an independent government, but he was also
> fighting for a peculiar way of life, for the
> defense of his home, and as it often seemed
> to him, for life itself.[75]

Since the South believed it was fighting for justice, its
righteousness was "somehow proved by account of the energy
with which (its cause) was pursued."[76]   After the war, the
nationalistic spirit helped soldiers on both sides to
emerge as principled American fighting men.   John Fox, Jr.,
in *The Little Shepherd of Kingdom Come*, wrote, "Every man
on both sides was right--who did his duty."[77]   Writing in
his poem *Gettysburg*, George Edward Vickers says:

> 'Tis not a fight where alien standards seek
> A place to glorify the pride of conquest:
>   the life streams
> Of blue and gray alike the same source bespeak,
> Though kinship defers to duty, and there seems

No common tie 'twixt those who yon mad combat wage;
How close they were in former days a century's
    thrilling annals tell.[78]

The new American soldier was found on both sides of
the struggle. According to Elbridge S. Brooks, "The War
for Secession was a revelation to the world of American
courage and American endurance."[79] Likewise, John H.
Wallace suggested that "The world has been convinced that
no opposing armies could have displayed such courage and
valor unless a principle precious to manly hearts was involved."[80] Rev. George H. Corey's description of Civil
War impetus could be applied to many American wars:

> We made war the instrument of justice, the
> herald of liberty. When the war is waged
> for a principle, for benign institutions,
> then the war-wave rolls with the impetus
> and weight of an idea and the energy of
> moral enthusiasm.[81]

Both sides expected a new condition of national life to
emerge out of the war: the North, reborn and purified
from the sin of slavery, and the South, a nation free
from the oppression of the North.

Walter Millis suggests that something else was born
out of the Civil War experience: a new age of violence.
The ideas of glory present at Bull Run when men still
fought face to face were quite different from the trench
warfare around Petersburg in 1864. Gradually personal
combat became less important, and mechanized warfare,
"total" war (Sherman's march to the sea, for example),
was predominant.[82] Thus, the Civil War marks a crucial
shift in the manner of war and in ideas of warrior
heroism. Yet, even after such a shift, old ideas of
martial glory persisted tenaciously. According to Robert
Penn Warren, the Civil War was both transitional and

foreshadowed future American wars:

> Between 1861 and 1865 America learned how
> to mobilize, equip, and deploy enormous
> military forces--and learned the will and
> confidence to do so. For most importantly,
> America emerged with a confirmed sense of
> destiny, the old sense of destiny confirmed
> by a new sense of military and economic
> competence. The Civil War was the secret
> school for 1917-18 and 1941-45.[83]

The change in warfare brought with it a change in
perceptions of the war. W. Fletcher Thompson suggests
there was a shift in the mode and the sense of perception:
"Artists themselves were encumbered with an antiquated
artistic concept of war that sacrificed realism for
stereotyped heroics....They were due for a rather rude
shock."[84] The various groups of artists were not prepared for the disaster at Bull Run and found that traditional images did not capture the realism of battle.
Henri Lovie, one of the gifted sketch artists of the war,
was the first to publish his sketches of dismembered
bodies. His realistic sketches of the horror of war at
Shiloh signaled the end of innocent idealism about war
for western writers and brought war home in a new way to
readers of popular magazines. As sketch artists were
turning toward realism, the development of photography
made war "real" in a different way. Led by Matthew Brady,
photographers took shots of the carnage and utter desolation of the battlefield. In addition to Brady's work,
Alexander Gardner's photographs concentrated almost totally
on the dead and on the horrors of war. His photographs of
the Antietam battlefield in 1862 before burial was com-
pleted made a great impression on the public.

Bell Wiley suggests that combat in the Civil War was

an "intimate elemental thing, with the infantry bearing
the brunt, and artillery and horse-mounted cavalry
fighting, normally in rear support."[85]   While this was
true throughout the war, notably in the first three
years, the Civil War was becoming a mechanized war, and
combat was undergoing change.   In his poem, "A Utilitar-
ian View of the Monitor's Fight," Herman Melville says:

> Hail to victory without the gaud
> Of glory; zeal that needs no fans
> Of banners; plain mechanic power
> Plied cogently in War now placed--
>   Where War belongs--
> Among the trades and artisans.
> ....
> War yet shall be, and to the end;
> But war-paint shows the streaks of weather;
> War yet shall be, but warriors
> Are now but operatives; War's made
>   Less grand than Peace,
> And a singe runs through lace and feather.[86]

Melville saw the transformation from wooden ships to iron-
clads as symbolic of the shift to the machine age, and
part of the dream of a pastoral American republic was
gone:

> And the Iron Dome,
> Stronger for stress and strain
> Fling her huge shadow athwart the main;
> But the Founder's dream shall flee.[87]

The mechanization of warfare supplied armies with
weapons capable of mass destruction, but commanders were
often tied to traditional views of combat.   The infantry
charges at Fredericksburg, Cold Harbor, and Pickett's
famous charge at Gettysburg showed the futility of this
kind of warfare.   Europeans would apparently not learn

this lesson until the terrible slaughter on the western
front in World War I. The emergence of mass death raised
the question of the meaning of the warrior's sacrifice.
The individual deaths of John Brown, Elijah Lovejoy, and
Uncle Tom had meaning, but could the thousands of soldiers
slaughtered on one battlefield bear witness to the power
of redemptive sacrifice, or bear witness to the utter
futility of dying in battle? Walt Whitman's encounter
with suffering "provided the most dramatic illustration
of how the ante-bellum sensibility confronted the horrors
of the Civil War."[88] Whitman could speak of the death of
individual soldiers, but could not give "formal expression
to his sense of the war as an anonymous 'slaughterhouse,'
not only because his readers could not assimilate such an
insight, but because, ultimately, he could not accept it
himself."[89]

Like Whitman, Mark Twain sensed the crisis of meaning
involved with mass death. In *A Connecticut Yankee in King
Arthur's Court*, published in 1889, Twain shows a single
Yankee armed with gatling guns, mines, etc., destroying
the knights of Arthur and putting an end to chivalry. As
in the Civil War, the dead

> did not exist as individuals, but merely as
> homogeneous protoplasm, with alloys of iron
> and buttons. The chivalry of medieval Britain
> and of nineteenth-century America were both
> swept away by the machine of war 'like chaff
> before the gale.'[90]

Perhaps the interpretations of mass death by Louisa May
Alcott in *Hospital Sketches* and the stories of Ambrose
Bierce illustrate the "most meaning" that writers of the
period were able to conceive. Alcott wrote, "When the
great muster roll was called, these nameless men might be
promoted above many whose tall monuments recall the barren

honors they have won."[91] The war stories of Ambrose
Bierce describe his lost illusions. In his descriptions
of the dead,Bierce believed that

> existence was an essentially destructive,
> rather than creative, process, not only
> because it led to the meaninglessness of
> death, but also because experience taught
> the futility of all human hopes and human
> ideals. Once such illusions have been
> systematically exposed, what remains is
> the paralyzing horror at the heart of
> things.[92]

These contrasting images of the meaning of mass
death are present in each World War and in our latest
conflict in Vietnam. The use of nuclear weapons carries
the question of meaning one step further. Not only do we
have to try to give meaning to _mass_ death, we have to try
to understand the meaning of extinction.

Images of sacrifice, heroism and glory were not
abandoned by most, but the American imagination had yet
to develop ways of satisfactorily mythologizing persons
and events connected with the new kind of warfare. As
Daniel Aaron notes, "It took time...to adjust to the enormous scale of the War and to tally its material and human
cost. Traditional notions of heroism had to be modified
when instruments of precision killed by remote control."[93]
The new idea of heroism was aptly expressed by Connecticut
novelist John W. Deforest, "'The man who does not dread to
die or to be mutilated is a lunatic'--but 'the man who,
dreading these things, still faces them for the sake of
duty and honor is a hero.'"[94]

Images of mass death brought images of mass heroism.
The heroic soldier was now one who stoically accepted his
duty and endured the horrors of war. The common soldier,

often before seen as a crusader, was also seen as a man of
discipline "doing his job."[95] Many stressed the uniqueness of the volunteer soldier and portrayed him as a descendant of the men of '76. Speaking in an era when both
sides were praised for their deeds, John C. Ridpath says
that the Confederate soldier "rose from the earth when the
tocsin was sounded, and went forth to battle with the same
motives and same heroic devotion as did the Boys in Blue."[96]
He portrays the citizen-soldiers as balanced warriors,
suggesting that "even in the pitch of battle and the license
of the camp they kept their hearts void of offense towards
man and God."[97] Further, like the Minutemen before them,
once the war was over the soldiers "lost at once [their]
war-like character and melted away among the people from
whom [they] had sprung."[98]

Like Emerson's Minutemen, these warriors were often
perceived as "set apart" by their battle experience.[99]
Ambrose Bierce rose from an eighteen-year-old enlistee to
major, and fought in many campaigns. He believed that
veteran soldiers were different from civilians. They were

> hardened and impenitent man-killers to whom
> death in its awfullest forms is a fact familiar
> to their every day observation; who sleep on
> hills trembling with the thunder of great guns,
> dine in the midst of streaming missiles, and
> play cards among the dead faces of their
> dearest friends.[100]

Diaries and letters of Civil War soldiers illustrate the
initiatory process in combat. A Confederate soldier at
Bull Run comments on the initial fear and nervousness generally felt before a battle, and then "'with your first
shot you become a new man.'"[101] Another soldier comments
on the ecstasy of battle, "'There is something grand about
it--it is magnificent....I feel elated as borne along with

the tide of battle.'"[102] Bruce Catton, remembering old
veterans he knew in his childhood, observes that

> These old gentlemen, drowsing out the greater
> part of their lives in the backwoods, had
> once been lifted beyond themselves by an ex-
> perience which perhaps was all the more
> significant because it was imperfectly under-
> stood.[103]

The apocalyptic view of history molded the war into
an act of purification, a cleansing war. America was guilty
of sins against God and his order, and only a blood sacrifice would be regenerative. In an 1861 sermon, Octavius B.
Frothingham saw soldiers' death as Christ-like:

> Christ was 'a regenerative principle...
> embodied in the form of a young Galilean,'
> and the 'deaths of noble young men in
> battle...are the snapping open of so many
> brave caskets, and the dropping into the
> fruitful soil of humanity of the quick
> seeds of a new national and human life.'[104]

Cyrus Bartol understood the war as purgatory for the Union.
He offered a prayer that

> this American community of States may ex-
> perience from the hand of God a remission
> by virtue of the shedding of so much blood.
> Innocent blood, indeed, it has often been;
> but innocent blood, willingly poured out
> by the lovers of country and mankind for
> others' deliverance--how effectual it is
> to the awakening of all that is holy in
> the human soul![105]

In a memorial service dedicated to an officer who fell at
Vicksburg, the biblical text was John 15:13, and the minister asked that as Jesus died to regenerate mankind,

Americans died for their country, "Who, next to our Savior, is our greatest benefactor and friend?" In eulogizing the fallen Captain, the minister said:

> He has fallen in the performance of a great
> and solemn duty....These trees and hills will
> be clothed a fresher green; these homes will
> be more secure, and better worth living in;
> these schools will be filled with a freer and
> more docile succession of pupils....A nobler
> race will walk our streets for generations
> yet to come...because of the life which he
> and others like him have lived, and the death
> which they have died.[106]

In 1865, Horace Bushnell gave his famous address at Yale saying, "According to the true economy of the world, so many of its grandest and most noble benefits have and are to have a tragic origin, and to come as outgrowths only of blood."[107] In an oration delivered in 1866, John Davidson observed, "The flag of our nation flaps its pure folds in every breeze, not torn and tattered by war, but purified by the death of our heroes and cleansed in their blood, from the smallest taint of the dark pollution of slavery."[108]

The sacrifice of soldiers was the price for the continued life of the country. Gail Hamilton said that though death is natural, "only once in a generation comes the sacrificial year, the year of jubilee, when men march lovingly to meet their fate and die for a nation's life."[109] Walt Whitman had a similar, if more sophisticated, idea. He understood the contradictions of war as part of a spiritual dialectic. The sacrifice of a soldier was part of a communal sacrifice, and each individual lived on in the renewed existence of the nation. Thus, in addition to renewing the life of the country, the warrior fulfills his life. He is immortal in either transcendent life or in the

fame his sacrifice has brought him. Mrs. George Pickett,
wife of the famous Confederate general, wrote:

> With those names that are emblazoned upon
> the pages of history go the spirit and the
> force and the courage of the thousands of
> nameless heroes who reached the last great
> height of sacrifice and left the memory of
> the private soldier as a priceless legacy
> to their country.[110]

Cornelia J. Jordan, in *Echoes From the Cannon*, commented:

> Forget them? No, never while honor
> And truth and devotion shall shed
> The light of a halo immortal
> Round the brows of our patriot dead.[111]

Likewise, William Barrows declared during the war, "At
every mound where a soldier rests, the American citizen
and the historian of the preserved Union shall read this
inscription: HE SAVED THE REPUBLIC. Let them rest in
their beds of honor. Their names and their memory are
safe."[112]

In *War Poems of the Southern Confederacy*, there is a
picture of the Confederate monument dedicated to the memory
of North Carolina soldiers. The monument portrays a dying
soldier crowned by fame. Whether gaining immortality for
self or paying for the regeneration of the nation through
his blood, the soldier was often portrayed as eager to make
the sacrifice. Edward Bellamy gives this description of a
regiment going to war:

> The imposing mass, with its rhythmic movement,
> gives the impression of a single organism....An
> afflatus of heroism given forth by this host of
> self-devoted men communicates itself to the most
> stolid spectators....Eyes glaze with rapturous
> tears as they rest upon the flag. There is a

thrill of voluptuous sweetness in the thought
of dying for it. Life seems of value only as
it gives the poorest something to sacrifice.
It is dying that makes the glory of the world,
and all other employments seem but idle while
the regiment passes.[113]

Several important images emerge from this material.
Contrary to traditional belief that America has viewed
history progressively, we are able to detect what Eliade
calls the urge for a "universal conflagration." The new
world will emerge only after the old is destroyed by the
Civil War. Eliade states, "The basic idea is that, to
attain a higher mode of existence, gestation and birth must
be repeated."[114] As the Revolutionary War brought America
into being, the Civil War will allow her to begin again;
America will be reborn through war. Rev. Milton Badger,
welcoming the troops home in Madison, Connecticut, on July 4,
1865, said as much in his statement, "We go back...and con-
nect the beginning with the end--the birth of the nation
with its second birth."[115] The second birth began with the
events at Fort Sumter. Echoing a popular feeling, Elbridge
J. Cutler declared in his Phi Beta Kappa poem at Harvard in
1861:

Then a red flash, like lightning,
Across the darkness broke,
And, with a voice that shook the land,
The Guns of Sumter spoke:
Wake, sons of heroes, wake!
The age of heroes dawns again,
Truth takes in hand her ancient sword
And calls her loyal men,
Lo, brightly o'er the breaking day
Shines freedom's holy star!
Peace cannot cure the sickly time--
All hail the healer, war![116]

As the Civil War brought memories of the first birth of
America, it brought adherence to the powerful models of the
Revolution. Henry Adams recalled his youth in the 1850s in
Boston, "'One lived in the atmosphere of the Stamp Act, the
Tea Tax, and the Boston Massacre.'"[117] Wendell Phillips be-
lieved the war was a repetition of the Revolution, an "up-
rising of the plain people of the North, 'the cordwainers of
Lynn, the farmers of Worcester, the dwellers of the prairie'
against the 'rebellious aristocracy' of the South."[118] The
soldiers were indeed the sons of the sons of the fathers.
In giving the 4th Michigan their colors in 1861, Mrs.
Josephine Wilcox reminded her audience:

> You are the sons of brave men, who under this
> banner achieved the glorious victory of our
> national independence....We are the daughters of
> the brave women of '76...our trial has come, our
> spirits waken and we feel the blood of heroes
> stirring in our veins. The eyes of the world are
> placed upon our republican institutions.[119]

Twenty-four years later, Elbridge Brooks took comfort in
looking back at the war, noting that though the circumstances
of war changed, the American soldier exhibited all the virtues and courage "as when in the days gone by he stood for
liberty at Lexington and Bunker Hill."[120] John Davidson observed that like the Minutemen, "The Army of the Union was
formed almost in a day. It marched, it conquered, and in a
day it melted away into the citizens of the Republic, and
formed the bone, sinew, mind and muscle of the nation."[121]
Stephen Vincent Benét spoke similarly of the Confederates:

> Army of Northern Virginia, fabulous army,
> Strange army of ragged individualists,
> The hunters, the riders, the walkers, the
>   savage pastorals,
> The unmachined, the men come out of the ground....[122]

Perhaps the most symbolic celebration linking the
images was the dedication of the Concord Civil War monument
on April 19, 1867, the ninety-second anniversary of the
battle of Concord Bridge. As for the original Minutemen,
the community gave thanks in remembrance of their sacrifice
and blessed the soldiers "who came forth from all our peaceful homes, our husbands and brothers, our Fathers and
Sons."[123]

Because of their action in war, the Minutemen of '61
were seen as responsible for the new life of the nation.
As Rev. Badger said, "We needed a baptism of blood. We
have had it. We awake to the newness of life."[124] In
another sermon, William Henry Furness declared:

It baffles the imagination, to depict the glories
of the age which, amidst the bloody confusion of
this hour, is opening upon us, the new world,
which is coming into existence arrayed in a
millennial splendor.[125]

Davidson stated, "America today stands ransomed, redeemed,
regenerated, reunified, disenthralled."[126] Cyrus Bartol
believed that a new race would arise from the conflict. He
hoped that their ideas would be so purified that "all
citizens of all the sections of our soil shall be able to
live together in forgiveness, love, and peace!"[127]

Robert Penn Warren believes that the Civil War was our
Homeric period. He suggests that "We look back nostalgically
on the romantic image of some right and natural relation of
man to place and man to man, fulfulled in worthy action."[128]
If one event symbolizes this "right relation" in the Civil
War's Homeric action, it is Gettysburg. Walter Millis notes
that since Waterloo there has not been a single decisive
battle with the finality exhibited there. War, he believes,
was losing its "one virtue--the power of decision."[129] This
may be quite true, and the accuracy of Millis' statement can

be seen more clearly in examination of the wars of the
twentieth century. Still, every martial cosmogony must
have a center, a place from which the new creation will
spring. Consequently, Gettysburg has been symbolized as
the turning point of the war, the crucial moment in the
struggle for rebirth.

The little Pennsylvania community of Gettysburg is
one of America's sacred places. The battle and regenerative
blood shed on its ground sanctified the battlefield. As
J. Frank Hanly observed, "The sunlight does well to linger.
It will never again find these fields and hills the same.
It will return, but they shall be different."[130] Hanly
describes the fighting, noting that the battle is the agony
of the birth of one nation and the death of another:

The very air is quick with pain. The valley,
choked with war. The din is incessant. The
confusion, indescribable. Wild, discordant
sounds rend the air--the rattle of rifles;
the scream and crash of bursting shells; the
shouts of commanders; the roar of cannon; the
cheers and cries of enraged and struggling
divisions. Men run hither and yon; rush to
and fro; come in contact with one another,
fight like maniacs; hand to hand; shout,
struggle, fall and die, shrieking with mortal
agony.   Air, earth and sky, unite in one
universal wail of pain and agony.[131]

At the consecration of the Gettysburg cemetery (the
occasion of Lincoln's Gettysburg address), Edward Everett's
oration compared the warriors involved in this momentous
battle to those of Marathon, a battle which decided whether
Greece would live or die. Commenting on the cemetery,
George Gross declared, "Here sleep those 'unnamed demi-gods'
of the rank and file....At our feet lies an army!"[132] After

visiting Gettysburg, Stephen Vincent Benét wrote:

> No men had fought
> There but enormous, monumental men
> Who bled neat streams of uncorrupting bronze,
> Even at the Round Tops, even by Pickett's boulder,
> Where the bronze, open book could still be read
> By visitors and sparrows and the wind....[133]

In his poem *Gettysburg*, George Vickers captures the cosmic importance of the battle:

> Here was the nation's test; man's highest, greatest rise
> In the ebb and flow of war; here human will
> And effort lost their semblance and attained the size
> Of God-like striving, where each hand but vied to fill
> The earth-pores with the other's blood, while half the
> World did pause
> With horror dumb and wait the issue.[134]

Gettysburg was a battle revealing the true courage of the American warrior. Fifty years after the battle, Speaker of the House Champ Clark stated:

> It was not Southern valor, or Northern valor.
> It was, thank God, American valor; that valor
> which caused our Revolutionary Fathers to throw
> their gage of battle in the face of the son of
> a hundred kings....The soldiers of the North
> and the soldiers of the South were American
> freemen all, fighting like heroes for what they
> considered right. As such I honor them. As
> such I teach my children to cherish them.[135]

In the three days of Gettysburg, one moment stands out above all others. George Ripley Stewart puts it well: if "Gettysburg provides the climax of the war, then the climax of the climax, the central moment of our history, must be Pickett's charge."[136] The charge, the glorious assault by Pickett's fifteen thousand men across the field separating

Seminary Ridge from Cemetery Ridge, provided all the traditional images of intimate combat, heroism, and decisiveness.   The "High-Water Mark" was the symbolic center of
our history.   Would the ridge be held?   Would there be a
new birth?   Henry S. Burrage describes the spot, now quite
near the Soldiers' Cemetery:

> The grounds embrace about seventeen acres on
> Cemetery Hill...it is the ground which formed
> the apex of our triangular line of battle, and
> the key to our line of defences.   It embraces
> the highest point on Cemetery Hill, and over-
> looks the whole battlefield.   It is the spot
> which should be consecrated to this sacred
> purpose.[137]

The spot was the sacred center of the battle.   James W.
Eaton says:

> The decision of the Rebel commander was upon
> that point; the concentration of artillery fire
> was upon that point; the din of battle developed
> in a column of attack upon that point; the
> greatest effort and greatest carnage was at
> that point; and the victory was at that point.[138]

The hand-to-hand combat at the "Bloody Angle" was the point
and moment of national rebirth.   The soldiers of each army
lay on the stone wall,

> almost in an embracing position.   Gray shoulder
> against blue shoulder, their colors and their
> blood blending together upon the altar of the
> stone wall, resurging as one the stars and the
> stripes and 'The Spirit of Gettysburg.'[139]

Thus, Hanly declares:

> Out of the baptism of fire and blood and the
> holocaust of carnage and of woe the Union is
> rising, rising undismembered and unbroken,

sublime in the unity of its forging purpose,
glorious with the splendor of future endeavor,
and luminous with achievement.[140]

The sacred spot of Gettysburg has been cared for by
Pennsylvania and the United States government. Both have
worked to keep the natural features of the battlefield as
they were in 1863. Burrage stated that "Stone walls were
rebuilt and the woods, cut off in the intervening years,
were renewed, thousands of young trees being planted for
this purpose."[141] Gettysburg is a field of monuments.
Since the Soldiers' Cemetery was dedicated in 1863, many
states have erected memorials. The field now contains over
two thousand monuments and markers. As Bolton suggests,
"The sight of these regimentals, flags and graves translates
to us the day of sacrifice."[142]

Martial megaliths provide an imperishable remembrance,
but the battle has been remembered in many ways. On
August 13, 1885, the Pennsylvania Department of War held a
reunion at Gettysburg. A sham battle was staged, increased
maintenance of the field was pledged, and Confederate
markers were allowed to be placed in the field. Similar
battle re-enactments and commemorative oratory took place
on the anniversaries of the battle. On one such occasion,
old veterans from both sides slowly walked out the drama of
Pickett's Charge, and "the excitement rose to such a pitch
that the Philadelphians refused to be driven from the wall
even symbolically, and a conflict with walking sticks en-
sued."[143]

The government set up tent cities for the veterans on
the fiftieth and seventy-fifth anniversaries, and paid ex-
participants train fare to attend the reunion. The high-
light of these reunions, at least for the photographers,
was the handshake between veterans over the stone wall
where they had fought in 1863.[144] At the end of the

seventy-fifth reunion, the last for most of the veterans,
Jack McLaughlin captured the tone of veneration with which
these veterans were regarded.   "The special reunion trains
had been pulling out since early morning, and now, as the
final train moved away, the living link with this part of
America's past faded."[145]   Even if the living link with
Gettysburg was gone, the symbolic link was not.   Other
remembrances began shortly after the war.   The introduction
to *The Union Sergeant* states, "It is the only drama founded
on the facts and thrilling incidents in the history of the
Fighting Sixth Regiment Mass. Vols,--the only one giving a
correct representation of the fight at Gettysburg."[146]

In 1884, Paul Philippoteaux displayed his "Cyclorama"
of the battle of Gettysburg.   Done with meticulous detail,
it was four hundred feet long and fifty feet high.   The experience of viewing the cyclorama (from an elevated plat-
form) was supposed to transport one to the center of the
battlefield, and the three days of fighting unfolded before
the viewer.   The *Boston Globe* reported, "Entering the
building specially erected for it, going through a dim
passage and mounting a flight of stairs, the visitor coming
centrally into the view experiences a thrill of wonder and
delight."[147]

More recently, Paul Spehr noted that in the movie
"The Battle of Gettysburg" (1956) the conflict was "re-
created through the use of narration, background music, and
views of statues, monuments, and gun emplacements on the
battlefield."[148]   William Frassanito matched photographs
taken after the battle with contemporary views of the
battlefield.   His book "recreates the battle almost as if
it were a contemporary news event--the reader is transported
to the battlefield by the photographs and through the
analysis of the photographs to the action itself."[149]
Frassanito comments on his intentions:

By including modern photographs taken from the original camera positions, I have attempted to impart a feeling of time transcended...to heighten the viewer's awareness that the moments captured by Gardner, Brady, and the other photographers were, and are, as real as the moments now being experienced in reading these very words.[150]

Some writers have also described a nostalgia for those heroic and decisive days. Hanly, writing in 1912, notes that Pickett's Charge would be impossible then, since the automatic weapons of the twentieth century would destroy the soldiers, and they would not even see their enemy. Eaton, writing in 1962, laments, "In a day of pushbutton warfare, when the next war will be fought from guided missile control panels, it is difficult to imagine the awesome beauty of Pickett's Charge."[151]

The events and remembrance of Gettysburg illustrate many of the motifs we have mentioned in regard to the Civil War generally. It was the moment of greatest courage, greatest sacrifice, the moment when America was reborn through the actions of her volunteer warriors. That the Civil War is remembered in so many ways shows the capacity for the War as symbolic experience. Bruce Catton believes the War has "given us a common tradition, shared memories that go to the very roots of our existence as a people."[152] Robert Penn Warren sees the War as our only "felt history," "history lived in the national imagination."[153] Important in that imagination is the figure of the volunteer warrior, persisting as a founder, savior, son of the Fathers throughout the experience of a transitional war; a war which introduced new problems for the traditional perception of war, difficulties which would become readily apparent in the World Wars of the next century.

The "Splendid Little War" with Spain rehearsed all
the traditional images. As Carl Sandburg wrote, "Over all
of us in 1898 was the shadow of the Civil War and the men
who fought it to the end."[154]   The memories of the Civil
War in the half-century that followed focused on the
romantic aspects of war, not the horrible price of war.
Thomas Leonard writes:

> By the end of the century three points of view
> marked recollections of the Civil War. The
> most popular memoirs softened and idealized
> combat....Some articulate military theorists
> remembered that the South had been ravaged,
> but they did not challenge the contention
> that the struggle had been a noble one. The
> realists evoked the violence in order to
> praise the men who endured it.[155]

As the human cost of war was quickly idealized, so,
too, did the old image of personal combat as the height of
battle reappear. Quickly forgotten were the technical ad-
vances which made Pickett's Charge unrealistic (though
romantic) even in 1863. In 1899, Elihu Root, recently
appointed Secretary of War, said, "The American soldier
today is part of a great machine which we call military
organization."[156]   Millis notes that this view was not
wholly acceptable at the time. Nostalgia for personal warfare was common. Many writers tried to show the distance
between fighting men and modern weapons in the Spanish-
American war. "Technology was perceived as something that
stood between the sailor and his enemy; it made man lose
control, shielded him from danger, and so compromised the
heroism of his fight."[157]   However, new war technology was
not seen as evil. On the contrary, the development of new
weapons was seen as a force which would bring peace by increasing the death potential of weapons. Even peace groups

in the late nineteenth century lauded modern weaponry. Josiah Quincy declared, "When the arts of destruction have won their final victory...the wars which call them into activity must of necessity cease."[158]

If the status of war technology did not suffer in the latter part of the nineteenth century, the perception of the warrior did. Some believed soldiers and sailors would be "liberated" from structures of traditional warfare and be able to become more flamboyant. Others saw correctly that the new technology of war could insulate warriors from their own identity in battles, see themselves as the servants of war-machines, and become remorseless, guiltless creatures. The disastrous results of war technology would not be apparent until the World Wars. The old images of the warrior would largely persist in spite of the changes in the nature of war.

Part III

The Doughboys:

Persistence and Tension in Classic Martial Imagery

Americans in the nineties had endured several decades
of crisis. Labor upheavals, massive waves of immigration,
and the closing of the frontier all contributed to a crisis
mentality. Frederick Jaher suggests that images of battle
were common in different areas of national life. Ignatius
Donnelly saw a crisis emerging from a war between producers
and financiers; Jack London, from a battle between labor and
capital; Brooks Adams, Homer Lea and others, from a struggle
for survival between Anglo-Saxons and inferior races. Cataclysmic thought was a common feature of American life at
the time. Especially significant in the public mood as it
formed opinions in the Spanish-American war period was the
image of war as a necessity for racial survival. Jaher
writes:

> America was facing a world simmering with
> conflict, ready at any moment to erupt into
> total war. Vigilance and preparation were
> necessary to ensure triumph--and triumph the
> nation must have, for defeat meant annihila-
> tion. [159]

To a people sensitive to the moral essence and message
in the information they received, the Spanish rule in Cuba,
consistent with the whole history of Spanish conquest, presented the American people with a clear example of evil at
work. Gerald Linderman argues persuasively that it was

Senator Redfield Proctor's speech to the Senate on March 17,
1898, and not the Maine tragedy, which was the key element
in public opinion and official decision on the necessity of
war. His speech "rendered totally unambiguous the morality
of the situation....He offered war founded on an undivided
humanitarianism."[160] *Scribner's Magazine* put it succinctly,
"What was this country's duty in the sight of God? (War,)
For humanity's sake."[161] General Miles, in the introduction
to *Harper's Pictorial History* of the war, felt that Europe
learned that America has "heroic and sympathetic patriotism
that impels us to respond to the cry of the oppressed
wherever it may be heard." Prophetically, if also not
eagerly, he stated, "The day has not yet arrived when the
sword has ceased to be a great factor in the world's destiny."[162] Spain was portrayed in the press as a brutal
oppressor, committing countless atrocities upon the Cuban
people, who in the early months were seen as rebels much in
the manner of our ancestors of '76.[163] Thus, we faced Spain
in a "crucial" war as a united country, swelling with pride
at the re-awakening of national patriotism, and the willingness to sacrifice for the country, but also for the principle
of liberty.

Some saw war as just the tonic for national life. Henry
Watterson, editor of the *Louisville Courier-Journal*, declared:

> From a nation of shopkeepers we become a nation
> of warriors....We risk wars, but a man has but
> one time to die....In short, anything is better
> than the pace we were going before these present
> forces were started into life.[164]

Novelist Robert W. Herrick wrote:

> War is a great developer as well as a great
> destroyer of life. Nothing else, it would seem
> in our present stage of development presses the

cup of human experience so full of realization
and understanding as battle and death.[165]

Walter Hines Page asked in the *Atlantic Monthly* if a new
generation did not need a great adventure, whether a "life
of quiet may have become irksome, and may not be natural to
us," heirs of an active Anglo-Saxon heritage.[166]   There
was concern for both the race and the nation.   Roosevelt
and Homer Lea were concerned that the United States would
be left behind in the struggle for national survival unless
martial virtues were emphasized.   Lea, a crippled adventurer
and militarist, believed war a biological necessity, since
nations were controlled by the laws of struggle and survival.
Writing in the years before World War I, he thought that
immigration was weakening America, and in 1912 called for
war with a "clarion call for the 'Saxon People' to arouse
themselves to the somber consequences of their neglect and to
break away from the pleasant security of their delusions."[167]
This manner of thought was widespread in the Spanish-American
War years.   War, though a terrible necessity, was often
viewed as an uplifting experience for the Anglo-Saxon race
and for America.

Of course, war was perceived as personal.   In 1895,
Oliver Wendell Holmes could declare to the graduating class
at Harvard that war's message was divine, and that "Out of
heroism grows faith in the worth of heroism."[168]   Roosevelt
viewed war and combat in traditional terms.   One charged the
enemy, and the training and racial superiority of Americans
would bring victory.   Some would fall, but the surviving
veterans would "rehomogenize" America and strengthen
America's martial spirit.[169]   Soldiers often shared this
belief in the strengthening qualities of war.   Linderman
points out:

> The "boy of the country town" still thought of
> warmaking as personal expression and scarcely

at all as concerted group action. Face to
face with the enemy, the individual was the
integer of meaning. It was he testing himself.[170]

Soldiers in the Spanish-American War were still seen
as crusaders, and viewed themselves as on a mission, an adventurous testing of their manhood, if not for the proclaimed ideals of the war. The warrior could still be
heroic, though war technology raised disturbing questions
about traditional notions of heroism. The Splendid Little
War did nothing to alter drastically American perceptions
of the warrior as liberator and protector. He did not in
this war found a new world, but was perceived as spreading
the light of liberty to others less fortunate, and radically
altered the future perception of America's understanding of
her mission to the world. An optimistic and powerful country
whose benevolent warriors were the beacon of liberty would
face the World War and the challenge to the traditional image
of the warrior.

World War I illustrates both the continuing change in
the image of the warrior, and also the persistence of traditional ways in which Americans symbolically remember the
warrior. Existing side by side are romantic views of war
and the warrior, and the gradual realization that modern war
reduced the warrior to a cog in a machine and rendered
heroic sacrifice useless and meaningless. Americans had been
exposed to these dimensions of war during the latter years of
the Civil War, yet had been able either to incorporate new
experience or simply to ignore it and retreat into traditional
categories of interpretation. As Paul Fussell shows in *The
Great War and Modern Memory*, World War I created a crisis of
perception for Europeans, who had no categories capable of
absorbing the carnage and slaughter of trench warfare. The
loss of a generation of young men made romantic memory of the

war next to impossible for Europeans, but Americans faced
the war from both a geographical and psychological distance
and had to absorb a less awesome scale of death. Postwar
disillusion would be powerfully expressed by the writers of
the twenties, but part of the anger was directed not only at
the war, but at the failure to secure the aims of the war.
To a greater extent Europe felt the impact of total war.
America lost the illusion of idealism as a practical force,
Europe lost an incomprehensible number of young men. Yet
Americans did fight and die, and total war was visible;
thus, the symbolic tensions faced in the Civil War returned
once again.

It is common to speak about America's involvement in
the Great War as a crusade, a battle of Armageddon, and an
end to the optimistic view of the moral order of the universe. The image of the war as crusade and the warrior as
crusader is a useful one, although by limiting the image of
war and the warrior to this category, we may ignore the
tensions that arise during the war. The Great War was both
crusade and task, the warrior both crusader and worker, no
longer fighting for a sacred mission, but doing a job he had
been told to do, as a part of a war machine. People struggled
to maintain traditional categories and archetypes while the
horror of modern war was demanding changes in perception. By
briefly noting these tensions, we will see the power of traditional images and the problem of assimilation that modern
warfare brought. World War I was truly the last of the
nineteenth-century wars and the first total war.

America entered the war as a country above the conflict.
To fight, issues would have to be clear, evil clearly lo-
cated. In his speech to Congress asking for war, Woodrow
Wilson declared that Germany was conducting warfare against
mankind. America would fight with the coolness of the traditional American warrior:

We must put excited feeling away. Our motive
will not be revenge or the victorious assertion
of the physical might of the nation, but only
the vindication of right, of human right, of
which we are only a single champion.[171]

The ideal of self-determination and triumphant democracy was not all that brought America into the war. The
war was also a conflict to save western civilization from
the Hun. In the *Chicago Tribune*, John T. McCutcheon's
cartoon entitled "Hope of Civilization" showed doughboys
marching beneath a huge American flag. Joseph Pennell's
lithographs of war work in America and England conveyed one
basic message, according to H. G. Wells: "The motif of the
supreme effort of Western Civilization to save itself and
the world from the dominance of the reactionary German
Imperialism that has seized the weapons and resources of
modern science."[172]

The propaganda campaign of the British and the demonization of the Germans are often and accurately cited as
pushing America closer to war. Other images were also at
work, affecting America's view of war and the warrior.
Thomas Leonard says that "The invasion of the United States
was the most seriously studied military problem in the Pro-
gressive Era."[173] Not only was it a seriously studied
military problem, but a graphically portrayed incentive to
preparedness. Yet, if the motive was preparedness, the
effect of invasion fantasies would naturally urge people
to see the warrior as a protector and savior, fighting not
only for freedom or western civilization, but for the very
life of his country.[174] While these fantasies urged people
to turn toward war and the warrior, they brought home the
horrors of modern war. A Joseph Pennell poster showed a
bombed and charred Statue of Liberty with New York burning
in the background, and German submarines and aircraft moving

toward the city. The message reads:

    That Liberty Shall Not Perish

    From The Earth.

    Buy Liberty Bonds.

    Movies, a powerful medium by 1914, contributed to the
fantasies. In 1915, *The Battle Cry of Peace* showed the invasion of New York by a "foreign enemy." In this controversial film, the Germans were not identified by name, but
the picture of the enemy was the "prototype for the later
propaganda figure of the Hun."[175] In *Defense or Tribute*,
released in 1916, our Founding Fathers return and see the
peril of the country:

    Flashbacks picture the oppression of Jews, the

    Roman conquest of Gaul, and the Terror during

    the French Revolution, and lead to the audience

    being asked point blank: do you want invasion

    and conquest?[176]

The film ends with a re-creation of the Charge of the Light
Brigade--in this case, America bumbling her way to death
through unpreparedness. *The Fall of a Nation* (1916) reveals
treasonous pacifists and eventual invasion. Many other preparedness films told of plots of the Germans and Japanese,
and the atrocities committed by Germany in the war.[177]

    Popular fiction also portrayed invasions. J. Bernard
Walker's *America Fallen!* in 1915 and Cleveland Moffett's
The Conquest of America in 1916 illustrated what Germany
would do to America after the European war had been concluded.
The symbols were powerful: the invasion of New York and
Boston, the capture of Washington, the helplessness of Americans facing the German war machine.[178] The images took root
in public perception. Thomas Moran, a historian at Purdue,
saw Germans "coming across the Rio Grande and sweeping up
through the Middle West. Which would you rather do--fight
the Germans in Indiana and Illinois or fight them on the

Western front?"[179] Even in 1918, Rev. Herbert S. Johnson
of the Warren Avenue Baptist Church, Boston, could say:

> I can see the time coming, when, unless we
> cease the camouflage, a strong man can't
> make his way through the streets of Boston
> because of the debris of a German bombard-
> ment. I can see the time when our women
> will be attacked by German soldiers, as the
> women of Belgium and France have been.[180]

Thus, as the *Charleston News and Courier* wrote in
1917, "It is a war of self-defense, a war for the preservation of America itself. We are helping to preserve democracy in Europe because, if feudalism triumphs in Europe,
democracy as we have known it cannot survive in America."[181]
It was as defenders of America as well as soldiers of freedom that Americans went to fight. Though soldiers were
going "over there," they were somehow blessed with a sacred
power because of our righteous cause.[182] They were crusaders fighting in a holy war. A Baptist minister declared,
"I look upon the enlistment of an American soldier as I do
on the departure of a missionary for Burma."[183]

Just as the Great War became a holy war, and the Germans became, as Mildred Aldrich said, "the most absolute
synonym of evil that history has ever seen,"[184] the war became total war for America in a new sense. The distinction
between soldier and civilian blurred. Everyone could become
a soldier in the Lord's Army. Wilson suggested as much in
his draft message of June, 1917: "It is not an army that
we must shape and train for war; it is a nation...."[185]
Cartoons captured this sentiment well. James Montgomery
Flagg's cartoon entitled "Tell That to the Marines" shows an
angry American, a modern Minuteman, taking off his suit
jacket, a newspaper lying on the ground, its headline proclaiming, "Huns Kill Women and Children." J. H. Cassel in

the *New York World* depicted Uncle Sam beating a drum, calling forth the masses from all corners of the country to
battle on the eve of a glorious new day.   George Hecht
suggests that

> All these cartoons impart an heroic spirit to
> the interruptions of normality. They seek to
> establish in the modern mind the logistical
> fact that modern war involves the mobilization
> of the total resources of the nation.[186]

Though Americans moved toward war with caution, they
also belied that caution with their admiration of war.
Stanley Cooperman suggests that Americans saw the war as
righteous and the soldiers "as honorable, courageous
soldiers marching, with divine guidance, toward a destined
future."[187]   Romantic views of the war and the warrior were
not only present in preparation for war, but during our involvement.   Trench warfare, air war, and mass death brought
by outdated infantry tactics did not destroy the romantic
images of war.   Thomas Leonard notes that Americans could
question what they saw in battle and wait for the romantic
version of events to appear.[188]   In the early years, war was
still viewed as a sport with rules that the Germans unfortu-
nately violated frequently.   Edwin H. Blashfield's poster
"Carry On" is typical of the romantic and sporting view of
war.   An American foot soldier leads others in a charge. The
lead soldier is followed by Columbia with her sword drawn,
holding an American flag, and she is followed by an American
eagle ready to strike.[189]

For many, war was a rebirth of our heroic age, and
images of past wars were points of martial orientation.
Congressman James Beck saw Verdun as both Calvary and Geth-
semane.   The casualties "seemed proof that miracles of heroism
were possible in that decadent, commercial age."[190]   Americans
arriving in France were cast by writers as heirs of the

Revolution or represented the raw, manly power of the America West.[191] Charles Grasty, a reporter for the *New York Times*, viewed the landing of American troops as "'the return of the Mayflower, armed.'"[192] The famous comment attributed to General Pershing, "Lafayette, we are here," implied the completion of the circle of civilization and celebrated the triumphant return of the powerful soldiers of God's Army to a still corrupt and war-torn Europe.

The impact of war and the perception of the warrior were largely shaped by war narratives written between 1914-1918. As I mentioned, the public had a glory-filled idea of war. Cooperman comments, "It was the fife and drum of the local military exercise rather than the filth of no man's land which captured and delighted American imaginations."[193] In 1917 and 1918, while Hemingway, Cummings, Dos Passos, et al., felt the shock and the horror of the war and consequently could not interpret the war in romantic or heroic terms, heroic accounts of the war were widely and avidly being read by many Americans. The chief literary antecedent which provided traditional views of war was still *The Red Badge of Courage*. Written in 1895, Stephen Crane's Civil War novel provided an appropriate vehicle for Americans to imagine both the horrors and the virtues of warfare. Henry Fleming, the hero of the novel, enlists with unrealistic images of the glories of battle. Soon confronted with the harsh realities of army life, he begins to doubt his ability to face battle. He flees from a battle, but eventually returns to perform bravely. His "red badge of courage" is not a physical wound, but the inner battle that he won. Crane writes, "He had been to touch the great death, and found that, after all, it was but the great death. He was a man."[194] Crane describes the impersonality of battle and the desolation of the battlefield that so resembled the character of warfare in World War I. Still, people could be assured that war was

a "test" for a young man; it was a structured event, having
beginning and decisive end, and it had a purpose which
could be plainly understood; it was a purifying and a redemptive experience. Cooperman believes that

> There is perhaps no sharper indication of the
> general naivete toward warfare than the fact
> that *The Red Badge of Courage* was an image of
> reality for young men...setting out in 1917
> to earn their own badges of courage and man-
> hood.[195]

Winifred Kirkland wrote in *The Atlantic Monthly* of May,
1918, that "one approaches in reverence the revelations of
trench warfare."[196] If many Americans agreed, and indica-
tions are that they did, these narratives provided a powerful impetus for the persistence of traditional views of war.

By 1914, however, people could do more than read about
war or listen to stories about war. They could <u>see</u> war in
film. Timothy Lyons writes:

> Films in 1915 which used war as a central
> conflict in the narrative managed to add to
> the influence the American public was re-
> ceiving, contributing to the simplistic,
> "romantic" view of war gradually being adopted
> by the populace.[197]

Serials were of great importance in this period. They were
short and climactic, clearly portraying heroes fighting for
national honor and security against evil and "unnatural"
villains. After America entered the war, George Creel's
committee on Public Information further shaped American
perceptions by giving assistance in the production of patriotic films. Pacifist films were banned, and even news
photographs were censored. The "results were as sweet and
tame as the censor pleased, showing a very strange war where
mud and blood hardly existed."[198]

Americans were aware of the new conditions of warfare, often through these romantic accounts, yet the concept of mass heroism kept the shattering effect of the war from Americans. Three major motifs persisted in our thought through the war, motifs that we have examined earlier: war experience as personal initiation; war as sacrificial event; war as redemptive for the nation. William Stidger wrote in *Soldier Silhouettes* that Americans must look beyond the wounds and death of battle into the soldier's soul, "for no boy goes through the hell of fire and suffering and wounds that he does not come out newborn."[199] Floyd Gibbons, the Ernie Pyle of World War I, spoke of the valor and courage of American soldiers as they mounted infantry charges and, after being wounded himself, saw in the hospital

> The new melting-pot of America. Not the
> melting-pot of our great American cities
> where nationalistic quarters still exist,
> but a greater fusion process from which
> these men had emerged with unquestionable
> Americanism. They are the real and the new
> Americans--born in the hell of battle.[200]

William C. Dawson says of soldiers that the average citizen was re-made by fighting. He was like "St. Paul...after he had his vision of the opening heavens on the road to Damascus."[201] Combat was viewed as not only a positive experience, but as an experience with tremendous spiritual potential. Echoing *The Red Badge of Courage*, many narratives speak of the transformation of worthless civilians, cowards perhaps, who find their "real selves" in battle. Through acts of individual heroism, they share in collective glory, often dying a heroic death after saving their comrades.

Consequently, the horror of war, far from destroying old heroic images, added to them. The more terrible, the

more of a challenge to "take it," the greater the potential for heroic action in a war of horror. The war experience also served to purify all warriors, not just to
transform "bad" civilians into good soldiers. The men
emerging from the war would not be "soft" atrophied products of western civilization, but strong men, products
of an ennobling war. Ministers argued that the holy war
brought not only spiritual strength but salvation to
soldiers. Dr. Ernest M. Stires of St. Thomas's Church,
New York, declared, "They will find God. They will dis-
cover their souls." He believed the war made Christians
of the soldiers. At war's end, one would be able to see
"the very faces of the victorious soldiers were ennobled
by the beauty of the ideals for which they fought."[202]

Battle not only brought rebirth, but gave to the individual the opportunity to make the great sacrifice for
his country. *The Chicago Evening Post* noted in July, 1917,
that freedom was bought with blood and "preserved and
widened through the fires of war--you cannot keep it if
you will not fight for it."[203] The war narratives showed
Americans eager to fight and, if need be, to die. The
righteousness of the cause took away the fear of death.
Floyd Gibbons writes, "If death awaited at the end of the
road, then those men were marching toward it with a song."[204]
Death would be a noble sacrifice, and the narratives show
many soldiers hoping that if they have to die, it be a right
kind of death. An American flyer identified with the ideal
and the style of death when he said, "to die, rather than
betray the cause of right and justice, this is not to die,
but to become immortal."[205] Sacrifice brought the individual
immortality, a glorious death ordained by God. Sacrifice
also provided the fertile ground for peace, for the new world
of peace and liberty to emerge out of the last war. A powerful expression of this thought is the War Memorial at Widener

Library, depicting peace springing up from the unburied
bodies of the war dead.

A series of posters printed in *Life* magazine during
the war points out the parallel attitudes toward war in the
American mind. The image of war appears as a shroud of
death, a devil raised from hell, or a barbarian Mars summoned for the destruction of the earth. Indeed, this <u>was</u>
largely America's view of war before we became involved
both psychologically and militarily. By the time of our
entrance, the war was viewed as a redemptive act, not only
for the country, but for the world, and sacrifice was the
noblest form of death. Again, images appeared suggesting
that Americans expected war to produce a new birth of the
individual <u>and</u> the nation. Dawson writes of a soldier, "He
thanks God not because of the carnage, but because when the
wine-press of new ideals was being trodden, he was born in
an age when he could do his share."[206] Even atrocities
could be dismissed as necessary for the rebirth of the
world:

> We must help in the bayoneting of a normally
> decent German soldier in order to free him
> from a tyranny which he at present accepts
> as his chosen form of government.
> ....
> We must aid in the starvation and emaciation
> of a German baby in order that he, or at
> least his more sturdy little playmate, may
> grow up to inherit a different sort of
> government from that for which his father
> died.[207]

Irvin Cobb wrote in *The Glory of the Coming* that all
the nations were transformed by the war. Belgium suffered
as did the Christ; Britain turned from fat and slothful to
trim and militant; France became a model of how the free

world fights; and America, by uniting with the "Old World,"
brought hope for a new world. A *New York World* cartoon,
The Dawn of Tomorrow," shows Uncle Sam looking on a new
day; a rainbow breaks through the clouds of war declaring
"That War May Be Ended." *The Atlantic Monthly* entitled a
section of the magazine "The Great War" during the war
years. After the war, the section was changed to "The New
World." None of these images is new or reveals anything
more than similar examples found in the Revolution or the
Civil War. Yet from these few examples we can see that
the traditional images of war as ennobling and regenerative
experience and the warrior as a sacrificial savior and
liberator persist in different situations of war in America.

Traditional images of war and the warrior did not remain without opposition during the war. The English artist
C. R. W. Nevinson complained that war panoramas were no
longer possible, largely because "shining armor" and
picturesque uniforms had disappeared. Men fighting tried
for good reason to be invisible, to blend in with the land.
Further, warfare was carried out on land, sea, and in the
air, spreading the panorama to new bounds. Of great significance was the artists' realization that the machine, not the
warrior, was now the decisive factor in the war. Nevinson
declared that a war which violated convention demanded art
which also violated convention. A "more synthetic method
is needed to express the essential character of this cataclysmic war."[208] In a similar vein, Albert Gallatin said,
"War pictures of today have almost no roots in the past;
the pictorial recorder of modern warfare has had no sign-
posts to guide him."[209] In an introduction to a recent
BBC series on art and war, T. G. Rosenthal gives a reason
for this artistic dilemma:

> The trench warfare of 1914-1918, the concen-
> tration camps, the bombing of Hiroshima have

ravaged the twentieth century psyche but they
have not directly produced paintings or sculpture able to match in grandeur the horrors of
those cosmic insults to civilization.[210]

The devastation of the western front made romantic images
absurd to many. The power of the destruction was often
eloquently expressed:

You go to the front, and for days you see only
destruction, disease, decay. Nothing growing,
nothing blooming, nothing constructive. It is
not so much the flying death that is terrible;
it is the rotting dead. Trees rotting, houses
rotting, crops rotting, machines rotting, horses
rotting, men rotting.[211]

Curiously, war objects of all kinds--model planes, tanks,
soldiers--were to be found in the home.

Images of war penetrated the most traditional
places in the most elemental disguises....The
more unlikely the juxtaposition of the martial
or the patriotic with the practical, the better--
Union Jack knickers on a pantomime dame, a bull-
dog stamped on the butter, hats in the forms of
Imperial eagles made of real feathers.[212]

The popular arts did not express in their items and arti-
facts of the war the reality of horror that other artists
felt. Some artists portraying the wounded of the war on
a poster, for example, created a fantasy world of bright
hospitals "where bandages went becomingly round the head
over a slight scalp wound and most bullets went in at the
shoulder--what Siegfried Sassoon described as 'wounded in
a mentionable place.'"[213] It was left to the American
writers of the post-war period to try to express to Americans the multitude of passions and changing sensibilities
the war gave rise to.

Our distance from the war did not lessen the horror
for American writers.   Protest expressed itself in shock at
the scale of the slaughter, the meaninglessness of death,
and the dehumanization of combat.   Ernest Hemingway offers
a good example of this kind of protest in *A Farewell to
Arms*:   "I had seen nothing sacred, and the things that were
glorious had no glory and sacrifice was like the stockyards
at Chicago if nothing [was] done with the meat except bury
it."[214]   No act of skill or bravery was significant on the
battlefields of Europe.   Indeed, to continue the reversal,
the "good soldier" was most likely the one who would die
meaninglessly, dutifully obeying the order to go "over the
top."   Kenneth Lynn writes, "A desolate sense of alienation
is the special mark of the best American fiction to come
out of World War I."[215]

If Hemingway protested the hypocrisy of idealism in
war, Dos Passos protested the dehumanization, the alienation
of the war.   Yet nowhere is the sense of futility of war and
the victimization of the impotent warrior better expressed
than in Dalton Trumbo's *Johnny Got His Gun*.   Joe Bonham
emerges from the war with no face or limbs, not reborn but
"dead" because of his ordeal.   He sees the soldier as a
slave and sees himself as a portent of the future.   His
facelessness and general helplessness illustrate the general condition of the warrior in a total, mechanized war.
The varieties of protest literature generally view war as
an empty, chaotic, meaningless, horrible event, one that
rendered the individual impotent in battle, and far from
reborn, "dead" to the rest of the world, with which he could
only communicate in silence, uncomprehending silence.

Perceptions of modern warfare and the warrior moved in
two parallel and disparate directions: war as heroic or
futile, the warrior as savior or victim.   The warrior was
portrayed as reacting with both heroic gesture and with

shock on the western front. While Arthur Empey wrote his
best-seller *Over the Top* during the war, one of the most
famous of the war narratives, other writers not associated
with literature of protest were using words like putre-
faction, decay, stench, to describe the battlefield. As
Cooperman says, the battlefield was an "open burial
ground." He writes that

> A clear imagistic pattern emerges in the World
> War I novels as a group: human beings are
> seen as animals (sheep, cattle, even...goats)
> or insects; the war environment is seen as
> machine, or monstrous organism (dragon, pre-
> historic bird, lion). The war is also viewed
> in terms of absurdity as a "circus" or fly-
> paper.[216]

The images of sheep, goats, cattle, or insects do not
depict heroic or courageous animals. They bring to mind
herds, passive groups driven unthinking to the slaughter.
So it was for many viewing the fighting. Combat, or the
non-combat danger of war (random shelling, mines, gas,
etc.), became an impersonal experience. The soldier was
often killed outside of combat by an unseen enemy. Cooperman
notes that "In place of heroes there were faceless masses
of men butchering each other with little or none of the
personal tests celebrated in epics."[217]

The Great War was not an arena for traditional warriors. "Dashing leadership has counted for little; organ-
izing ability and scientific military thinking for everything," declared *Collier's* in 1916,[218] and along with the
belief in the utility of mechanized warfare went the
assumption that technology made warfare more humane. Even
the slaughter on the western front failed to shake the
belief that submarine warfare, air warfare, and poison gas
were somehow diminishing the death rate. Leonard writes,

"By the early 1920s the faith that would sustain weapons
work was reaffirmed: technology made war briefer, more
humane, and less frequent."[219]

    If technology was the dominant force, warriors would
have to change. The appearance of the warrior had "evolved"
away from the personal. Not only was he part of a machine,
but even his appearance was machine-like, or monster-like.
"The advent of gas and gas masks meant a return to a
caricaturing of the human visage that went beyond the
wildest nightmares of the surrealists."[220] One soldier
wrote home, "'It is a war of machines and machinery and
officers and privates are mere cogs.'"[221] Leonard also
points out that some soldiers were proud of their status
as "living bayonets" and found fresh excitement in this
kind of war. To some, the machine-like quality of the war
was apparent, at least in their reporting, at an early
date. Will Irwin, reporting on the entry of the Germans
into Brussels in 1914, wrote:

> We had seen three days of the German army by
> now; and it seemed to me...that the whole
> world had turned into a gray machine of
> death--earth and air and sky. The gray
> motor-cycles and automobiles streaked past,
> the mufflers cut out, chugging the message
> of death. Overhead, the gray biplanes
> buzzed with a kind of supernatural power.
> The very singing of the regiments, as they
> swung in behind the baggage-wagons, seemed
> no more a human touch. It was mechanical,
> like the men who sang--the music of a music
> box.[222]

Yet even in the inhumanity of mechanized warfare,
the heroic image persisted. It shifted its stance from
the shining warrior of past wars, but did not disappear.

In England, Bruce Bairnsfather's comic figure "Old Bill" symbolized the common soldier as a warrior hero. "Fed-up, unkempt soldiers collectively turned into a new heroic image, which contained a truth and a humanity missing in vapid stereotypes of 1914."[223] The corresponding change in the popular arts would come in the United States in World War II, with the emergence of Bill Mauldin's Willie and Joe. Yet even for Americans, mass heroism was a popular image in the narratives of World War I. Thus, if emphasis was given to the individual at all, it was given to the common soldier. Dixon Wecter concludes that the "Art produced by the Great War...spoke far less of martial glamour, or trumpets and gold braid, than of the homely bitter detail, the simplicity and vices and courage of an average man."[224]

There was, of course, one refuge for traditional ideas of warfare, the air war. Combat was still personal, marked by duels and acts of chivalry. The Lafayette Escadrille revealed a nostalgia for the time of personal combat by placing an Indian in "full war cry" on their planes. A flyer wrote, "This flying is much too romantic to be real modern war with all its horrors. There is something so unreal and fairy like about it which ought to be told and described by poets."[225] Though the air war was still a clean war of personal combat, the desire for this kind of war reveals how powerfully its loss was being felt, as the inhuman horrors of modern war dawned on warriors of all types. The men of the Lafayette Escadrille were expressing nostalgia for traditional warfare as they fought the last "traditional" battles in one of the newest forms of warfare.

The Great War was a modern war in practice, and a nineteenth century war in popular view. 1914 was a year of heroic views of war and traditional strategy, soon

changed by the realities of the mechanized field. Yet
public perception of the war, especially in America, continued to find individual heroes like Sergeant York and
Eddie Rickenbacker, and also appreciated the mass heroism
of the trenches. The horror of the western front made
sacrifice and courage all the more sacred for some and
destroyed categories of interpretation for others. Post-
war American writers condemned the war, the futility of
the sacrifice, and the society which led the country into
war. The warrior was now often part of the machine of
war, and as such, lost a sense of mission. The mission
belonged to the machine; the warrior was the passive
operative doing a job that had to be done. Still, this
view was not completely dominant even after the war.
Jack Spears writes, "As the realities of W.W.I receded
from public consciousness the romanticized glamor of it
began to appear in the movies about it."[226]

    Indeed, the two strands of perception regarding the
warrior as savior and as nameless victim merged into a
romantic and yet realistic symbol, powerful enough to
capture many Americans: The Unknown Soldier. As he lay
in the Capitol Rotunda, at the heart and the symbolic
center of the nation, *The New York Times* reported that
from the dome of the building "the brooding figure of
Freedom watched, too, as though it had said 'Well Done'
to the servant, faithful unto death, asleep in the dim
chamber below."[227] There have been Unknown Soldiers of
other wars, too, as graves in Arlington from the Civil
War will attest, and no doubt in almost all wars there
were unidentifiable casualties, but for the first time in
America a nameless soldier would represent all the nation's
war dead. In one sense he was yet another unknown in the
mechanized world of modern warfare; in another he was a
triumphant symbol of traditional romantic war images:

protection, sacrifice, devotion to country. At the burial
and memorial service on November 11, 1921 (Armistice Day
anniversary), President Harding rehearsed these themes:

> We do not know the eminence of his birth, but
> we do know the glory of his death. He died
> for his country, and greater devotion hath no
> man than this.

He went on to say that the Unknown Soldier went to fight
with no hate, except for war. "In the maelstrom of destruction and suffering and death he fired his shot for
liberation of the captive conscience of the world."[228]

For millions of Americans the Unknown Soldier was the
tragic symbol of sacrifice in an ennobling war.[229] This
symbol reveals the persistent veneration of our warriors
and the power of traditional images even in the time of
modern warfare. The mass heroism of the American warrior
during the Great War found its place in American memory
in the Tomb of the Unknown Soldier. Future wars would
have their unknowns placed at Arlington, but not with the
same symbolic effect as the first. He represented a
multitude of images, nostalgias, lost illusions and dire
warnings about the place of war and the warrior in future
American wars.

CHAPTER THREE

FROM HOMELY HERO TO EXECUTIONER:
WAR AND THE WARRIOR IN MODERN AMERICA

PART I

THE HOMELY HERO:

THE TASK OF HEROISM IN WORLD WAR II

During the Great War, romantic martial images existed
in increasing tension with new images of mass death and
machine warfare. The classic role of a warrior was kept
alive in public memory, yet the face of the warrior was
changing. Nevertheless, the shattering effect of the loss
of a generation of men was the nightmare Europe had to deal
with, not America. The war did little to alter perception
of the classic American warrior. For England, the Great
War was "All encompassing, all pervading, both internal and
external at once, the essential condition of consciousness
in the twentieth century."[1] Paul Fussell demonstrates the
continuing presence of the war in modern memory, yet for
Americans the Second World War was the "creative" event
that the Great War was for Europeans.

As is generally noted, we went to war in 1941 with our
"eyes open," speaking and acting pragmatically rather than

ideally, ready to right a grim but necessary war, not to
prepare for the millennium. The war was not the first this
generation had faced. The Great Depression had often been
referred to as a threatening foreign enemy, and both Hoover
and Roosevelt used war symbols to spur the nation to action.
In his inaugural address on March 4, 1933, Roosevelt said
that the nation must move "as a trained and loyal army
willing to sacrifice for the good of a common discipline."[2]
In *The Battle for Democracy*, Rexford G. Tugwell viewed the
Depression as one of the moral equivalents of war, believing
it could "steel" one in much the same way. Illustrating the
power that the Great War <u>did</u> have on American consciousness,
Leuchtenberg believes that almost all New Deal acts owed
much to the experience of that war.

> Imaginative wartime experiments with garden-
> city ideas paved the way for the greenbelt
> towns of the thirties, while the rural re-
> settlement and subsistence homestead projects
> of the New Deal reaped the harvest of seeds...
> planted in the war years.[3]

The Civilian Conservation Corps was "mobilized" and viewed
as a new army going to domestic war. A report in 1933 was
rich in war imagery:

> The big drive was begun. Uncle Sam has
> thrown full C.C.C. strength into the front
> lines of the forest....The entire reforesta-
> tion army has landed in the woods--and has
> the situation well in hand.
> In all sectors the reforestation troops are
> moving ahead. Battle lines of the gypsy
> moth are beginning to crack and fall back....
> Forest fires are being repulsed on all
> flanks the moment they show their smudgy
> red heads through the trees.[4]

Many Americans viewed the Great Depression as the war against internal evil, and World War II as the war against external evil, a war of necessity fought with no illusions. Ray Abrams has chronicled the painful struggle of the churches prior to the war after their ecstatic response to World War I. From 1939 to the end of 1941, there was division on the merits of the war, which was seen largely as a sinful enterprise. Pearl Harbor brought an end to argument for most Americans. *The Christian Century*, previously a forceful voice for non-intervention, declared, "Our country is at war. Its life is at stake." War was an "unnecessary necessity, therefore a guilty necessity."[5]

Yet when we entered the war, we entered wholeheartedly, almost, it seems, with a sense of relief, for the forces of good and evil had long since been recognized.[6] Though allegedly the crusading spirit of the Great War was absent, the concept of Holy War was not completely dormant. Roosevelt's war speech on December 9, 1941, echoed familiar themes in the American approach to war. Our force would be "directed toward ultimate good as well as against immediate evil," for the goal is "far above and beyond the ugly field of battle."[7] Thus, from the beginning Roosevelt declared the hope of regeneration through war, and stated in Wilsonian terms the transcendent principles we were fighting for. The war would be directed against recognizable evil: a total war. As the narrator in the radio play, "The Price of Free World Victory," declared, "No compromise with Satan is possible....Strong in the strength of the Lord, we who fight in the people's cause will not stop until that cause is won!"[8]

Representative Charles A. Plumley delivered a radio message in 1942 in which he called forth Lincoln's spirit to inspire a great war effort. He interpreted World War II as the first worldwide civil war, a continuation of the

never-ending struggle between right and wrong. As Americans,
we had the fate of the world in our hands. To illustrate,
Plumley recited this poem:

> The High Crusade whereon we have embarked calls
> forth the free.
> In hosts, with spears and flaunting flags arrayed;
> Not for one dragon's end, one victory.
> One last great war, but to unending war
> Without, within, till God's white torch supreme
> Melts the last chain: and the last dungeon door
> Swings slowly wide to the triumphant dream.[9]

The revival of the crusading ideal was not only limited to
the occasional individual. Stewart Alsop wrote:

> To fight the war which sooner or later we shall
> be called on to fight we need a crusading faith,
> the kind that inspired the soldiers of 1917,
> setting forth to war to make the world safe for
> democracy.[10]

Walter Lippman understood the war as an opportunity for
America to fulfill her destiny in the world. Henry Luce
stated in "The American Century" that war could be a transforming agent as he thought it had been in England. It was
right and proper for America to use her power in any way
that she saw fit. James Reston, in *Prelude to Victory*,
stated that the war <u>must</u> become a national crusade, through
which we could gain the virtues of the simple Christian
life we had lost.

For some, the war would be a clarification of the
nature of America. War was still a "baptism of fire," not
only of the individual, but of the nation. Jonathan
Daniels, editor of the Raleigh *News and Observer* and
eventual Assistant Director of Defense Mobilization and
administrative assistant to Roosevelt, observed:

In an America grown magnificently male again
we have a chance to fight for a homeland....
Here is the time when a man can be what an
American means, can fight for what America
has always meant--an audacious, adventurous
seeking--for a decent earth.[11]

The awakening war would transform America into a male
country. As in traditional societies, the regenerative
function in times of war no longer belongs to the female.
It is the warrior, still partially understood as a crusader,
who is responsible for the rebirth of the nation and for the
preservation of the transcendent principles which have been
imperiled. Returning to Europe again in 1944, American
forces were launched on D-Day by General Eisenhower, who
declared:

You are about to embark upon the Great Crusade,
toward which we have striven these many months.
The eyes of the world are upon you. The hopes
and prayers of liberty-loving people everywhere
march with you....You will bring about the
destruction of the German war-machine, the
elimination of Nazi tyranny over the oppressed
peoples of Europe, and security for ourselves
in a free world.[12]

Roosevelt ended D-Day with a prayer on the combined radio
networks, a prayer for the soldiers who "set upon a mighty
endeavour, a struggle to preserve our Republic, our religion,
and our civilization, and to set free a suffering humanity."[13] We fought, Roosevelt said, not for conquest, but
for peace and justice against the "unholy forces" of the
Axis. On the western front, D-Day was the symbolic opening
of the martial struggle for the rebirth of a free Europe.
Soldiers, as saviors and liberators, were the agents of rebirth. Bob Hope captured the apocalyptic drama of the moment:

What has happened during these last few hours
not one of us will ever forget....You sat up
all night by the radio and heard the bulletins,
the flashes, the voices coming across from
England, the commentators, the pilots returning
from their greatest of all missions--newsboys
yelling on the street....It seemed that one
world was ending and a new one beginning, and
that history was closing one book and opening
a new one, and somehow we knew it had to be a
better one.[14]

The drama of D-Day changed the rhythm of American
life. Church bells, factory whistles, automobile horns,
even a modern Paul Revere announced the "good news."
Geoffrey Perrett writes:

Stores quickly closed or did not bother to
open. Streets were generally deserted.
Sports events were cancelled....Strikers
went back to work. Red Cross blood dona-
tions soared. The turning in of defense
bonds dropped, while bond sales turned
steeply upward.[15]

From these few examples we meet familiar motifs. America
went to war realistically, but not as some would have it,
one-dimensionally. This war, like every war, interpreted
traditional martial symbols in contemporary context, and
like every war, had as its central figure the warrior, responsible for the life of the nation.[16]

John Blum calls the G.I.'s of the Second World War
"homely heroes," heroes who became patriotic models. These
heroes in part selected themselves by the classic warrior
virtues of courage and self-sacrifice, and by the task of
"working" at war. Like the Minutemen, the G.I.'s were perceived as unmilitaristic heroes, capable of victory because

of the power of the American ideals which inspired them.
They were often seen as "pioneer stock," and underdog
heroes.   The soldiers, heirs of the experience of the
thirties, were seen like their predecessors, as hard workers.
The G.I. was indispensable, even in a technological war.
"Only Bill and his buddies could get in there, on foot, the
way God made them."[17] General Marshall wrote, "A well
trained man with a good rifle--there you have the real
fighting man."[18] Stewart Holbrook laments the lack of
attention given to the infantryman, the "old-fashioned
fighting man." Echoing motifs familiar to us, he writes:

> They fight grimly, filled with more personal
> hate perhaps than are machine fighters, and
> often with the fury that comes with primeval
> battle, that of hand-to-hand combat. This
> is the kind of fighting our ancestors knew.[19]

Classic battle ecstasy of foot soldiers was valued over the
"cool" emotions of machine fighters. Winston Churchill,
though underestimating the value of air power, believed that
a brave foot soldier "with his rifle and bayonet is still
the master of his country's fate."[20]

Writers and reporters helped shape the image of the
G.I. in America. Perhaps the most beloved correspondent of
the war was Ernie Pyle, whose column appeared in 310 papers
six times a week, with more than twelve million readers.
Pyle assured Americans:

> As for our foot soldiers...you need not have
> felt any shame or concern about their ability.
> I saw them in battle and afterward and there
> was nothing wrong with the American soldier.
> His fighting spirit was good. His morale was
> okay. The deeper he got into a fight the more
> of a fighting man he became.[21]

The courage of this fighting man was a revelation of classic American courage. At Tarawa, Robert Sherrod wrote that American soldiers proved themselves as willing to die as the most fanatical Japanese, and predicted that "the road to Tokyo would be lined with the grave of many a foot soldier."[22] As Tarawa proved, the American G.I. was adaptable to war under any conditions. In a *Life* article, "Experience by Battle," John Hersey commented on paintings of combat by various field artists. The paintings of Rendova, New Georgia, by Aaron Bohrod illustrated the "rot, the confusion and the fears of fighting in a primeval world....Let it be said to the eternal credit of our men that they live in this jungle, and fight in it too, cheerfully."[23]

As classic warriors of America, the G.I.'s were the twentieth century Minutemen, capable of equaling any five in battle, but displaying their humanity after the fighting had stopped. Ernie Pyle wrote that

> They weren't warriors. They were American
> boys who by chance of fate had wound up with
> guns in their hands, sneaking up a death-laden
> street in a strange and shattered city....And
> even though they weren't warriors born to the
> kill, they won their battles. That's the
> point.[24]

The G.I. was a civilian soldier, reluctantly marching off to battle. However, once there, he was, thanks to his moral superiority, a fierce warrior, a "conscript yeoman--a competent but fundamentally an amateur and transient warrior."[25]

The transient warrior has also been characterized as the "unhappy warrior." All he desired was to return home to the American way of life. In addition to being a savior and a liberator, the G.I. was a preserver. Blum comments,

"The hero of World War II stood for blueberry pie and blond
sweethearts, for the family farm and for Main Street, for
perseverance and democracy--for Americanism as a way of
being."[26] The war was a different kind of crusade, the
warrior on a somewhat different mission. War was to be endured, withstood, and heroism arose out of the social responsibility of the individual soldier. The tone of the
mission is well stated by Merle Miller in his report on Sgt.
Kevin McCarthy, who was

> no storybook soldier. He does not pretend he
> enjoys war. He's been in the South Pacific
> for almost a year and a half now, and he wants
> to hear American spoken again. First, however,
> he recognizes that a war must be won.

McCarthy said of his mission in war, "It's like going to
the dentist; you don't like it, but it has to be done."[27]

The G.I. became a hero as much for his endurance, for
his preservation of home and country, as for his martial
achievements on the battlefield. Heroism became an accepted
part of the job. The grim G.I. was a new kind of hero--dirty
and bedraggled, sometimes comical, yet still seen as the
soldier of the Lord, doing the sordid job of wiping out
hideous evil. His grim determination was emphasized. Sgt.
John Bushemi wrote, "Even the dead marines were determined
to reach Tarawa's shores."[28] Bill Mauldin, whose Willie and
Joe captured the reality and bitter humor of the world of
the infantry, wrote in *Life* that "G.I. Joe" was fighting the
war to end a life he hates. The reward for a successful
mission is "pushing the enemy back over a cold rocky mountain
[to] follow up and push him over the next one."[29]

Besides popular books by Sherrod and Pyle, other combat
literature shaped American perception of the soldier.[30] War
movies, especially those starring Humphrey Bogart, were
popular. In *Casablanca* (1943), Bogart portrayed a cynic who

discovers social concern during the war. Instead of going
to Casablanca with Ingrid Bergman, he goes with Claude Rains
to a Free French garrison to fight. The same motif of conversion appears in *To Have and Have Not* (1944) and *Passage
to Marseilles* (1944). In *Sahara* (1943), Bogart played a
tough and ingenious tank commander, responsible for his men
and also very much the rugged and grim American warrior.[31]

Underlying the popular portrayal of the G.I. as a
"homely hero" was the classic warrior motif of the savior,
ready to sacrifice his life for his country. The G.I. was

> part of an army that left its bootprints on
> three continents, a hundred islands--deep in
> history. With his allies he saved the world;
> and hoped to God he'd never have to do it
> again.[32]

The G.I. was not the only classic form of the warrior
in the war. The airman was seen by some as the elite warrior, a "new human type, which literature will soon learn
to know."[33] As an educated warrior, the airman faced combat
without the primeval ruthlessness of his Nazi and Japanese
enemies. He was akin to a medieval knight; his plane "was
his snorting steed, the heavens his battleground, and his
combat with enemy warriors highly personal."[34] The airman
in World War I was a similar kind of figure, but air warfare
was not then seen as crucial to the war effort, and to a
large degree the pilot was a peripheral warrior. In World
War II, the airman was symbolic of the technology used to
master the frontier of space. Thus, while the G.I. fought
to preserve a way of life, the airman was fighting a "futuristic" kind of war. He was not the grimy soldier who endured war, but the glamorous warrior who enjoyed personal
combat. In addition to being chivalrous warriors, the air-
men helped to bring about the advent of total war and
altered perceptions of the warrior in America.

The development of air power further diminished dis-
tinctions between war and peace. All people were "warriors"
during World War II. Americans, though spared the horrors
of war on their land, mobilized as a nation of warriors. The
New York State Council of Defense stated that it was a civilian's war and <u>all</u> must join in the fight. By July, 1942,
over seven million Americans volunteered for civil defense;
by mid-1943, over twelve million.[35] In the April 6, 1942,
issue of *Life*, we see how civilians modeled their mobilization efforts on the figure of the warrior. The American
Legion called for formation of a guerrilla army to be raised
from twenty-five thousand deer hunters. In Tillamook, Oregon, farmers organized in order to

> defend their heritage with bullets and the
> frontiersman's lore. Sworn to die fighting
> if need be, they plan to hide their dairy
> herds deep in the woods, to combat forest
> fires started by incendiary bombs, and to
> harry the invader who dares penetrate their
> trackless timberlands. To a man they are
> dead shots.[36]

The common worker was in some small sense a hero of
this war. Robert Young, in the 1942 film *Joe Smith,*
American, was a classic example of this kind of civilian
warrior. He played an aircraft worker who was working on a
new bombsight. Enemy agents kidnapped him, tortured him,
and threatened him with death if he did not give them information about the sight. Smith endured their torture and
eventually escaped, and then led police to the hideout.
Despite being blindfolded when kidnapped, he had remembered
turns in the road and the sound of a calliope. "Thus Joe,
the common workman, displayed uncommon attributes in resisting the Nazis...not unexpected of Hollywood's war heroes."[37]
The civilian warrior was called upon to "fight" by being an

efficient worker, to "sacrifice" various material goods to
win the war on the home front, and thus do a part in winning the larger war.[38]

Yet the soldier, sailor, and airman in the field of
combat were acting in a world more conducive to warrior
virtue than any civilian in America. Marie Bonaparte wrote
of the warrior in World War II:

> The fact of being called up, dedicated to the
> dangers of war and death have suddenly trans-
> formed the hitherto commonplace citizen into
> someone sacred: in receiving his call-up or
> reading the poster mobilising his group, the
> aura of the "sacred" begins to invest him.[39]

The war provided the stage of classic battle initiation.
We have noted that General Patton viewed himself as a high
priest of battle, attempting to instill the gift of controlled battle ecstasy into his men. He was not the only
one to speak of this. Ernie Pyle saw men who experienced
"the taste of primitive passion--the ferocious frankness of
the blow struck with one's hand--the direct call and the
straight response."[40] An army chaplain who noted that
soldiers are overcome with "blood-lust" believed that "war
never leaves a soldier where it found him."[41] Combat set
apart the warrior as it had for centuries in many different
cultures. His martial actions made him different. Pyle
noted the difference between soldiers and civilians; civilians worked abstractly for war to end, soldiers destroyed
the enemy. Of the soldier Pyle said, "He was truly at war.
The rest of us, no matter how hard we worked, were not.
Say what you will, nothing can make a complete soldier except battle experience."[42]

Warriors were called upon to make the final and regenerative blood sacrifice for the nation. Throughout the war
there were specific battles which highlighted not only

individual sacrifice, but sacred and regenerative battles:
the war's last stands.   1942 provided Americans the epic moral
victory of Bataan and Corregidor.   In a radio play, "The
Epic of Bataan," the narrator told Americans:

> They were rookies, most of them.
> This was their first war.
> They crouched at the noise at first.
> And handled their guns like farmers.
> But they caught on fast.
> ....
> Riding out to meet the Jap tanks
> with the head-hunting Igorots tied to the turrets
> to guide them! And above, heroic and alone,
> the last four P-40 fighter planes riding out
> with their grinning pilots: with their patched wings
> and tired motors, riding out to give 'em hell![43]

The heroic defeat was, of course, caused by shelling,
disease and starvation, not by Japanese superiority in warrior spirit.

> Our fathers of the living past,
> these are your sons! Remember them
> with Bunker Hill and Valley Forge.
> Tom Paine, Jefferson, Lincoln: your words live again!
> Your words are poems shining on our bayonets
> and our bayonets are fixed![44]

Lt. Colonel Warren J. Clear had been one of the last to
leave Corregidor before its capture. Upon his return to the
United States, he spoke on the Army Hour radio program about
the bravery and heroism of our troops, and of the unique
fighting spirit of the American warrior. This report brought
a deluge of phone calls to NBC, an overwhelming response from
listeners who had been able to "see" a last stand in a way
they could not view the Alamo or the Little Big Horn. The
men of Bataan became heroic models for the nation. "It was

defeat without despair. Because now the nation had the
example of those 'grim, gaunt men of Bataan' to serve as an
incentive to greater home effort."[45] As Custer had provided
a model of heroic and sacrificial death for an earlier generation, the homely heroes of Bataan and Corregidor now
served as models of endurance, bravery and sacrificial
death.

Also serving as models of American bravery during a
1942 last stand were the marines of Wake Island. Arthur
Pope, Chairman of the National Committee for National Morale,
wrote, "They lifted our chins, they squared our jaws and
stiffened our backs...they gave us morale."[46] A series of
movies which appeared shortly after the war began popular-
izing various last stands. In *Wake Island* (1942), Robert
Preston and Brian Donlevy appeared as archetypal American
warriors, declaring, "We've got to destroy destruction.
That's our job." As the Japanese landing boats approached
the shore, the instructions to American soldiers were "Don't
fire until you see the whites of their eyes."[47] The fall of
the island was never shown; rather, Robert Preston and
William Bendix were heroically fighting from their foxhole
against hordes of the enemy. *Wake Island*'s ending "elicited
determination and vengefulness rather than despair."[48] The
1943 movie *Bataan* conveys much the same message. Bataan was
a "victory" because American troops delayed the enemy for so
long. Robert Taylor, one of a squad of men gradually being
picked off by the Japanese, says, "It doesn't matter where
a man dies, so long as he dies for freedom."[49]

Lingeman details other themes in various last stand
movies: the young kid who is killed, Japanese atrocities,
and the redemptive sacrifice of many in the face of a powerful and terrible enemy. The popularity of the movies drama-
tized and included the audience in these sacrificial battles.
The rhythm and attraction of war could be shared in a unique

way--as fiction and reality merged to lift the viewer into
a different time and space. The use of movies to convey
certain attitudes toward war and warriors, even if painfully
obvious at times, was also strikingly effective. More than
in any war to date, public memory could be molded through
film as well as by books and various forms of still art.[50]

The American warrior was the hero of the last stands,
as was Crockett at the Alamo and Custer at the Little Big
Horn. Yet it was not only in last stands that blood sacrifice was made, but in many heroic battles. Robert Sherrod,
walking the beaches at Tarawa, saw the formidable machine
gun emplacements every five yards, and in one he saw four
dead Japanese and two dead marines. He thought that the
marines in the first wave had given their lives so that
others would land. "They also gave their lives for one
hundred and thirty million other Americans who realize it,
I fear, only dimly."[51] The importance of battles was often
seemingly measured by the cost in dead and wounded. Tarawa
had the dubious distinction of having the highest number of
casualties and the highest ratio of dead to wounded in the
war. Pondering the tremendous casualties, Sherrod thought:

> Until now I haven't considered Tarawa in the
> light of history. It only seemed like a
> brawl--which it is--that we might easily have
> lost, but for the superb courage of the marines.
> But....Maybe this is history.[52]

The war in which these last stands and heroic sacrifices
took place was not always portrayed as a grim and dirty business. The image of glorious war and the romantic warrior
lived on in magazine advertisements.[53] Ads utilized visual
images of battle and thus clarified motives for fighting
while suggesting that their product was indispensable for
the war effort. Often ads declared that soldiers were
fighting for the "American Way," for the opportunity to lead

the "good life." For example, a Warner and Swasey ad
asked, "Will you ever own another car?...Another radio?
Another gleaming new refrigerator? Those who live under
dictators merely dream of such possessions."[54]   Combat
appeared pleasurable, with Americans easily killing scores
of the enemy. The war was glorious:

> From the breathless pace of aerial combat to
> the majesty of naval confrontation to the
> churning hell of land warfare, one encounters
> a kind of lyrical rapture on virtually every
> page.[55]

Fox believes that the war was portrayed as the final
test of the American way of life, a way of life symbolized
by the warrior who was fighting to preserve the recognizable
world, his home. These magazine warriors were innocent but
brave Americans, full of "Yankee ingenuity" and the valor of
the combat soldier. They were cool and calm in battle.
They were defiant in the face of the enemy, having the self-
confidence of the free warrior. They were classic cool warriors in a war of high adventure, a war which was molded in
a certain way by illustration:

> Physical devastation of the land was illus-
> trated in vibrant columns of smoke and flame
> reaching cathedral like to the sky, while on
> the ground of the massive fresco moved men
> and machines. Within such illustrations the
> reader might well have caught the flavor of
> epic drama: the Lightning, dueling to the
> death with the Gustav high above the earth,
> became a kind of Promethean figure; the
> nose-gunner, locked in combat with a "tor-
> rent of hot Nazi steel," assumed a Rolandean
> cast: PT-150, its "dauntless deeds unexcelled
> by legendary heroes," came to seem clearly
> Odyssean.[56]

The portrayal of war in these ads was dangerously unreal. Pilots seemed to have a carefree attitude toward the
enemy, and victories hardly appeared to take much effort at
all. For example, in a Thompson Products ad, an American
submarine destroyed a number of Japanese ships with great
ease.   One battleship, meanwhile, took on a whole fleet.
"It was all over in seven minutes! American paint wasn't
even scratched."[57]

Both those with realistic and those with glorious
images of war expressed hope for a new world which would
rise out of war's ruins. Less a millennial dream, this
hope still echoed the familiar image of war as progenitor.
General Douglas MacArthur spoke during the ceremonies con-
cluding hostilities in September, 1945:

> It is my earnest hope and indeed the hope of
> all mankind that from this solemn occasion a
> better world shall emerge out of the blood
> and carnage of the past.[58]

The new world, according to some, should be modeled
after America. The *Saturday Evening Post* wrote: "We can't
see why Europe shouldn't be satisfied with making a United
States of itself."[59] Advertising also promoted a new world:
a consumers' paradise, a land of futuristic cities. An ad
in *Fortune* magazine showed a soldier looking at the devastation of war, and beyond that down the "road ahead" gleamed
the America of the future. Ads portrayed a better world
because of air research. A United Airlines ad stated, "Out
of war sacrifice will come a new era of opportunity for
all."[60]

A new era did come about during the war, but it was a
new era of total war. The fanatical pre-war devotion of
Billy Mitchell to air power and his thesis that the "vital
center" of enemy morale was the civilian center of a country
led to the refinement of total war. Defended as a doctrine

that would end war quickly, Walter Millis believes that it
led to the destruction of Guernica, Hamburg, Tokyo, Hiroshima, and Nagasaki. Air war was not only a part of total
war, but part of the continuing move toward mechanical warfare. Brendan Gill, writing in the *New Yorker*, reported a
conversation with a B-17 bombardier, a veteran of thirty
missions over Germany. The airman said that he was a cog
in a big machine, doing an unpleasant job that had to be
done. Warriors were often seen as part of a machine, continuing the image that we noticed in the First World War.
George Gray argued that "The modern soldier, sailor and
airman are in effect practicing scientists."[61] Warfare had
changed, and of necessity so had the warrior. John Hersey
wrote, "Once upon a time, a man had to have sinew in his arm
and heart to be a warrior....To be a warrior now, a man generally needs professional training in supersonics or aero-
dynamics or even politics."[62] Machines were perceived as
uniquely suited to American martial experience. We were a
nation of "tinkerers," and machines became our allies. An
ad for a Caterpillar diesel exclaimed that of all wars,
"this one comes nearest to being made to our measure."[63]

While romantic images of war and the warrior persisted
throughout World War II, particularly in popular arts and
continued fascination with the epic drama of heroic and
sacrificial battles, the evolution of modern warfare made
traditional romantic views difficult and perceptibly altered
images of war and the warrior. As warfare became a job
rather than a mission, a scientific endeavor to be carried
out by professionals rather than by heroic combat, images
of the enemy also underwent alteration. George Gray believed that the enemy was a part of the environment, a
problem for scientists dealing with a disastrous phenomenon
of nature. Enemies appeared in a variety of images in each
theater of war. Ernie Pyle wrote:

> In Europe we felt that our enemies, horrible
> and deadly as they were, were still people.
> But out here I soon gathered that the Japanese
> were looked upon as something subhuman and
> repulsive; the way some people feel about
> cockroaches or mice.[64]

While Germans were associated with unequivocal evil and
portrayed as sadists, Japanese were seen as subhuman. A
radio show host declared:

> Listen! Have you ever watched a well-
> trained monkey at a zoo! Have you seen
> how carefully he imitates his trainer?....
> The monkey...actually seems to be human.
> But under his fur, he's still a savage
> little beast!
> Now consider the imitative little Japanese![65]

Novels of the war did not portray the Japanese as an ideological threat, like the Germans, but rather as animals.
Only Kantor's *Don't Touch Me* and Michener's *Sayonara* show
the Japanese to be human beings. Though the ideological
threat in novels seemed to be strongest from the Nazis, the
Japanese were a more powerful emotional symbol of the enemy.
The image of rodent or imitative little animal was the
strongest. A war float in a parade entitled "Tokyo--We Are
Coming" portrayed an "American eagle leading a flight of
bombs down on a herd of yellow rats which were trying to
escape in all directions."[66] *Time* reported that on Iwo
Jima marines were called "rodent exterminators."[67] The
Japanese were portrayed as stupid creatures, much like
"animal slaves," and as shrewd, living "only to obey their
superiors' orders to kill as many guys as possible."[68]
Conversely, Americans often saw it as their task to kill as
many Japanese as possible, and the craft of killing became
valued <u>in itself</u>, not for any transcendent goal. *Time*

reported that after "four years of war one of four Americans
tacitly admitted that his primary concern was not to secure
surrender, but to kill as many Japanese as possible."[69]
Stuart Holbrook described the action of one of America's
warriors:

> He...rammed another clip into his gun, and
> moved again, still forward, still heading
> for that Jap army, that army of millions of
> yellow men that must be exterminated before
> the people of Gainsville, Georgia, the people
> of the United States, could live in peace
> again.[70]

Holbrook's warrior, though "exterminating" for a sacred
purpose (the purpose of the Allies in the war), seems dangerously close to an executioner, for whom killing is an end in
itself--no longer regenerative, not different, really, from
murder. We shall meet this phenomenon again in Vietnam,
where we will see the degradation of the symbolic action of
ritual killing to the act of murder and the related phenomenon of the body count.

While enemies have often been seen as alien, "other"
than one's own group, absolute war removed the ritual boundaries surrounding war and the warrior's regenerative act of
killing.[71] As war became the central experience of the
twentieth century, and populations, not only armies, were
"warriors" of some kind, enemies were not just "out there,"
nor did they always serve as heroic adversaries. Often,
they were there simply to be killed.[72] As restrictions van-
ished from warfare, the enemy became harder to identify.
Malcolm Cowley writes:

> Soldiers made little distinction among the
> occupied, the liberated, and the Allied
> countries, since the people in all of them
> were foreigners--that is, frogs, limeys,

heinies, ginsoes, yellow bastards, wogs,
flips, or gooks.[73]

Total war also did not allow the victorious warrior
any way to disengage from the contaminating effects of
battle, i.e., to ritually purify himself after the war.
Total war meant total contamination. In a number of novels
about the war, a virulent strain of American fascism emerged
as a new enemy: the by-product of the brutality of modern
warfare. The army company of anti-Semites in Irwin Shaw's
The Young Lions and, of course, General Cummings in Mailer's
The Naked and the Dead typify this face of the enemy.[74]
Different enemies brought different conceptions of total
war. John O. Killens's *And Then We Heard the Thunder* is a
story about a black company and their adventures in America
during the war. Solly Saunders, a member of the company,
initially believed in the war, but eventually came to see
that American fascists were the real enemy. He exclaims,
"There is no peace. There is no peace till freedom. You
can't make a man a slave and him live in peace with you."[75]
On the other side, Mailer's portrayal of Pvt. Roy Gallagher
offers us a vision of a reactionary white man, who, while
willing to fight, uses the war to prepare for the total war
after. So, in addition to the persistence of classic warrior motifs and glorious views of war, total war, the modern
experience of war, demonstrates the perceived mutation of
the warrior into an executioner, and the appearance of the
enemy in one's own culture.

Total war and the murder of a subhuman enemy are not
creative acts. While themes of regenerative sacrifice and
rebirth persisted into World War II, the war was also seen
as a barren, uncreative event. Sgt. Mack Morriss wrote of
combat in the Huertgen forest: "Behind them they left their
dead, and the forest will stink with deadness long after the
last body is removed."[76]   Even at Iwo Jima John Lardner

could write:

> This place where thousands of men of two
> nations have been killed or wounded in
> less than three weeks' time has no water,
> few birds, no butterflies, no discernible
> animal life--nothing but sand and clay,
> humpbacked hills, stunted trees, knife-
> edged kuna grass in which mites who carry
> scrub typhus live, and a steady, dusty
> wind.[77]

The portrayal of the battlefield more closely resembles
descriptions of World War I locations than the fertile
fields of Gettysburg. Archibald Macleish wrote early
in the war that though it was easy to imagine what defeat
would bring, victory as a creative force was hard to
imagine.[78] Novels of the war often stressed the continued fight against various forms of evil rather than
the birth of a new world. Indeed, in some novels the war
aborts rather than creates. In *The War Lover*, Buzz Marrow
exists only for war. Daphne, the major woman in the story,
says:

> He can't make love,...because love has
> to do with birth, life. When he gets
> in bed, he makes hate-attacks, rapes,
> milks his gland; and thinks that makes
> him a man.[79]

For many writers, the reality of the war was fear
and power--the eternal fact, according to Hassan, was
death. Yet there was little "usable content" in the
terror of war.[80] The convergence of technology and the
military reduced soldiers in both wars to a "sense of
littleness, almost of nothingness....The dimensions of
the battlefield reduced his subjective role, objectively
vital though it was, to that of a mere victim."[81] For

many, neither war nor the warrior were creative forces.
War as an experience unbounded by time or space provided
no framework of classic martial behavior through which the
warrior could act within recognizable categories nor be
assimilated to archetypal martial heroes.

In almost every instance of combat, warriors have
undergone a certain "numbing" effect by either inflicting
or suffering death. Yet killing in traditional societies
was strictly regulated by ritual and was part of the given
world--often viewed as necessary for life itself to continue. Even with the development of mass armies there
were attempts to regulate killing. In America, ritual
killing in war was purposeful; death was sacrificial, regenerative. We have seen that images of war and the
warrior have been symbolically framed by various kinds
of public memory: various literary forms, heroic art,
battle recreation (ritual consecration of sacred space
and time), and other popular forms of perception. The
content of persistent warrior motifs remained unrecognizable
as long as traditional categories were available for use
in interpretation. When the warrior could not be framed
in traditional ways, war was seen as barren and wasteful,
the warrior became passive, a victim in a military machine.

Traditional categories succeeded in molding the image
of the American warrior in popular perception, but at the
same time could not absorb the changes brought about by
modern warfare. Thus, in the Civil War, trench warfare
and mass death brought troubling ruminations about the
nature of sacrifice and heroic death at the same time
that the glory of regenerative sacrifice and the heroism
of Pickett's charge were being proclaimed. The traditional
motifs were resilient; thus, their continued life through
both world wars, when the phenomenon of total war was demanding a reshaping of perception of war and the warrior.

Consequently, classic symbols of war and the warrior were degenerate cultural forms, applied to the war experience in most cases, rather than evoked from that experience. Ironically, new kinds of contact with war (newsreels, radio, and the documentary film) have not deepened American understanding of war. Thus, "comprehension seems to be reduced in proportion to the increased exposure of war experience."[82] The need for new images has been noted by many. Katherine Kuh, commenting on visual arts during the Second World War, hinted at the difficulty by calling for new visual symbols which were necessary to show the "complete and drenching horror, the sadism, and the utter waste of war."[83] She noted that both man and nature had been reduced in stature in war art, for with the advent of aerial perspective, the artist could now look down as well as across the landscape. Man and nature were "dwarfed by altitude and speed [in] a new mechanical perspective."[84] Further, many artists failed to deal with the modern war, opting for older romantic views of warfare. Also, there was a nostalgia for the world at peace, and portrayals of dream worlds. It is no accident that the Fantasist school arose in New York during the war. Yet, even in a withdrawal to a world of inner fantasy, painting unconsciously was haunted by a war that required interpretation. E. P. Richardson wrote:

> Painting in the United States since the close of
> the 1939 war, has been haunted by apparitions:
> the ghosts and demons of Stone Age man have
> risen to stalk into the twentieth century. It
> was only a coincidence, but a singular one, that
> while American soldiers fought a terrible war in
> the jungles of New Guinea, the demonic images of
> Papuan art rose from the museum cases and walked
> among the enthusiasms of the studio.[85]

Part II

The Impotent Hero:

The Post-War Experience

One event stands unique in the American experience
during World War II, an event that did indeed give birth to
a "New World": the use of the atomic bomb. The use of the
bomb raised some moral outcry, but basically Americans
thought it justified.[86] Though followed by a wave of apocalyptic warnings, the bomb made little impression on Americans. No one else had it, it was not initially perceived
as that different from conventional weapons, and scientists
minimized the deadly effects of radiation.

This view changed radically with the appearance of
John Hersey's "Hiroshima" in the August 31, 1946, issue of
The New Yorker. Recreating the experience of the bomb from
the survivor's view, it created a sensation. The magazine
became a collector's item. The article was reprinted in
newspapers and read in four half-hour broadcasts over ABC.
It was published as a book in 1946, became a best-seller, a
Book-of-the-Month Club selection. Michael Yavenditti wrote
that *Hiroshima*

> provided a generation of students with their
> most moving--and often their only--representation
> of an atomic bombing from the point of view of
> those who survived it.[87]

According to Yavenditti, Hersey succeeded in transferring
the "experience of atomic attack from the traditional categories of war horrors to a more unique level...qualitatively

different from other kinds of bombings."[88] Hersey's portrayal of A-bomb victims allowed Americans to sense the
horror of the bomb's effect on the residents of Hiroshima
in a way that no other account had. It was only through
descriptions of suffering and death that one could begin to
grasp the effect of radiation poisoning, or of the complete
destruction visited on the city. There had been, of course,
other cities annihilated or wounded by conventional bombing:
London, Rotterdam, Dresden, Tokyo, etc. In some, the loss
of life was greater than in Hiroshima. Yet the emotional
impact of the atomic bomb was different--among the victims
and, when the truth was known, among the victors. Robert
Jay Lifton suggests that the A-bomb brought "a sense of
totality, a sense of ultimate annihilation--of cities,
nations, the world."[89] He details the attempts by Japanese
writers to respond to A-bomb experience, attempts which met
little success. Miss Yōko Ōta, the best-known writer of
A-bomb literature, told Lifton, "There is no pattern and no
category for the atomic bomb experience....One can find no
words to describe it."[90]

Americans made few attempts to interpret this experience until a decade after it. Hersey's account gave Americans a window into the human suffering resulting from the
bomb, but his was not an interpretive acccount. Thus, the
difficulty of shaping the A-bomb experience into usable
categories is illustrated by the literature about it. The
terror of the apocalypse forced even science fiction to
transfer utopias to worlds far away after we had ostensibly
destroyed this one. Tales of future war were often trans-
ferred to other galaxies--in the stories of Asimov, for ex-
ample--for the contemplation of future war on this planet
was incomprehensible. I. F. Clarke noted that the imagination could do nothing "with the shape of the total war-to-
come except to describe the end of civilization."[91] The

bomb and the following technological advancements made the
redemptive image of science in war a horror of technological
development. The bomb "made the body universe a place of
fear," according to Allan Ginsburg, an Orwellian world where
technology controls man, who is fallen and without redeemer.[92]

The existence of atomic weapons and the reality of
total war made all peoples warriors and turned everyplace
into a potential battlefield. Warfare was now the natural
condition of life. It might be hot war or cold war, but it
would continue, it seemed, endlessly. For example, Richard
Nixon suggested in *Six Crises*, "The natural and inevitable
condition of the world is one of basic antagonism."[93]
President Truman, in a speech before Congress on March 12,
1947, spoke of the antagonistic paths confronting humanity:

At the present moment in world history nearly
every nation must choose between alternative
ways of life....One way of life is based upon
the will of the majority, and is distinguished
by free institutions, representative government,
free elections, guarantees of individual liberty,
freedom of speech and religion, and freedom from
political oppression.

The second way of life is based upon the will of
a minority, imposed upon the majority. It re-
lies upon terror and oppression, a controlled
press and radio, fixed elections, and suppression
of personal freedom.[94]

The United States was, in the view of many, the key to
the first way of life. America must ensure that the new
world is brought into being, despite a seemingly endless
line of evil forces aiming to abort the new birth. In 1949,
Hanson Baldwin, writing in *The New York Times*, said, "We alone
may be able to avert the decline of Western Civilization

and a reversion to nihilism and the Dark Ages."[95]

The gradual realization that the <u>real</u> war had not ended in 1945, and the emergence of Russia as a nuclear power, led many Americans to recall nostalgically the recent heroic age, the world war. The popularity of the television series "Victory at Sea" reveals this nostalgia. The series, shown repeatedly in many cities until 1961, restated themes of liberation and preservation in a time of perceived Communist threat. Adept use of war film revealed American and Allied courage. Exalting the sacred mission of the war, the message was clear. "If they were strong men in battle then, we must be so in the future when our turn comes to defend the cause of freedom."[96] The high moral purpose of the war assured American warriors rebirth, as befits the heroes of freedom. On the other hand, film showed only the despair and grief of the Japanese. Leonard Graves, the narrator, speaks to dead Japanese: "Welcome home, young man....You are home, but you will never know anything but a long, endless night."[97]

The search for heroic archetypes in past wars was accompanied by the search for heroic cold warriors. Confrontation between warriors was reduced to non-apocalyptic events. In spy stories Smersh and Spectre became the enemies. Clarke writes:

> Now the professional warrior in the struggle
> between East and West is the secret agent,
> licensed to kill, whose only connection with
> real life is the fact of the cold war.[98]

Mickey Spillane's Mike Hammer was a warrior fighting against the evils of Communism. James Bond fought epic battles with a variety of enemies, and like classic warriors, was "entrusted with the mammoth task of safe-guarding an entire civilization; the free world depends on his actions."[99] Comic strip heroes joined these literary heroes to fight Communism.

> Buzz Sawyer, flying for the Navy, was busy
> coping with "the sinister machinations of a
> World Power," Terry left off fighting the
> Pirates and warred on the Red Chinese...L'il
> Abner helped liberate Lower Slobovia...and
> Daddy Warbucks and his buddies blew up
> "enemy" planes carrying H-bombs.[100]

As Terry of *Terry and the Pirates* said, "The only good Red
is a dead Red."[101]

Thus were the dangers of nuclear warfare "limited" by
portrayals of personal combat between professional warriors
of each side. Still, the best these warriors could do was
preserve a cold war status quo, since victory now conjured
up images of death and destruction for the victor as well
as the vanquished.[102]

Warriors also appeared in the military phase of the
Cold War, the fighting in Korea. Admiral Tarrant in
Michener's *The Bridges at Toko-Ri* declared that America is
in "an unending war of many generations."[103] This is an
apt description of the Korean conflict. It was not the
irruption of war in a time of peace, but a "hot" conflict
in the period of Cold War. Much of the concern was to
limit the war, to re-establish parameters of warfare now
that total war and human life were incompatible. Indeed,
General Omar Bradley said that Korea was "a preventive
limited war aimed at avoiding World War III."[104] This nega-
tive conception of warfare was anathema to some, who stuck
to old categories. Eight Republican senators declared in
1951 that "It is too much to expect that our people will
accept a limited war. Our policy must be to win. Our
strategy must be devised to bring about decisive victory."[105]

The policy of limited war was unintelligible to one of
America's greatest heroes, Commander of the Army Douglas

MacArthur.[106] Like Patton, the hero of the return to the
Philippines was a casualty of the changing nature of war
and the emergence of the professional warrior. Technological warfare had been the arena of the professional even in
World War II, and was now dominant in Korea. In many
Korean war movies, civilians were portrayed as powerless
and vulnerable.

> Into the breach to contain the powerful foe--
> at least on the screen--stepped the professional
> warrior, prepared to smash the Communists but
> disciplined enough not to proceed further than
> ordered.[107]

Secret agents like John Wayne in *Big Jim McClain* (1952) or
officers like Gregory Peck in *Night People* (1954) emphasized the importance of professionals. Peck declared:

> These are cannibals, Mr. Leatherby...head-
> hunting, blood-thirsty cannibals out to eat
> us up....Anything that burns me is an amateur
> trying to tell a professional what to do....
> These decisions have to be made by soldiers.[108]

Ironically, as the technocrat became the new symbol
of the military in America, classic ambivalence toward the
warrior returned. He was now, because of his cool, his pro-
fessionalism, a threat to the governmental function, a
threat to the civilian ruler. This worry is illustrated by
Fletcher Knebel and Charles W. Bailey's novel *Seven Days
in May*, the story of a military plot to take over the government. General James Mattson Scott, the chairman of the Joint
Chiefs of Staff and the leader of the coup, is, of course,
the ultimate offspring of Mailer's General Cummings, who predicted that a military order of life would eventually triumph
in America.

Total war called for carefully trained professional
soldiers who would see the need for military solutions to

conflicts or else utilize their expertise in limiting conflict, and it also invited the demise of the warrior as a
heroic figure, for no sacrifice or revelation of bravery
could ultimately be the decisive act.   The question of
existence and salvation no longer lay with the actions of
the warrior, but with the possibility of nuclear destruction.
Common soldiers in literature turned to their own preservation as ultimate meaning and often spoke of the absurdity
of war.   Yossarian in Joseph Heller's *Catch-22* is the model
absurd hero.   For him, winning is not important, only living and dying, for war is the arena of destruction, not
creativity.   Yossarian lives in an insane world, surrounded
by all the evils of the modern war machine, and discovers
that the only heroic action which counts is his own survival and eventual desertion.   Hans Morgenthau echoes part
of the logic of *Catch-22* and other war novels of the absurd,
"To defend freedom and civilization is absurd when to defend
them amounts to destroying them."[109]
The dawning of the nuclear age and the complexity of
technological warfare made it difficult for the warrior to
appear as a powerful regenerative figure.   He no longer
seemed the central actor in the drama of war.   Yet the realization that Americans faced a warlike environment of long
duration evoked nostalgia for the clarity and decisiveness
of the warrior's actions.   Hence, many searched for warrior
functions in various areas of cold war life, and many hoped
that the memory of heroic warriors would still inspire a
nation of civilian warriors to carry on the battle between
competing ways of life.

Part III

The Executioner:

The Experience in Vietnam

The various events, lessons and experiences of World
War II and the Cold War years contributed to the world view
of the "Best and the Brightest" during the formative years
of our Vietnam involvement.[110] Many fragments come to mind:
Munich, Pearl Harbor, Hiroshima, the hysteria over the
"loss" of China, the death camps, postwar reconstruction,
the Berlin airlift, the domino principle, and the continued
American belief in a threatening, dualistic world. Yet,
the images constructed no longer adequately coincided with
the world out there.[111] It is within the context of these
images that John Shy's rhythm of American war would be
destroyed and the warrior would take on shapes never popularly associated with classic American warriors.

The emotions of involvement in Vietnam "came to us
gradually," Peter Stromberg observed, "affected us slowly,
gathered occasionally for a climactic moment, and then
faded slowly like the pain from a toothache."[112] Indeed,
the impact of war was not present. There was no Pearl
Harbor or major aggression against recognizable places, no
armies rushing across borders. There was no psychic or
symbolic jump from peace to war (except, of course, the
vote on the Tonkin Gulf resolution). Though proclaimed
the victim, the attacked in Tonkin Gulf, America did not
feel attacked. The rhythm of life did not miss a beat.
John Mueller, noting trends of popular support for wars

in Korea and Vietnam, wrote that

> The enemy is less obviously "evil," progress in
> battle is more difficult to measure and compre-
> hend, the American entrance into the war is less
> easily rationalized, and the end of the war is
> more likely to prove puzzling and unsatisfying.[113]

Even Senator J. William Fulbright, during his Vietnam hearings, confessed that he could find no adequate models to
help define America's entrance into or conduct of the war.
He found it difficult to comprehend. "I have never en-
countered such a complex situation," he confessed. "It is
not clear-cut, like Korea or like the Second World War....
This is a subtle thing. This is not comparable to the
bombing of Pearl Harbor."[114]

For some of the soldiers, at least those who have
chosen to write about their experiences, it is obvious
that models and memories of past heroic wars failed to
suffice. The tone of their writing conveys both absurdity
and alienation. Not only was the form or script of the
war somehow different, the explanations put forth to justify
their presence were untrue. Lifton writes that these purposes,

> repelling outside invaders, or giving the
> people of the South an opportunity to choose
> their own form of government--are directly
> contradicted by the overwhelming evidence a
> GI encounters that he is the outside invader,
> that the government he has come to defend is
> justly hated by the people he has come to
> help, and that he, the American helper, is
> hated by them most of all.[115]

The American soldier, trained to be the aggressor,
fought the war on the Viet Cong's terms. The enemy used
passive tactics rather than classic forms of combat and

failed to fit "any of the traditional American notions of
what a formidable adversary should look like."[116] They
were too small, often women, and had no uniforms. The ex-
tensive use of booby traps, "traps for the booby," in
which the victim is his own executioner, and mines, elicited Phillip Caputo to report:

> We _were_ making history: the first American
> soldiers to fight an enemy whose principal
> weapons were the mine and the booby trap.
> That kind of warfare has its own peculiar
> terrors. It turns an infantryman's world
> upside down. The foot soldier has a special
> feel for the ground. He walks on it, fights
> on it, sleeps and eats on it; the ground
> shelters him under fire; he digs his home
> in it. But mines and booby traps transform
> that friendly, familiar earth into a thing
> of menace, a thing to be feared as much as
> machine guns or mortar shells. The infantry-
> man knows that at any moment the ground he is
> walking on can erupt and kill him; kill him
> if he's lucky. If he's unlucky, he will be
> turned into a blind, deaf, emasculated, leg-
> less shell. It was not warfare. It was
> murder...walking down the trails, waiting for
> those things to explode, we had begun to feel
> more like victims than soldiers. So we were
> ready for a battle, a traditional, set-piece
> battle against regular soldiers like our-
> selves.[117]

The "distorted" action of the enemy--running, hiding, setting ambushes, constant sniping, plus the terrors Caputo
describes--fit no pattern of warfare Americans read about
or saw in films. Yet, novels of the war occasionally show

warriors consciously trying to model themselves after a
classic conception of the American warrior. Sgt. Slag
Krummel in *One to Count Cadence* speaks of his long military
heritage and says, "I was raised for a warrior. What else
would you have me do?"[118] Soldiers perceived themselves as
heirs of the western folk-heroes. John Wayne, for example,
became a popular model. Wayne symbolized the courage and
humaneness of classic American warriors. He embodied the
animating virtues of the American mission, for he always
killed in a sacred cause: the continued life of the nation,
and his foes were always clearly evil; his martial actions
were always directed toward appropriate enemies.

    Even in the difficult situation that was Vietnam, the
classic image of the American warrior was put forth as it
had been in other wars. Captain John A. Hottell wrote that
the team spirit and will to survive in Vietnam could moti-
vate the soldier "to acts of courage that match the valor
of his predecessors who, in other times, may have had a
cause for which to fight."[119] A journalist for *Life* sketch-
ed the heroic services of a navy lieutenant in 1965. Lt.
Meyerkurd was portrayed as aggressive and resourceful in
battle, and respected even by the enemy. He was kind to
kids,--"You'd think he was out here on a goodwill tour,"--
and when he died, he died doing his duty, sacrificing himself for a stronger Vietnam.[120] Thus could the *Army Times*
report that of the soldiers in Vietnam, "Each was a
modern-day heir to a sober tradition which commenced with
Bunker Hill and Concord Bridge."[121] Some of the soldiers,
however, bitterly rejected any classical formulation. Tim
O'Brien, a Vietnam veteran, wrote:

    We weren't the old soldiers of World War II.
    There wasn't any reason to write a "Guadal-
    canal Diary," no valor to squander for
    things like country or honor or military

objectives....Horace's old do-or-die aphorism--
"Dulce est decorum est pro patria mori"--was
just an epitaph for the insane.[122]

Newsweek commented after the war had long since ended
for our soldiers that Vietnam "produced no national heroes
at arms, no Sergeant York, no Audie Murphy--it assembled a
mixed bag of historical footnotes--men as disparate as Abbie
Hoffman, William Calley, and Daniel Ellsberg."[123] A different war not only failed to produce heroic warriors, but
produced situations which prohibited many from viewing
sacrifice or combat as redemptive or regenerative. The
very nature of this war created what Lifton called "atrocity
producing situations." The infamous "body count," the
statistical count of "enemy" corpses as indicative of success in Vietnam, has become for some observers the most
important symbol of the corruption of American warfare and
the warrior's mission. General Maxwell Taylor, at the
Fulbright Hearings in 1966, accurately expressed the military outlook on the body count: "We are looking for these
people and destroying them at the greatest rate that has
ever taken place in the history of the struggle."[124] That
these deaths were seen as part of the virtuous mission and
were classified as "combat deaths," when in fact many civilians were killed, is evidence of the counterfeit nature
of the mission.[125] As General Lucian K. Truscott has
written, the number of enemy dead has always been a statis-
tic of war, but never "the sole criterion by which to de-
termine which side was 'winning.'"[126] Phillip Slater con-
tends that the body count reflected "total war" within the
boundaries of American mythology. The implicit assumption
behind the killing was "So many today, so many tomorrow,
and one day we will have killed all the Communists in the
world and live happily ever."[127]

In previous wars, both soldiers and the public have generally viewed the killing of the enemy as regenerative, necessary for the survival and rebirth of the nation. Killing in combat, even the mass casualties of bombing in World War II, was seen as part of the symbolic process of war. In Vietnam, the popular phrase, "If it's dead, it's VC," reveals the degeneration of ritual combat killing to the illusory quantitative principle of death. One does not recognize the enemy and kill him in combat, but first kills him and then proclaims him enemy. Adolf Jensen in *Myth and Cult Among Primitive Peoples* explains the change, applicable to the American situation in Vietnam as well as in archaic societies:

> If killing is a sacred act which involves re-
> wards, its root meaning will be corrupted by
> the primitive (though human) deduction that
> the more killed the more benefits are engen-
> dered.[128]

For many, the sacrifices, the spilling of regenerative blood, became an absurd act in a meaningless war. Death was largely a matter of chance. Novels continued this twentieth century theme. In *Incident at Muc Wa*, a soldier declares:

> It's all a matter of statistics now. So many
> men, so many cubic meters of air, so many
> bullets flying across. There's not a damned
> thing I can do to better my chances.[129]

Though this theme is not unique to America's Vietnam involvement, death has a different meaning than it did in other wars. Fictional conceptions of lethal death portray the people of Vietnam as the shadowy, faceless agents of American death. Fiction also portrays the natural environment of Vietnam as a threat; the vegetation, heat, rain, disease, insects, even the language ("monkey talk") are

seen as ominous and evil.   The effect of modern weapons,
though present in other wars, also added a potent dimension
to the war in Vietnam.   Caputo writes:

> And the mutilation caused by modern weapons
> came as a shock....I could not believe those
> bloody messes would be capable of a resur-
> rection on the Last Day.   They did, in fact,
> seem "more" dead.   <u>Massacred</u> or <u>annihilated</u>
> might better describe what had happened to
> them.[130]

Perhaps in Vietnam the lack of a sacrificial framework made
the dead seem "more dead" than in other wars.

Many novels of the war portray characters who sacrifice for a friend or even a principle, but not for country.
This attitude is also found in soldiers' accounts and in
other non-fiction about the war.   Ron Kovic, Michael Herr,
Tim O'Brien and Phillip Caputo express cynicism and contempt regarding sacrifice for the stated mission in Vietnam.
The real mission was survival and the endurance of the ro-
tation.   Stories of death in one's last few days, as reflected in Joe Haldeman's *War Year*,   illustrate the meaninglessness of death and the absurdity of sacrifice.   Caputo
states it succinctly:

> I thought grandly in terms of noble sacri-
> fices, of soldiers offering up their bodies
> for a cause or to save a comrade's life.
> But there had been nothing sacrificial or
> ceremonial about Sullivan's death.   He had
> been sniped while filling canteens in a
> muddy jungle river.[131]

Likewise, the parents of Michael Mullen could not find the
means of symbolizing his death in Vietnam.   C. D. B. Bryan
writes in *Friendly Fire*:

When a young man is killed in a war, his
parents console themselves that he gave his
life for some higher ideal, that he died in
the service of his country and that his awful
sacrifice is recognized and appreciated by a
grateful country and citizenry, but how could
Gene and Peg Mullen comfort themselves over
their son's death in Vietnam?....Peg and Gene
could not help thinking how none of these
people's sons had had to go....What's more,
the Mullens sensed that the general attitude
among their son's contemporaries was not that
Michael had been a patriot, but rather that
he had been a poor, unfortunate scapegoat who
hadn't had enough sense or enough pull not to
get caught. "I don't need to be here! I
don't need to be here!" Michael had protested
that night he telephoned from Des Moines. "I
simply didn't need to be drafted!"[132]

Vietnam produced warriors concerned and disillusioned
about their mission. It produced war narratives which reflect the clash between a memory of classical American
warrior models and the reality of a war which frustrated
all attempts made to symbolize it in traditional patterns.
The literary memories are often angry ones in which the
soldiers seem as much at war with the American mythology
that sent them to war as with the shadowy figures of the
enemy. Indeed, Vietnam gave birth to a situation that was
impossible to interpret in traditional ways: My Lai.
There have been, of course, numerous My Lais in our
national past. Some, during the Philippine-American war,
for example, even received a fair amount of publicity.
Yet the nurturing imagery of righteous warriors fighting
in God's cause remained strong and certainly represented

the majority view well into the Vietnam conflict. These
martial symbols were powerful enough to channel any discordant events into comfortable mythological categories.
However, My Lai occurred during a war that did not evoke
traditional symbolic responses easily; hence, the image of
the American warrior as murderer, while not unique in fact,
struck home with the power of a revelatory event.

My Lai is an event which, like Hiroshima and Auschwitz,
raises questions that go far beyond the massacre itself,
questions directed at the core institutions and values of
America. The process by which villagers were turned into
"the enemy" was an example of the soldiers bearing false
witness to their mission. Commenting on soldiers' discussions after the massacre, Lifton writes, "In all this
they were recreating My Lai, treating it as if it were a
great battle and a noble victory, and themselves as if they
were all-powerful warrior heroes who had magnificently
carried out their ordeal."[133] The logic of the war and the
transformation of the Vietnamese into "gooks" or "slopes,"
subhuman beings unlike "real" human beings, and the
accompanying lack of combat structure made My Lai all too
possible.[134] Lt. Calley expressed his vision of the enemy
as evil, pervading the alien world of Vietnam, the total
evil it was his mission to destroy. He said in his address
to the jury:

> When my troops were getting massacred by an
> enemy I couldn't see, I couldn't feel, and I
> couldn't touch--that nobody in the military
> system ever described them as anything other
> than Communism. They didn't give it a race,
> they didn't give it a sex, they didn't give
> it an age. They never let me believe it was
> just a philosophy in a man's mind. That was
> the enemy out there.[135]

Portrayals of My Lai and Calley illustrated the
radically divergent messages the symbol could communicate.
Some praised Calley, believing him to be doing his duty in
a "dirty" war; some perceived him to be the victim of a
national policy that refused to let their warriors win the
war; others believed him to be a scapegoat; for many, the
line between ritual killing and murder had been violated
at My Lai and the American warrior could now be visualized
as a murderer--an executioner.

Columnists viewed Calley in these symbolic terms.
Richard Hammer saw him as a symbol of "a divided and em-
bittered nation." James Reston called him an "anti-hero
for a war without glory or nobility and a symbol for a
time of moral confusion."[136] William Grieder in *The
Washington Post* reminded those who saw Calley as a hero
that he was

> held responsible by a jury of his peers for
> 'wasting' 22 lives. He picked up a baby,
> threw him into a ditch and shot him. He is
> the soldier who butt-stroked an old man in
> the face, then shot him at point-blank range
> and blew away the side of his head. Some
> hero.[137]

In the second week after Calley's conviction, Jacob Javits
declared that

> If the nation really is encouraged to believe
> that Calley is a hero--then we have changed
> as a people, during the course of this tragic
> war, even more disastrously than I had imag-
> ined.[138]

These protestations by columnists and political figures
reveal the fierce support for Calley among many Americans.
The American warrior was classically humane in battle, yet
a fierce fighter. Never was he perceived as a murderer.

For a military jury to find Calley guilty was not to find
guilt in one man, but to attack the sacred martial symbols
of America. After Calley was found guilty, over 100,000
telegrams and letters were sent to President Nixon, reportedly ten to one in favor of Calley. In a pro-Calley
rally in the Columbus, Georgia, Memorial Stadium, Rev.
Michael Lord said, "There was a crucifixion 2,000 years
ago of a man named Jesus Christ. I don't think we need
another crucifixion of a man named Rusty Calley."[139] A
South Carolina radio station played taps several times
each hour. Organizations printed "Free Calley" bumper
stickers. Jimmy Swan, a gubernatorial candidate in
Mississippi, linked Calley with Patton, MacArthur, Eisenhower, and Robert E. Lee. All, he said, were "turning in
their graves at the decision." An article appeared in
The Austin American Statesman in the form of an editorial
obituary, declaring that America refused to support her
soldiers and that the Americans who convicted Calley were
the same ones who had betrayed America throughout the war.

Perhaps the most interesting response to the My Lai
massacre and Calley's conviction was the popular record,
"The Battle Hymn of Lt. Calley." *Life* reported in April,
1971, that the record had sold more than two million copies.
Recorded by Tracy Nelson, the dramatic song opened with a
voice saying that this song was about a "little boy who
wanted to grow up and be a soldier and serve his country
in whatever way he could." Then, to the tune of America's
most sacred martial music, "The Battle Hymn of the Republic," the hymn begins:

My name is William Calley, I'm a soldier of
this land,
I've vowed to do my duty and to gain the upper
hand,
But they've made me out a villain, they have

stamped me with a brand
As we go marching on.
. . . .
When I reach that final campground in that land
Beyond the sun, and the Great Commander asks me
"Did you fight or did you run," I'll stand both
straight and tall, stripped of medals, rank and
gun, and this is what I'll say: Sir I followed
all my orders and I did the best I could. It's
hard to judge the enemy, and hard to tell the
good. Yet there's not a man among us that would
have understood. We took the jungle village
exactly like they said. We responded to their
rifle fire with everything we had, and when the
smoke had cleared away a hundred souls lay dead.
. . . .
When all wars are over, and the battles finally
won, count me only as a soldier, who never left
his gun, <u>with</u> <u>a</u> <u>right</u> <u>to</u> <u>serve</u> <u>my</u> <u>country</u> as
the only prize I've won.[140]

The song portrays the tragic fall of an American warrior hero who has lived up to the creed of the Minutemen
and has fallen victim to the betrayal of his misguided or
treacherous countrymen. <u>Why</u> so many were misguided or
treacherous is not thought to be a serious problem.   Since
they were, and warrior "virtue" was not appreciated, there
is a significant desire to revive the spirit of old American wars, old American heroes, whose action was correctly
perceived as heroic, just as Calley's <u>should</u> be. Consequently, Calley was a symbol for all persuasions: a tragic
hero, a scapegoat, a product of this particular war, an
executioner.

At a time when many Americans failed to see the Vietnam conflict as a regenerative conflict--indeed, often saw

it as a by-product of more pervasive American sins--the
revelation of the My Lai massacre seemed to confirm the
worst fears about the nature of the war and the American
mission in Vietnam. America had been born in war, and the
nation's most profound acts of preservation had taken place
through conflict. Warriors, whether Chevaliers or Minutemen, had always been popularly perceived as humane warriors, New World warriors, who gave evidence through the
success of their martial actions that the cause in which
they fought was sacred. Times of war had often provided
opportunities to allow Americans to celebrate the mythology
of conflict and victory that revealed the divine interest
in this national experiment. Even in times of serious dis-
sension regarding unpopular wars, voices of protest were
muted by military (i.e., providential) victory. Warfare
revealed the character and the destiny of the nation, yet
the lack of consensus about Vietnam called into radical
question not only the actions of a few soldiers accused
of murder, but probed the dark side of the nation's past
and the appropriateness of a mythology of martial victory.[141]

In *The Trial of the Catonsville Nine*, one of the de-
fendants speaks of the murderous past of America:

We wish to say lastly
Why we went to Catonsville
Americans know
that their nation was born in blood
we have expanded our frontiers
and pacified the Indians
in blood.[142]

For many, the deaths of the My Lai victims were symbolic of the barren nature of all death in modern warfare,
especially in Vietnam. Michael Novak expresses those
sentiments in his comments about Calley:

> The Battle Hymn of Lieutenant Calley may turn
> out to be exactly the battle hymn the Republic
> most needs at this moment: redemption wrested
> from the limp bodies of children and women in
> a godforsaken ditch.[143]

My Lai, then, presented Americans with an atrocity of its
own making, almost a microcosm of the war. We possessed
no structures of interpretation to make sense of it. The
nation's mythology would not accept it.[144] The editors of
Newsweek stated it plaintively:

> Mindful of the comforting image of Americans
> at war--the friendly GI handing out candy bars
> to ragged victims even while mopping up an
> enemy-held town--the massacre at Song My seems
> to escape comprehension.[145]

The shocking pictures of the massacre shown in *Life*'s
December 5, 1969, issue did not help Americans to comprehend the meaning of the event. The playwright and ex-
soldier David Rabe noted that people often objected to the
pictures of the event rather than to the event itself.
Indeed, in the December 12, 1969, issue, *Life* printed some
of the reaction to the pictures. They ranged from shock
and outrage at the event to shock and outrage at the pictures. Some saw the report as another plot to weaken our
fighting morale. Winn reports similar reactions. An Ohio
mother said, "I can't believe that a massacre was committed
by our boys. It's contrary to everything I've ever learned
about America." Another correspondent said, "I can't believe our boys' hearts are that rotten."[146]

There was no acceptable way to depict these events or
to accept guilt within the framework of American martial
mythology. Like the European writers facing the slaughter
in the trenches during the First World War, conventional
images failed to convey more than warring voices either

proclaiming the fall of a hero or outrage toward an
executioner. Even the most precise image, the photograph,
could not convey the "sight" of My Lai to Americans.[147]

The aura of My Lai and its implications hovered over
all veterans, deservedly or not. Oral histories of the
war by Mark Baker and Al Santoli abound in purgative
atrocity stories. For example, one GI spoke about the
enjoyment of killing:

> I was literally turned on when I saw a gook
> get shot. When a GI got shot, even if I
> didn't know him--he could be in a different
> unit than me--that would bother me. A GI
> was real. American get killed, it was a
> real loss. But if a gook got killed, it
> was like stepping on a roach.[148]

The image of GI's as "Baby-Killers" has never before been
part of the Minuteman symbol, and yet it has been one of
the powerful martial symbols to emerge out of the war in
Vietnam.

The portrayal of Vietnam warriors in film reveals the
degeneration of traditional perceptions of the American
warrior. They are victims, executioners, alienated drug-
crazed veterans continuing the war on the streets of America, but they are never heroes in the classic mold. There
were no Audie Murphys or Sergeant Yorks or George Pattons.
In fact, the only film hero to emerge out of the war (with
the possible exception of Michael in *The Deerhunter*) was
Billy Jack, and his heroic deeds were carried out in
America. None of the movies presents the traditional
story of martial victory inspired by sacred ideals. No
great act of martial heroism leaves audiences assured that
this battle or death or sacrifice brings the nation closer
to the new world. Even the most recent films such as *The
Deerhunter*, *Coming Home* and *Apocalypse Now* cannot move

beyond spectacular battle scenes communicating surrealistic
images of the war, the human tragedy brought about by the
war, and halting attempts to convey "hidden" truths about
the war. In no sense are these elaborate films traditional
American war movies. They offer no sense that war is
creative, nor do they portray warriors as the principal
agents of the nation's sacred mission.[149]

Heroic action in movies about Vietnam is limited to
The Green Berets, and specifically to John Wayne. Consequently, traditional symbolization of the American warrior
took refuge largely in one popular medium: country and
western music. Jens Lund reports that in January, 1966,
five pro-Vietnam war songs were on *Billboard*'s country hit
list. Stonewall Jackson, for example, sang "The Minute
Men Are Turning in Their Graves,"

They'd rather go to prison than heed our
country's call,
The Minute Men are turning in their graves.
Washington and Jefferson are crying tears of
shame,
To see these men who'd rather live as slaves.[150]

By far the most popular song of the war was Barry Sadler's
"Ballad of the Green Berets." The single was released on
January 12, 1966, and the album of the same title a week
later. Sadler sang the song on the Ed Sullivan Show on
January 30, 1966. Coupled with Robin Moore's book *The
Green Berets*, the single record sold two million copies in
the first five weeks, the album over one million. By
March, the song was number one in *Billboard*. No clearer
indicator could be given of the nostalgia of the American
people for an old American warrior, and no clearer instance
given to show the lack of classical martial imagery in
Vietnam: the valor of the warrior drawn not from the
battlefield, but from the nostalgia of a tradition-laden
song.

Country music both mythologized the warriors fighting in Vietnam, and as protest against the war grew, satirized and sneered at the protestors. Sheb Wooley's "The Love In" and Don Bowman's "San Francisco Scene" laughed at the counter-culture, and seemingly in answer to "Where Have All the Flowers Gone?" Bill Anderson sang "Where Have All the Heroes Gone?" He laments the "fame" of draft resisters and asks where are the classic heroes like John Wayne, Douglas MacArthur, and even the Yankee Clipper, Joe Dimaggio. In a more militant vein, Merle Haggard sang "The Fighting Side of Me,"

> If you don't love it, leave it, let this
> song that I'm singing be a warning, when
> you're running down this country man you're
> walking down the fighting side of me.[151]

This song inspired the oft-seen "America--Love It or Leave It" bumper stickers, and Haggard continued his attack in 1969 with his famous "Okie From Muskogee."

As the war became less popular, country music turned more to the reality of the war. Hugh X. Lewis reflected this shift in "War is Hell," as did Gene Wyles' "Reporters of Wars." An exception is Pat Boone's "Wish You Were Here Buddy," in which war is seen as an exciting event. He sings "We're dodging real bullets and man it's a lot of fun."

Pro-war songs have received much less attention than have more famous protest music. Songs by Bob Dylan, Pete Seeger, Peter, Paul and Mary, Joan Baez, et al., received more air time nationwide and are seen as representing an authentic symbolic alternative to the war. By the same token, country music vigorously defended our participation in Vietnam and our traditional view of the heroic warrior. It also contains the residue of many of the themes we have become familiar with.

Popular arts in America displayed the conflict that
was going on in America concerning the war. Francine Gray
wrote:

> The very obscurity of this war's motives
> incited the majority to clutch more fiercely
> than ever to its old myths of American
> innocence and Edenic perfection, while the
> minority floundered in self-flagellation.[152]

In response to protest marches, thousands marched in Washington on April 4, 1970, in a "March For Victory." Ralph
Moellering reported that advance publicity made use of a
famous martial symbol of America--the marines raising the
flag on Iwo Jima. No doubt many Americans could still say
with Raymond Tymeson, "My son gave his life fighting for
freedom....Where you stand, there stands America. Where an
American stands, there stands freedom."[153] Yet many more
found the images of regenerative sacrifice and fertile war
unsatisfactory. C. D. B. Bryan has captured this feeling
in his moving account of the death of Michael Mullen in
Vietnam, the ensuing battle between his parents and the
government, and their conversion to the anti-war movement.
Bryan speaks about the response from the Mullens' neighbors
to Michael's death:

> These men were part of "the great Silent
> Majority" President Nixon had referred to,
> and they wept as much out of confusion and
> frustration and rage as they did out of
> grief for the Mullens' loss. From kinder-
> garten through the twelfth grade in their
> Iowa schools they had pledged their allegiance
> to the flag, been taught to love their country,
> respect their government. To them, American
> history was of Genesisic simplicity, its early
> Presidents Old Testament prophets whose lives

were parables of selflessness and virtue....
Of course, they thought themselves patriotic.
Of course, they believed that a man has a duty
to serve his country. Many of them, a majority
had fought in the Second World War, a war which
had had front lines and battlefields and winners
and losers, where success could be measured,
enemy territory absorbed behind ribbons and pins
and flags on the carefully kept maps back at home.
These men had been young then, thinner and tougher,
and they remembered how, moving through the liberated cities and villages, they had been greeted
as heroes, how the grateful citizens had gifted
them with flowers and wine, how the pretty young
dark-haired girls had climbed up the armor-plated
sides of their half-tracks and Sherman tanks to
be kissed. It was a war which had confirmed the
image they carried both of America and of themselves: strong and generous, invincible and
humane. And of course, they had been scared....
But they had done it....They had returned as
young lions, brave warriors, to be celebrated
and praised...and absorbed and confused...and
frustrated and forgotten as their war became
American history, superseded by the new crises...
in Korea and Hungary and Berlin...and now in
Vietnam....The death of Michael reminded them how
powerless they had become. These sudden crises...
unnerved them because they no longer felt they had
access to the facts--whatever they might be--facts
which they were no longer sure they would want to
know even if there were someone around who was
willing to tell them.[154]

The inability of the symbolism of sacrifice to allow patriotic mourning reveals the more general inability of martial symbolism to resolve the tensions inherent in perceptions of modern warfare and the Vietnam war in particular. As a result, there was never a sense of appropriate ending to the war, no final victory to consecrate the sacrifices, not even a last stand that would impart the lesson of martial heroism and bless the animating ideals of the mission. On the contrary, warrior sacrifice was often perceived as a payment for American guilt. "America did not enlist in the war for life," *Time* stated in 1975. "There cannot be an infinite cycle of protests, recriminations, and guilt. The U.S. has paid for Vietnam--many times over. A phase of American history has finished. It is time to begin anew."[155] Likewise, President Ford, at his news conference of May 6, 1975, said that the lessons of Vietnam were obvious and had been learned by all Americans. Thus, warrior sacrifice did not contribute to a rebirth of any kind, but atoned for the guilt of America. Warrior sacrifice has generally been interpreted as a creative event, redeeming the nation from the threat of external evil. Rarely have Americans perceived martial sacrifice as a means of atoning for internal guilt.

Many warriors experienced the lack of a sense of ending. Unlike veterans of other wars, warriors often returned alone to a society profoundly ambivalent about their presence. Warriors returned as outcasts and scapegoats, victims of the fractured symbol of the American warrior. They returned to a nation divided by perceptions of the war and the worthiness of the American mission in the world. The controversy about the significance of the war raged about the veteran, who stepped from a hot war in Vietnam into an ideological war, a civil war, in America. Naturally, one veteran lamented,

A lot of vets back here in the World just
picked up rifles and started shooting people.
I can understand that. They could not adjust.
They just threw us back into a place that we
were untrained to live in. They should have
had to train us to come back into the World.
It took me <u>years</u> to understand that I'm part
of the United States.[156]

Many warriors, of course, returned peacefully, and
adjusted, according to Tim O'Brien, "too well." Many felt
the rage, confusion, isolation and impotence of unresolved
contradictions in the midst of a society that wanted only
to ignore their stories. Jay Jeffrey speaks of his own
sense of contradiction, "If I believe in America, I must
feel guilty for letting it down, if I am critical of
America, I cannot understand why I fought and saw so many
killed."[157]

Returning warriors bore the brunt of the collective
desire to forget Vietnam. Yet no national trauma is forgotten; it is only repressed. Caputo notes the <u>conscious</u>
<u>act</u> of forgetting the war:

There are no monuments to its heroes, no
statues in small-town squares and city parks,
no plaques, nor public wreaths, nor memorials.
For plaques and wreaths and memorials are
reminders, and they would make it harder for
your country to sink into the amnesia for
which it longs.[158]

The warriors did not forget, but, as Shad Meshad
(Chief of the Vietnam Veteran Resocialization Unit
at Brentwood V.A. Psychiatric Hospital) writes, "The
main thing that America refuses to look at is the Vietnam
veteran."[159] As the nation moves further away from the war
years, this attitude has begun to change. The war is

becoming part of a usable past, the veteran capable of being seen as honorable, even heroic for his duty and sacrifice, however unwise or ill-conceived the national mission might have been.

As a result, war stories are again best-sellers. As we have seen, the literature produced by the warriors reveals men conscious of the martial models that shaped them, and often illustrates the attempt to reinterpret their mission and convey the "truth" of the war and the ideology that supported it in light of their radical disillusion. This struggle, many veterans suggest, may be the only regenerative event to emerge from these years. It is imperative, then, that we return to the veterans, for they still speak with the authoritative voice of the *Homo Furens*, the warrior baptized by fire. "It is in their memories," Peter Marin writes, "and in the possibilities of their speech, that the antidotes to our silence and fantasy lie."[160]

Voices of warriors sensitive to the power of martial mythology must be heard as symbols of wars and warriors are reconstituted in light of the Vietnam war. The continued development of technological warfare and the trauma of Vietnam contributed to the fracturing of traditional martial symbolism; but as various ideological groups begin to re-dream the American dream, these martial myths and symbols will be reshaped. And, if Walter Capps is correct that "the most profound social trends in the post-Vietnam era are based on images of America that Americans most wish to retain," it may be that our nostalgia for innocence and clarity of mission will allow traditional martial symbolism to absorb the discordant images produced during the Vietnam war.[161]

The persistent attractions of war and the evocative power of martial mythology are frightening in an era of nuclear warfare. Certain mythologies of nuclear war portray

it as a final purifying act through which the unbearable
tensions of history will be resolved. The bomb becomes a
deity, "capable not only of apocalyptic destruction but also
of unlimited creation."[162] Though the warrior would not
function on the nuclear battlefield, renewed imagery of cold
war and the threat of nuclear war have made everyone combatants living on a worldwide battlefield. As a result,
we find warriors in every area of life, for warfare is carried out incessantly, everywhere. Urban guerrillas certainly style themselves after ideological warriors of the
past, using language of sacred mission to describe their
total war on society, believing that their sacrifice will
further the cause and bring them the honor of revolutionary
immortality. Moral crusades, always steeped in martial
imagery, become even more intensely so since they are carried out under the powerful symbolism of nuclear apocalyptic.
The mission of the "New Right" is militant in tone and content, for these believers are involved in the "enduring warfare between truth and error, right and wrong, eternal life
and unending death."[163] The war is a holy war, though the
battlefield is domestic as well as foreign, and the war
calls for God's warriors to "move past the shelling, the
bombing and the foxholes and, with bayonet in hand, encounter the enemy face to face and one-on-one bring them
under submission to the Gospel of Christ, move them into
the household of God and call it secured."[164]
    As the symbolism of warfare and the actions of new cru-
sading warriors spreads into every area of life, it is not
clear if threatening symbolism of nuclear extinction or
reconciling symbolism of the "global village" will present
evocative alternatives to traditional martial imagery. If
we continue to perceive the world as essentially Manichaean,
and look to total wars and new crusaders for redemption, it
seems likely that these traditional symbols will move the
nation inexorably toward the tragedy of nuclear warfare.

FOOTNOTES

PREFACE

1. Gerardus van der Leeuw, *Religion in Essence and Manifestation*, Vol. 2 (New York: Harper and Row, 1963), p. 401.

2. J. Glenn Gray, *The Warriors: Reflections on Men in Battle*, with an introduction by Hannah Arendt (New York: Harper and Row, 1959), p. 33. The evocative power of the holy and the nature of human response are described in Rudolf Otto, *The Idea of the Holy* (New York: Oxford University Press, 1958).

3. There are numerous works that discuss the origins and significance of war. For example, see Robert Ardrey, *The Territorial Imperative* (New York: Athenum, 1966); Raymond Aron, *The Century of Total War* (Boston: Beacon Press, 1955); Paul Bohannon, *Law and Warfare* (New York: The National History Press, 1967); J. D. Clarkson and T. C. Cochran, *War as a Social Institution* (New York: Columbia University Press, 1941); Leonard Bramson and George W. Goethals, eds., *War: Studies From Psychology, Sociology, Anthropology* (New Work: Basic Books, Inc., 1964); Konrad Lorenz, *On Aggression* (New York: Harcourt, Brace and World, 1966); Sue Draves, *The Gestalts of War: An Inquiry into Its Origins and Meanings as a Social Institution* (New York: The Dial Press, 1982); Maurice N. Walsh, ed., *War and the Human Race* (Amsterdam: Elsevier Publishing Company, 1971); Elwin H. Powell, *The Design of Discord: Studies of Anomie* (New York: Oxford University Press, 1970); Alfred Vagts, *A History of Militarism* (n.p.: Meridian Books, Inc., 1959); Quincy Wright, *A Study of War*, 2 vols. (Chicago: University of Chicago Press, 1942).

4. Peter C. Rollins, "Victory at Sea: Cold War Epic," *Journal of Popular Culture* 6 (1973): 464.

5. Mircea Eliade, *The Myth of the Eternal Return: Or Cosmos and History*, Bollingen Series XLVI, trans. by Willard R. Trask (Princeton, New Jersey: Princeton University Press, 1971), p. 43.

6. Richard Slotkin, *Regeneration Through Violence: The Mythology of the American Frontier, 1600-1860* (Middletown, Connecticut: Wesleyan University Press, 1973), p. 3.

7. See Jan Van Baal, *Dema: Description and Analysis of Marind-Anim Culture* (The Hague: Martinus Nijhoff, 1966); H. G. Schulte Nordholte, *The Political System of the Atoni of Timor* (The Hague: Martinus Nijhoff, 1971); Adolf Jensen, *Myth and Cult Among Primitive Peoples*, trans. by Marianna Tax Choldin and Wolfgang Weissleder (Chicago: University of Chicago Press, 1963); Jacques Soustelle, *The Daily Life of the Aztecs* (Middlesex, England: Penguin Books, Ltd., 1964); Michael Harner, "Jivaro Souls," *American Anthropologist* 64 (1962).   For an excellent bibliography on archaic warfare, see William T. Divale, comp., *Warfare in Primitive Societies: A Bibliography* (Los Angeles: California State University, Los Angeles, 1971).

8. Johannes Pedersen, *Israel, Its Life and Culture* I-II (London: Geoffrey Cumberlege, Oxford University Press, 1940), p. 311.

9. Ibid., III-IV, p. 18.

10. Norman Cohn, *The Pursuit of the Millennium*, 2nd ed. (New York: Harper and Row, 1961), p. 20. For a good introduction to apocalyptic expection in America, see Ernest Lee Tuveson, *Redeemer Nation: The Idea of America's Millennial Role* (Chicago: University of Chicago Press, 1968).

11. Cohn, *Pursuit of the Millennium*, p. 59.

12. Robert Jay Lifton, *Home From the War* (New York: Simon and Schuster, 1973), p. 27.

13. Carol R. Andreas, "War Toys and the Peace Movement," *Journal of Social Issues* 25 (January, 1969): 96.

14. Mircea Eliade, *Rites and Symbols of Initiation*, trans. by Willard R. Trask (New York: Harper and Row, 1958), p. 84.

15. See Desmond Seward, *The Monks of War* (Hamdon, Connecticut: Archon Books, 1972); and Richard Drinnon, *Facing West: The Metaphysics of Indian-Hating and Empire-Building* (New York: Meridian Books, 1980), p. 56.

16. Both statements from Gray, *The Warriors*, p. 51 and pp. 23 and 27.

17. Werner Jaeger, *Paideia: The Ideals of Greek Culture*, trans. by Gilbert Highet, 3 vols. (New York: Oxford University Press, 1943-1945), I:5.

18. Homer, *The Iliad*, trans. by Richard Lattimore, 18. 94-99; 115-116.

19. F. E. Peters informs us that Alexander claimed descent from both Heracles and Achilles. See *The Harvest of Hellenism* (New York: Simon and Schuster, 1970).

Also recollecting the virtues of Achilles as justification for present behavior was Socrates, who said in *The Apology*:

> You are mistaken, my friend, if you
> think that a man who is worth anything
> ought to spend his time weighing up
> the prospects of life and death. He
> has only one thing to consider in
> performing any action--that is whether
> he is acting rightly or wrongly, like
> a good man or a bad one. On your view
> the heroes who died at Troy would be
> poor creatures, especially the son of
> Thetis. He, if you remember, made
> light of danger in comparison with
> incurring dishonor when his goddess
> mother warned him, eager as he was to
> kill Hector, in some such words as
> these, I fancy: "My son, if you
> avenge your comrade Patroclus' death
> and kill Hector, you will die your-
> self--next after Hector is thy death
> prepared."
>
> When he heard this warning he made
> light of his death and danger, being

much more afraid of an ignoble life
and of failing to avenge his friends.
(Edith Hamilton and Huntington Cairns,
ed., *The Collected Dialogues of
Plato*, Bollingen Series LXXI [New
York: Pantheon Books, 1963], p. 14:28
b-c.)

20. Georges Dumézil, *The Destiny of the Warrior*,
trans. by Alf Hiltebeitel (Chicago: University of
Chicago Press, 1969), p. 64.

21. Ibid., p. 107.

22. C. Scott Littleton, *The New Comparative
Mythology*, rev. ed. (Berkeley: University of California Press, 1963), p. 80.

CHAPTER ONE

1. Marcus Cunliffe, *Soldiers and Civilians: The
Martial Experience in America, 1775-1865* (Boston:
Little, Brown and Company, 1968), p. 68.

For good discussions of civilian-military relations,
see Arthur A. Ekirch, Jr., *The Civilian and the Military*
(New York: Oxford University Press, 1956); Samuel P.
Huntington, *The Soldier and the State* (Cambridge, Mass.:
The Belknap Press of Harvard University Press, 1957);
Louis Smith, *American Democracy and Military Power*
(Chicago: The University of Chicago Press, 1951); and
Alfred Vagts, *A History of Militarism* (New York:
Meridian Books, Inc., 1959).

For a discussion of the formative years of this tension
in America, see Richard H. Kohn, *Eagle and Sword: The
Federalists and the Creation of the Military Establishment in America, 1783-1802)* (New York: Free Press,
1975).

2. William Haller, *The Rise of Puritanism* (Philadelphia: The University of Pennsylvania Press, 1972),
p. 143.

3. As quoted in Haller, p. 189.

4. Roy Harvey Pearce, "The Significance of the
Captivity Narrative," *American Literature* 19 (March,
1949): 2.

5. Richard S. Slotkin, "Dreams and Genocide: The
American Myth of Regeneration," *Journal of Popular Culture*
5 (Summer, 1971): 41.

6. Slotkin, *Regeneration Through Violence*, p. 5.

7. Ibid., p.130.

8. See Richard Drinnon's interpretation of the Pequot
War in his *Facing West: The Metaphysics of Indian-Hating
and Empire-Building* (New York: Meridian Books, 1980).   The
dynamic evident here is strikingly similar to that described by Lifton in his discussion of Vietnam war veterans.
He writes:

> The syndrome draws upon, but in a basic way
> violates, Biblical imagery of the scapegoat.
> The sin (the war) is there, but it is not
> confronted by the (American) community as
> the Biblical ritual of atonement prescribes.
> Instead the scapegoat--or gook-victim--is
> made to bear the unacknowledged guilt of
> the victimizing community.
> (Lifton, *Home From the War*, p. 201.)

The polarization and contrast between absolute American
purity and the total depravity of the alien is apparently
present in the formative years of our ideology, and has
continued into our latest conflict.   Lifton believes the
soldier in Vietnam was both victim (Puritan captive) and
avenger, as exemplified in atrocities like My Lai.

9. Catherine Albanese, *Sons of the Fathers.   The
Civil Religion of the American Revolution* (Philadelphia:
Temple University Press, 1976), p. 106.

10. Ruth Miller Elson, *Guardians of Tradition:
American Schoolbooks of the Nineteenth Century* (Lincoln:
University of Nebraska Press, 1964).

11. Cunliffe, *Soldiers and Civilians*, p. 417.

12. Clive Bush, *The Dream of Reason: American Consciousness and Cultural Achievement from Independence to the Civil War* (Great Britain: Edward Arnold, 1977), p. 31.

13. Albanese, *Sons of the Fathers*, p. 145.

14. William Alfred Bryan, *George Washington in American Literature: 1775-1865* (Westport, Connecticut: Greenwood Press, 1970), p. 241.

15. Marcus Cunliffe, *George Washington: Man and Monument* (Boston: Little, Brown and Co., 1958), p. 213.

16. Thomas Andrew Bailey, *Presidential Greatness. The Image and the Man from George Washington to the Present* (New York: Appleton-Century, 1966), p. 79.

17. Quoted in William Alfred Bryan, *George Washington in American Literature: 1775-1865*, p. 68.

18. Frederick L. Harvey, *The History of the Washington Monument and the National Monument Society* (Washington, D.C.: Norman T. Elliot Printing Co., 1902), p. 12.

In his chapter "Sacred Places," Mircea Eliade informs us that a revelation of the sacred, i.e., the providential gift to the nation of Washington transforms the space in which this revelation takes place. Every consecrated place is a center, a place where the cosmic regions meet. George Washington brought creative and protective power from this center. For suggestive remarks, see Mircea Eliade, *Patterns in Comparative Religion*, trans. by Rosemary Sheed (Cleveland: The World Publishing Co., 1963), pp. 367-387.

19. Ralph Henry Gabriel, *The Course of American Democratic Thought* (New York: The Ronald Press, 1956), p. 94.

20. Ibid., p. 95.

21. Bush, *The Dream of Reason*, p. 34.

22. Ibid., p. 34.

23. Bryan, *Washington in American Literature*, p. 55.

24. Marcus Cunliffe, et al., *The American Heritage History of the Presidency* (n.p.: American Heritage Publishing Co., 1968), p. 138. The persistence of these symbols and the important figure of Columbia are not to be underestimated. For example, on a wall at the Epinal, France, War Memorial for American dead, there is a map showing the Allied advance in Europe following the August 15, 1944, landing on the Mediterranean coast. On the map appears the figure of Columbia leading Allied troops into battle with her sword, lightning coming from her shield. (H. Walker, "Here Rest in Honored Glory: The U.S. Dedicates Six New Battle Monuments," *National Geographic* 111 [June, 1957]: 764.)

The eagle, symbol of supreme authority in Europe, became a bald eagle in America. It was "hatched in the midst of war, the eagle clutched arrows in one claw, but an olive branch in the other." (Joshua C. Taylor, *America as Art* [Washington: Smithsonian Institution Press, 1976], p. 10.) The bald eagle became the dominant symbol in American design, from its use as an insignia for the Society of Cincinnati and its appearance on local and federal coins in the late 1870s to its continued use today. Taylor presents many pictures of Washington, often in the center of a pantheon of heroes, accompanied by Columbia and the eagle. Interestingly, in portraits of <u>President</u> Washington, he is often portrayed as a general. For another discussion of the development of American national symbolism, see Alton Ketchum, *Uncle Sam: The Man and the Legend* (New York: Hill and Wang, 1959).

25. Albanese, *Sons of the Fathers*, p. 165.

26. Charles F. Mullett, "The Classical Influences on the American Revolution," *The Classical Journal* 35 (November, 1939): 96.

27. Quoted in Bryan, *Washington in American Literature*, p. 123.

28. Bryan, *Washington in American Literature*, p. 87.

29. J. T. Headley, *Washington and His Generals*, 2 vols. (New York: Baker and Scribner, 1850), 1:23.

30. Bryan, *Washington in American Literature*, p. 136. Irving Allen in an article, "Providential Events in the Life of George Washington," cited six "miraculous events" that Washington (with the help of Providence) was blessed with. See Robert Haven Schauffler, ed., *Washington's Birthday* (New York: Moffat, Yard and Co., 1913), pp. 227-238.

31. Bryan, *Washington in American Literature*, p. 53.
Ruth Miller Elson notes that in schoolbooks Washington was
seen as commissioned by heaven as a savior, protected by
God. At the core of his heroism were his military acts.
Washington appears as a god in a book published in 1906,
Heroes Every Child Should Know, written by H. W. Mabie.

> The Almighty, who raised up for our hour
> of need a man so peculiarly prepared for
> its whole dread responsibility, seems to
> have put a stamp of sacredness upon his
> instrument.

Likewise, George A. Gordon in "Lessons From the Washington
Centennial," said,

> We cannot doubt in the case of Washington
> the fact of a divine call. Joshua was
> not more evidently called to command the
> armies of Israel than Washington to lead
> the forces of the United Colonies.
> (Schauffler, *Washington's Birthday*,
> pp. 76 and 96.)

32. Bryan, *Washington in American Literature*, p. 217.

33. Ibid., p. 154. See his chapter on Verse, pp.
121-170.

34. Ibid., p. 84. Bryan notes Joel Barlow's *The
Vision of Columbus* (1787) as an important epic suitable
to treatment of an event such as the Revolution, and the
centrality of Washington.

35. Headley, *Washington and His Generals*, 1:33.

36. Dorothy Burne Goebel and Julius Goebel, Jr.,
Generals in the White House (Freeport, New York: Books
for Libraries Press, 1971), p. 52. Valley Forge served
as a kind of purgatory for American patriotism. In his
Address at Valley Forge on June 19, 1798, Henry Armitt
Brown said Valley Forge was a "place of sacrifice, in
this vale of humiliation, in this valley of death, out
of which America rose regenerate and free." (Schauffler,
Washington's Birthday, p. 43.)

37. Bryan, *Washington in American Literature*, p. 158.

38. Headley, *Washington and His Generals*, 1:31.

39. Ibid., 1:39.

40.   Bryan, *Washington in American Literature*, p. 228.
Even in England,

> the whole range of history did not present
> a character, upon which the British press
> could dwell with such 'entire and unmixed
> admiration.' The long life of George
> Washington was not stained by a single
> blot.
> (McGrane, "Washington, Anglo American
> Hero," p. 9.)

As a perfectly balanced man, Washington became the model
American in every facet of life. He was a "nobler human
type" than any ancient hero, according to Charles W. Eliot.
Silas W. Deane wrote in a letter,

> Let our Youth look up to this man as a
> pattern to form themselves by; who unites
> the bravery of the soldier with the most
> consummate modesty and virtue.
> (Nettles, "The Washington Theme," p. 175.)

41.   Bryan, *Washington in American Literature*, p. 50.

42.   Albanese, *Sons of the Fathers*, p. 46.

43.   Gabriel, *The Course of American Democratic
Thought*, p. 97.

44.   Birthday oratory is examined well in Schauffler,
Washington's Birthday.

45.   Albanese, *Sons of the Fathers*, p. 161.

46.   Jasper B. Shannon, "The President: Rex,
Princeps, Imperator?" in Joseph M. Ray, ed., *The President:
Rex, Princeps, Imperator?* (University of Texas at El Paso:
Texas Western Press, 1969):1-18.

47.   Louis Smith, *American Democracy and Military
Power* (Chicago: The University of Chicago Press, 1951),
p. 34.

48.   For an interesting discussion of different kinds
of warriors who have tried to become successful in politics,
see T. Harry Williams, "The Macs and the Ikes: America's
Two Military Traditions," *American Mercury* LXXV (October,
1951):32-39.

49.   Stephen E. Ambrose, *Crazy Horse and Custer* (Garden City, New York: Doubleday and Company, 1975), p. 182.

50.   Ibid., p. 185.

51.   In addition to Ambrose, these books were helpful to me in constructing a picture of the life of Custer: Marguerite Merington, ed., *The Custer Story: The Life and Intimate Letters of General George A. Custer and His Wife Elizabeth* (New York: Devin-Adair, 1950), and Jay Monaghan, *Custer: The Life of General George Armstrong Custer* (Boston: Little, Brown, 1959); especially helpful for his career in the west were George A. Custer, *My Life on the Plains* (Norman, Okla.:   University of Oklahoma Press, 1962), and Elizabeth B. Custer, *"Boots and Saddles," Or, Life in Dakota with General Custer* (Norman, Okla.:   University of Oklahoma Press, 1952).

52.   Henry Nash Smith, *Virgin Land: The American West as Symbol and Myth* (Cambridge, Mass.:   Harvard University Press, 1970), p. 152.

53.   Taylor, *America as Art*, p. 143.

54.   There are, of course, other perceptions of native Americans.   The West was often seen as a potential home for a regenerate community, free from the corruption not only of the old European world, but from the corruption of eastern America.   Indians could still be moral antagonists, but also possible converts.   If one viewed the West as a place where a full communication with nature was possible, the Indian became the symbol of this virtue, the "noble savage."   It was not only in static categories that the Indian was seen.   Nineteenth century anthropological thought viewed the Indian as a degenerative form from past great cultures.

55.   The amount of material discussing controversial points about the battle is enormous.   Perhaps the best "road map" through various issues is W. A. Graham, *The Custer Myth: A Source Book of Custeriana* (Harrisburg, Pennsylvania: The Stackpole Company, 1953).

56.   For an excellent discussion about the shift in opinion, see Bruce Rosenberg, *Custer and the Epic of Defeat* (University Park: The Pennsylvania University Press, 1974), pp. 73ff.

57.   "First Account of the Custer Massacre," *Bismarck (N.D.) Tribune*, 6 July 1876.

58.   A. J. Donelle, comp. and ed., *Cyclorama of Custer's Last Battle* or *The Battle of the Little Big Horn* (New York: Argonaut Press, 1966), p. 19.   The idea of the army being at the picket line of civilization was not merely an old general's idea.   One of the subheadings in the *Bismarck Tribune* carrying the first account of the battle was "Is This the Beginning of the End?"

59.   *Boston Sunday Globe*, 20 June 1926.

60.   C. B. Galbreath, "George Armstrong Custer," *Ohio Archaeological Quarterly*, XLI (October, 1932): 631.

61.   Col. Ralph D. Cole, "Custer, the Man of Action," in ibid., p. 635.

62.   Eugene McAuliffe, *The Seventh United States Cavalry.   "Too Long Neglected"* (n.p.   March 1, 1957), p. 3.

63.   Rosenberg, *Custer and Defeat*, p. 97.

64.   Kent Steckmesser, *The Western Hero in History and Legend* (Norman: University of Oklahoma Press, 1965), p. 200.

65.   Frederick Whittaker, ed., *A Complete Life of General George Armstrong Custer* (New York: Sheldon and Company, 1876), p. 599.

66.   Ibid., p. 600.

67.   Rosenberg, *Custer and Defeat*, p. 219.

68.   Ibid., p. 1.

69.   Graham, in *The Custer Myth*, discusses several of these legends.   Rosenberg believes similar narrative elements are present in the other Last Stands he discusses, suggesting that various peoples have symbolized their tragic heroes in similar structural form.

70.   Rosenberg, *Custer and Defeat*, p. 150.

71.   Ibid., p. 3.   See his discussions in Chapters Three and Seven, especially.

72.   William F. Cody became one of the first to reenact the battle, accomplishing dramatically what Whittaker did in literary form.   In Cody's Wild West Show appearing before thousands in America and Europe, Custer's Last Stand was the climax.

73. J. R. Kelly, *The Battle of the Little Big Horn. Requiem for the Men in the Shadows* (n.p. 1957), p. 16.

74. Steckmesser, *The Western Hero*, p. 207.

75: Ibid., p. 211.

76. Ibid., p. 213.

77. Elson, *Guardians*, p. 327.

78. Ibid., p. 192.

79. Edward H. O'Neill, *A History of American Biography 1800-1935* (Philadelphia: University of Pennsylvania Press, 1935), p. 355.

80. For excellent discussion of Custer in popular memory, see Brian Dippie, *Custer's Last Stand: The Anatomy of an American Myth* (Missoula, Montana: University of Montana, 1976), and Don Russell, *Custer's List* (Fort Worth, Texas: Amon Carter Museum of Western Art, 1969).

The veneration of a living hero who had taken part in this battle is graphically illustrated by the tremendous interest in Comanche, the cavalry horse who survived the battle. Capt. Edward S. Luce recently wrote, "With blood dripping from his many wounds he consecrated that battlefield."

Comanche became a sacred animal. He was given a special stall, was never put to work, and always paraded with Troop I of the Seventh Cavalry on ceremonial occasions. He was mounted as a symbol of a cavalry horse and is on display in the National History Museum at the University of Kansas. There is further information about Comanche in Graham, *The Custer Myth*, and his story was popularized in the Walt Disney movie *Tonka*.

Even in the modern "cavalry," some are nostalgic for the old martial forms and see Comanche as an ancestor.

Now in our cavalry of today, we have what can be termed "iron horses," which wear armor at least twenty times heavier than that of the Middle Ages....Thus, evolution has changed the cavalry. There will be no more Comanches. But it is doubtful in any case whether another horse could show better the true spirit of the cavalry arm of the service. To even the modern cavalryman in an armored car or tank, "Comanche

still lives."
(Capt. Edward S. Luce, *Keogh, Comanche,
and Custer* [Ashland, Oregon: Lewis
Osborne, 1974], pp. 27-28 and 80.)

81.   Rosenberg, *Custer and Defeat*, p. 56.   The
importance of the pictures and other portrayals of Custer
should not be underestimated.   L. Kirstein writes,

> No one present at Custer's Last Stand
> survived to depict it, nor was the Maine
> caught by a *Life* photographer.   But these
> disasters and others less famous have
> taken their place in the American historic
> consciousness largely due to those very
> popular pictures that sprang up immed-
> iately to immortalize them....The lurid
> action, stylized into a tableau...has
> meant far more to our collective memory
> than documented memoir or careful history.
> (L. Kirstein, "American Battle Art:
> 1588-1944," *Magazine of Art* [March-May,
> 1944]: 147.)

82.   Recent revisions regarding Custer, especially
in works giving the "underside" of white America's treatment of native Americans by Dee Brown, Vine DeLoria, et
al., and the movie *Little Big Man* may change the status
of Custer and the perception of the Last Stand.   (Even
before historical revision began, Custer's popular image
had been questioned in the early sixties.   One of the
popular songs of the early sixties was entitled, "Please
Mr. Custer, I Don't Wanna Go."   Also, Johnny Cash sang:

> To some he was a hero
> but to me his score was zero
> and the Gen'ral he won't ride
> well anymore.
> (Brian W. Dippie, "Bards of the
> Little Big Horn," *Western American
> Literature* 1 [Fall, 1966]: 187.)

For any major change in the perception of Custer in the
near future, several elements have to be reckoned with.
First, as Rosenberg points out, Custer <u>lost</u> the battle,

> and to see his death and that of all the
> five companies with him symbolizing the
> most destructive aspects of white racism
> takes a greater suspension of disbelief
> than most Americans are able to muster.

Secondly, and more importantly, any change will have to
be a transformation of basic mythic and symbolic perceptions. In this respect, the Custer myth is like the
Hitler myth, "Hitler will remain the Siegfried who conquered the dragons of Europe and destroyed their 'treacherous' coalitions with the Judaic Nibelungs." (Rosenberg,
Custer and Defeat, pp. 205 and 283.)

That a warrior, esteemed throughout a war which saved the
Union, and immortalized by a mysterious, heroic and regenerative death which no Euro-American witnessed yet
everyone "felt" will be degraded by historical revision
alone, no matter how correct, is a dubious proposition.
Even during the Vietnamese conflict, the memory of the
"gallant Seventh" was present. On November 17, 1965, the
Laramie (Wy.) *Daily Boomerang* reported on a fight with
the enemy, saying,

> The brunt of the Communist attacks was
> taken by the 1st Cavalry's storied First
> Battalion, 7th Regiment--the unit that
> during the Indian wars was commanded by
> George Armstrong Custer. (Dippie, "Bards,"
> p. 193.)

     83. Significantly, Custer is often perceived to have
died on the top of the hill where the monument stands.
The persistence of the symbol of the hilltop as a signifi-
cant place in battle is still popular. The English War
Memorials Advisory Council stated shortly after World War
II,

> A hill to which in the course of one's
> daily round one can lift one's eyes in
> memory of the fallen, a hill which one
> can climb, away from the world's dis-
> tractions for periods of reflections,
> may well in rural areas where such land
> can be secured, form one of the most
> fitting of memorials.
> ("Hilltop as a War Memorial," *Royal
> Society of Arts Journal* 93 [August 31,
> 1945]: 524.)

The Little Big Horn takes its place beside other significant action on a hill or mountaintop. Moses received the
Commandments on a mountain, the Jews fought to the last
from the heights of Masada, Jesus said the Lord's Prayer
on a mountain. In American history, a persistent theme
has been the imagery from John Winthrop's "citie on a
hill" speech aboard the flagship *Arbella*. The statue

commemorating the Marines' raising of the flag on Iwo Jima is instantly recognized. Eliade tells us, "The mountain, because it is the meeting place of heaven and earth, is situated at the center of the world, and is of course the highest point of the earth." (*Patterns*, p. 100.) Thus, for the Custer epic, battle becomes a revelation of the sacred, a hierophany. The basic conflict of good and evil is present, and the hero sacrifices himself at the sacred meeting place, so that his mission may be complete.

84. Kelly, *Battle of the Little Big Horn*, p. 9.

85. John Field, "Patton of the Armored Force," *Life*, November 30, 1942, p. 116. Assistant Secretary of State William Lacy also said, "He was the modern J. E. B. Stuart, the eternal cavalryman." In Frederick Ayer, Jr., *Before the Colors Fade; Portrait of a Soldier*, with a Foreword by Omar N. Bradley (Dunwoody, Georgia: Norman S. Berg, 1971), p. 103.

86. Martin Blumenson, *The Patton Papers 1940-1945* (Boston: Houghton Mifflin Co., 1974), p. 840. Patton's celebrated shoot-out with two of Pancho Villa's men in 1915, while serving under General Pershing, helped form this image.

87. Vagts, *Militarism*, p. 479.

88. Blumenson, *Papers 1940-1945*, p. 847.

89. Charles R. Codman, *Drive* (Boston: Little, Brown and Co., 1957), p. 271.

90. S. K. Oberbeck, "Total Warrior," *Newsweek*, October 7, 1974, p. 98.

91. For Patton,

War was a passionate pursuit, a pursuit as coherent and profoundly satisfying as music is to a composer and painting to an artist. War made sense to Patton, and he lived it, thought it, and worked at it, ardent and unceasingly, every day of his life from earliest youth to his death.
(Robert Sharon Allen, *Lucky Forward* [New York: The Vanguard Press, Inc., 1947], p. 23.)

92.   William Bancroft Mellor, *Patton, Fighting Man*
(New York: G. P. Putnam's Sons, 1946), p. 13. For good
biographical information, see Martin Blumenson, *The Patton
Papers 1885-1940* (Boston: Houghton Mifflin Co., 1972);
Herbert Essame, *Patton: A Study in Command* (New York:
Charles Scribner's Sons, 1974); Ladislas Farago, *Patton:
Ordeal and Triumph* (New York: Ivan Obolensky, Inc., 1964);
Army Times, *Warrior: The Story of General George S. Patton*
(New York: G. P. Putnam's Sons, 1967). I have already
mentioned other works which contain helpful biographical
information: Ayer, *Before the Colors Fade*; Blumenson,
Papers 1940-1945; Codman, *Drive*; and Allen, *Lucky Forward*.

93.   Army Times, *Warrior*, p. 24.

94.   Blumenson, *Papers 1885-1940*, p. 723. The weight
of military tradition is well illustrated by the anthem
"The Corps":

> The Corps! Bareheaded salute it,
> With eyes up, thanking our God
> That we of the Corps are treading
> Where they of the Corps have trod--
> They are here in ghostly assemblage,
> The men of the Corps long dead,
> And our hearts are standing attention
> While we wait for their passing tread.
> We, sons of today, we salute you--
> You, sons of an earlier day;
> We follow, close order, behind you,
> Where you have pointed the way;
> The long gray line of us stretches
> Through the years of a century told,
> And the last man feels to his marrow
> The grip of your far-off hold.
> Grip hands with us now, though we see not,
> Grip hands with us, strengthen our hearts,
> As the long line stiffens and straightens
> With the thrill that your presence imparts,
> Grip hands--though it be from the shadows--
> While we swear, as you did of yore,
> Or living or dying to honor
> The Corps, and the Corps, and the Corps!
> (Army Times, *Warrior*, p. 25.)

95.   Both in Ayer, *Before the Colors Fade*, pp. 96-97.

96.   Ibid., p. 9.

97.   His flamboyance invited comparisons with Custer,
though Custer was much more impulsive and boyish in his

antics than Patton. Nevertheless, Patton provided a figure for popular adoration. One radio announcer described him, "A fiction writer couldn't create him. History itself hasn't matched him. He's colorful, fabulous. He's dynamite. On a battlefield he's a warring, roaring comet." (Blumenson, *Papers 1940-1945*, p. 524.)

    98. Essame, *Patton*, p. 208.

    99. Codman, *Drive*, p. 159.

    100. Patton was so aware of the power of an inspiring commander that he would practice his "war face" before a mirror.

    101. John J. Pullen, *Patriotism in America: A Study of Changing Devotions, 1770-1970* (New York: American Heritage Press, 1971), p. 137.

    102. Blumenson, *Papers 1885-1940*, p. 790.

    103. Ibid., p. 797. Likewise, his statue at West Point is characterized as exuding "command presence." Army Times, *Warrior*, p. 12.

    104. Blumenson, *Papers 1885-1940*, p. 757.

    105. Ibid., p. 796.

    106. Ibid., p. 757.

    107. George Smith Patton, *War as I Knew It* (Boston: Houghton Mifflin Co., 1947), p. 403. Patton made several allusions to sports when he spoke of discipline. He wanted automatic obedience, "so that when the quarterback gives the signal of life or death in the near day of battle, you will not think and then act, but will act and...think later--after the war." Blumenson, *Papers 1885-1940*, p. 500. Battle was the culmination, like the big game:

> Battle is the most magnificent compet-
> ition in which a human being can in-
> dulge...it brings out all that is best;
> it removes all that is base. All men
> are afraid in battle. The coward is
> the one who lets his fear overcome his
> sense of duty. Duty is the essence of
> manhood.
> (Army Times, *Warrior*, p. 113.)

The relationship between sports and battle is pronounced in Patton and may provide some clues to the location of the warrior figure in our time. Patton excelled at individual sports, such as swimming, riding, and track. Polo was also a game he played intensely. Essame says that Patton and Montgomery were both "ardent players of violent games." (*Patton*, p. 4.) Joseph Ellis tells us that one of MacArthur's sayings is inscribed on the arch of the cadet gymnasium at West Point. "Upon the fields of friendly strife are sown the seeds that upon other days, will bear the fruits of victory." (Joseph Ellis and Robert Moore, *School for Soldiers. West Point and the Profession of Arms* [New York: Oxford University Press, 1974], p. 198.)

It is no coincidence that Vince Lombardi, the Patton of professional football, served his apprenticeship under the legendary Red Blaik. Like Patton, he believed discipline and training were the keys to victory. Patton saw the connection between battle and sports as a quality of decisiveness. Battles and wars, like games, usually have a winner and a loser. Patton, like most Americans, thought it our right and our purpose to win whatever righteous battle we had embarked upon. In June, 1943, he spoke to his men, saying:

> We Americans are a competitive race. We
> bet on anything. We love to win. In
> this next fight, you are entering the
> greatest sporting competition of all
> times...for the greatest price of all--
> victory.
> (Blumenson, *Papers 1940-1945*, p. 269.)

Conversely, John Blum notes that war reporters stressed the athletic ability of war leaders.

> A culture that had made heroes of its
> athletes could hardly avoid making
> athletes of its heroes. Men who had
> found their boyhood models in Babe Ruth
> or Red Grange or Bobby Jones now served
> under Weaver or Clark or Patton...journal-
> ism did not create them, but it helped to
> make them appealing symbols for Americans
> in the service or at home.
> (John Morton Blum, *V Was For Victory:
> Politics and American Culture During
> World War II* [New York: Harcourt Brace
> Jovanovich, 1976], p. 58.)

108. Napoleon, like Patton, considered incompetent leadership "criminal." "The greatest crime that man can commit on earth [is] to kill on purpose men whose lives are entrusted to his direction and honor." Like Patton, T. E. Lawrence considered improper training "sinful." "To me an unnecessary action, or shot, or casualty, was not only waste, but sin." (Vagts, *Militarism*, pp. 15-16.)

109. Patton's view of training and battle is not always popular. Carl Cohen, writing about the proper use of the military in a democracy, believes that military life uncivilizes the recruit. Training assumes the American is

> by birth, training, and temperament ex-
> ceedingly civil...he is a civilian through
> and through. The corruption and degener-
> ation of military training may be imposed
> upon him, but it must always be imposed.
> (Carl Cohen, "The Military in a Democracy,"
> *Centennial Review* [Winter, 1963]: 92.)

Patton would probably answer that far from being degenerate, military training introduces men to the finest virtues that civilian life has not taught them, and proper training and battle experience will give them a moral stature superior to civilians.

110. Blumenson, *Papers 1885-1940*, p. 675. In a letter to his father in 1916, Patton said, "Only in epochs where the state is dominent [sic] has man advanced. Individualism is the theory of decay." (Ibid., p. 368.)

111. Ayer, *Before the Colors Fade*, p. 68.

112. George S. Patton, "War Letters," *Atlantic Monthly*, December, 1947, p. 34.

113. Blumenson, *1885-1940*, p. 16.

114. Blumenson, *Papers 1940-1945*, p. 906.

115. Ibid., p. 257.

116. Ibid., p. 611.

117. Patton, *War as I Knew It*, p. 8.

118. Ayer, *Before the Colors Fade*, p. 21.

119. Blumenson, *Papers 1885-1940*, p. 818.

120.   Patton, *War as I Knew It*, p. 404.

121.   Codman, *Drive*, p. 188.

122.   "Fighter's Words," *Time*, January 25, 1943, p. 61.
Patton assumed that the God of Battles was on his and
America's side. To his troops in Tunisia he said,

> The German is a war-trained veteran--
> confident, brave, and ruthless. We are
> brave. We are better equipped, better
> fed, and in the place of his blood-
> gutted Woten, we have with us the God
> of Our Fathers Known of Old.
> (Blumenson, *Papers 1940-1945*, p. 187.)

Time, in its "Religion" section, spoke about Patton's
prayers to God, especially his famous "Weather Prayer"
during the Battle of the Bulge. See issues of January 29,
1945, and January 10, 1949. Following is Patton's poem
"God of Battles," which he recited during the celebration
at the Coliseum, upon his return after the war.

> From pride and foolish confidence
> From every weakening creed
> From the dread fear of fearing
> Protect us, Lord and lead.
> Great God, who through the ages
> Hast braced the bloodstained hand.
> As Saturn, Jove or Woden
> Hast led our warrior band,
> Again we seek thy counsel,
> But not in cringing guise.
> We whine not for thy mercy-
> to slay: God make us wise.
> For slaves who shun the issue
> We do not ask thy aid.
> To Thee we trust our spirits
> Our bodies unafraid.
> From doubt and fearsome boding,
> Still Thou our spirits guard,
> Make strong our souls to conquer,
> Give us the victory, Lord.
> (*Los Angeles Times*, 10 June 1945, p. 2.)

123.   Cavaioli, *West Point and the Presidency*, p. 104.

124.   George S. Patton, "War Letters," *Atlantic Monthly*,
January, 1948, p. 56.

125. Martin Blumenson believes that Patton's rage, especially at the end of the war, was partially caused by subdural hematoma.

126. *New York Times*, 16 December 1945, p. 7.

127. Some observers heard him include the Russians.

128. Again, Patton relied on fate to support him, saying,

> I am destined to achieve some great
> thing--what, I don't know, but this
> last incident was so trivial in its
> nature, but so terrible in its effect,
> that it is not the result of an accident
> but the work of God. His Will be Done.
> (Blumenson, *Papers 1940-1945*, p. 439.)

129. Blumenson, *Papers 1940-1945*, p. 706. For detailed discussion of this unhappy period, see Ladislas Farago, *The Last Days of Patton* (New York: Berkley Books, 1982).

130. Codman, *Drive*, p. 141.

131. Herman Wouk, *The Caine Mutiny* (Garden City, New York: Doubleday and Co., 1952); and Norman Mailer, *The Naked and the Dead* (New York: Rinehart and Co., 1948).

132. Peter Aichinger, *The American Soldier in Fiction, 1880-1963* (Ames: Iowa State University Press, 1975), p. 54.

133. Ibid., p. 49.

134. Ellis and Moore, *School for Soldiers*, p. 161.

135. Ayer, *Before the Colors Fade*, p. 83

136. J. W. Montgomery, "Patton," *Christianity Today* 15 (October 23, 1970): 50-51.

137. Oberbeck, "Total Warrior," p. 98.

138. Blumenson, *Papers 1885-1940*, p. 4.

139. *New York Times*, 8 June 1945, p. 6; *New York Times*, 10 June 1945, p. 20.

140. *Los Angeles Times*, 10 June 1945, p. A.

141. Ibid., p. 1.

142. Mellon, *Patton*, p. 230.

143. Also, in 1946, The Philadelphia Sons of the
American Revolution honored George Washington and his
fourth grand-nephew, Patton, "one of the great immortals
of our country." (*New York Times*, 23 February 1946, p. 2.)

144. Blumenson, *Papers 1940-1945*, p. 840. Actually,
they did have a Patton. Colonel George S. Patton, Jr.
served in Vietnam in command of the 11th Armored Cavalry
Regiment. The *New York Times* headlined an article, "Son
of Patton Leads Tank Regiment in Vietnam." (31 July 1968,
p. 3.) He received the Distinguished Service Cross for
"exceptionally valorous action." (*New York Times*,
23 December 1968, p. 32.)

145. Bernard Weiner, "Patton," *Film Quarterly* 23
(Summer 1970): 61.

146. David Wilson, "Patton," *Sight and Sound* 39
(Summer 1970): 160.

147. Ellis and Moore, *School for Soldiers*, p. 162.

148. Patton was clearly a model and a nostalgic figure
for one important American, Richard M. Nixon. He was
enamored of the movie, viewing it several times. He was
particularly impressed with Patton's faith in the "Weather
Prayer." He applied it to Vietnam, saying, "We have every
chaplain in Vietnam praying for early rain. You have to
have the will and determination to go out and do what is
right for America." Nixon identified with Patton and his
crises. His associates in the White House "believe that the
emergence of Patton as a major figure in the Nixon pantheon
is a good sign--meaning that he will continue to hang tough
in the crunches." (Hugh Sidey, "Anybody See Patton?" *Life*,
June 19, 1970, p. 2B.)

Evans and Novak note that the decision to invade Cambodia
was made only after Nixon had watched *Patton* several times.
"The Impact of *Patton* on Nixon's Cambodian decision was felt
by every close advisor who was aware of the President's repeated viewings." See Rowland Evans, Jr. and Robert D.
Novak, *Nixon in the White House: The Frustrations of Power*
(New York: Random House, 1971), p. 252.

I deal with contemporary nostalgia for Patton in "Nostalgia
for Clarity: The Memory of Patton," *Studies in Popular
Culture* 5 (1982).

CHAPTER TWO

1. Walter Millis, *Arms and Men* (New York: Mentor Books, 1956), p. 23.

2. John Shy, *A People Numerous and Armed* (New York: Oxford University Press, 1976), p. 236.

3. John A. Logan, *The Volunteer Soldier of America* (Chicago: R. S. Peale and Company, 1887), p. 105.

4. Ibid., p. 105.

5. Ibid., p. 77.

6. Joel Barlow mentions in The Science of Liberty (from "Advice to the Privileged Orders," 1792) that equality in America results in numerous "operations." One of them is the ability to

> Make every citizen a soldier, and every
> soldier a citizen; not only <u>permitting</u>
> every man to arm, but obliging him to
> arm....It is because the people are
> civilized, that they are with safety
> armed.
> (Frederick C. Prescott and John H.
> Nelson, ed., *Prose and Poetry of the
> Revolution* [Port Washington, N.Y.:
> Kennikat Press, Inc., 1969], p. 174.)

7. Victor Hicken, *The American Fighting Man* (New York: The Macmillan Company, 1969), p. 177. Some of the well-known names are Gringo, Johnny Reb, Billy Yank, Roughrider, Doughboy, and G.I. Joe.

8. William Matthews and Dixon Wecter, *Our Soldiers Speak. 1775-1918* (Boston: Little, Brown and Company, 1943), p. viii.

9. The soldier's experience fits into this pattern. He separates by going into training. His initiation comes during the experience of battle. He is set apart after his return because of the sacred nature of his mission.

10. Dixon Wecter, *The Hero in America* (New York: Charles Scribner's Sons, 1941), p. 82.

11. Vagts suggests that von Steuben was responsible for the "considerate treatment of the common soldier [which led] to the beginnings of mass honor--a revolutionary idea." (Alfred Vagts, *A History of Militarism* [New York: Meridian Books, 1959], p. 100.)

Charles Hatch notes that Sgt. William Brown became the first common soldier to receive a "Badge of Military Merit," or Purple Heart. This award fell into disuse, but was finally reinstated in 1932. (See Charles E. Hatch, "Medal of Honor of the Revolution," *Virginia Cavalcade* 13 [1963]: 14-17.)

12. Ralph Waldo Emerson, *A Historical Discourse Delivered Before the Citizens of Concord, 12 September 1835 on the Centennial Anniversary of the Incorporation of the Town* (Boston: W. B. Clarke, 1835), p. 35.

Samuel Ripley Bartlett expresses a similar view in his *Concord Fight*:

> Dear Liberty herself once paused to think
> The best; then cast her robes of peace aside,
> And risked her all in War's uncertain tide.
> A second Marathon: a rustic few, unskilled
> Save in the arts by which their fields they tilled,
> Here smote the giant skill and laid him low,
> Humbled in dust, slain by a pigmy's blow.
> (Published in Boston: A. Williams and Company,
> [1860], p. 8.)

13. Matthews and Wecter, *Our Soldiers*, p. 4. The monument was finished in 1875. In addition to symbolizing the agrarian warrior, it represented one

> Who ventured life and love and youth
> For the greatest prize of death in battle.
> (*Proceedings of the Centennial Celebration
> of Concord Fight April 19, 1875* [Concord, Mass.:
> Published by the town, 1876], p. 16.)

14. Bartlett, *Concord Fight*, p. 24.

15. Prescott and Nelson, *Prose and Poetry*, p. 99.

16. John Witherspoon believed that the "state of a society...is what gives a particular color to the style." Republican states are often bold and ferocious; thus, Witherspoon suggests that warrior virtues are almost a biological part of the American personality and ethos. (Benjamin T. Spencer, *The Quest for Nationality* [n.p.: Syracuse University Press, 1957], p. 10.)

James Russell Lowell comments on the difference between
English and American soldiers:

> These men were brave enough and true
> to the hired soldier's bull-dog creed;
> What brought them here they never knew
> They fought as suits the English breed.

Of Americans he says:

> Their graves have voices; if they threw
> Dice charged with Fates beyond their ken,
> Yet to their instincts they were true,
> And had the genius to be men.
> ("Lines: Suggested by the Graves of Two
> English Soldiers on Concord Battleground,"
> in *The Complete Poetical Works of James
> Russell Lowell*, Cambridge Edition [Boston:
> Houghton Mifflin Co., 1897], pp. 96-97.)

17. Oscar Brand, *Songs of '76* (Philadelphia: M.
Evans and Company, Inc., 1972), p. 41.

18. Walter Muir Whitehill, *Amos Doolittle, 1754-1832.
In Freedom's Cause, A Portfolio of Revolutionary War En-
gravings by Amos Doolittle* (Chicago: R. R. Donnelley and
Sons, Lakeside Press, 1974), p. 13.

Oliver Larkin comments, "Amos neither possessed the skill
nor harbored the intention to glorify history. Yet there
was an eyewitness fidelity and conviction in these scenes."
(Oliver W. Larkin, *Art and Life in America* [New York:
Rinehart and Company, Inc., 1949], p. 58.)

19. Stow Persons, "The Cyclical Theory of History in
Eighteenth Century America," *American Quarterly* 6 (1954):
158.

20. Philip Davidson, *Propaganda and the American
Revolution: 1776-1783* (Chapel Hill: The University of
North Carolina Press, 1941), p. 183.

21. Arthur H. Buffington, "The Puritan View of War,"
Publications of the Colonial Society of Massachusetts 28
(April, 1931): 70.

22. Spencer, *Quest for Nationality*, p. 42.

23. For early American colonists, wars of purification had not only to do with defeating the enemy, but
also with purification of the sins of one's own group

which helped bring on this calamity of war. Douglas Leach
says:

> It is not easy for the modern generation
> to imagine such a public self examination
> as the Puritan colonies imposed on them-
> selves during King Philip's War. In our
> day the emphasis is at the opposite ex-
> treme. Thinking of our wars as crusades
> for righteousness, we feed ourselves on
> long lists of the enemy's sins rather
> than our own.

In speaking of the "triumph" of the Christians over the
Indians, Leach touches upon a basic element in all American
wars. "It would seem that the final triumph...depended not
so much upon military resources, although they were certainly
important, as upon a great moral victory over sin." (Douglas
Edward Leach, *Flintlock and Tomahawk* [New York: W. W. Norton
and Company, Inc., 1966], pp. 190 and 193.)

24. Davidson, *Propaganda and the Revolution*, p. 129.
Davidson quotes a newspaper which gave a description of what
slavery would be like. The element of chaos is certainly
present:

> He will debauch your Wives and Daughters,
> devour your Cattle, Swine, Corn and
> Poultry: He will set fire to your Woods,
> trample on the tender Plants in your
> Gardens, break down your Fences, and
> make your pleasant Fields desolate.
> Whenever he reigns among you, he will
> make Dastards of brave men, and Fools
> of the Fearful; Thieves of the Honest;
> and Whores of the Modest; Reprobates of
> the Religious; and Madmen of the Moral.
> In short there is no diabolical Change,
> which the infernal Monster, called
> SLAVERY, cannot accomplish.
> (Ibid., p. 130.)

25. Zabdiel Adams, "The Evil Designs of Men Made
Subservient by God to the Public Good; Particularly
Illustrated in the Rise, Progress, and Conclusion of the
American War," a sermon preached at Lexington, 19 April
1783, p. 14.

26. Leonard J. Kramer, "Muskets in the Pulpit,
1776-1783," *Presbyterian Historical Society Journal* 31
(December, 1953): 242.

27. Prescott and Nelson, *Prose and Poetry*, p. 89.
Regarding the effect of martial music, Arthur Schlesinger
wrote, "No one can gauge the effect of this musical propaganda, but its very existence suggests that it served its
purpose." ("A Note on Songs as Patriot Propaganda," *William
and Mary Quarterly* Ser. 3,11 [January, 1954]: 78.)

Vera Lawrence supports this claim in her notice of the
following from the *Boston Chronicle* of 1769:

> But when our country's cause the Sword demands,
> And sets in fierce array, the warrior bands;
> Strong martial music, glorious rage inspires,
> Wakes the bold wish and fans the rising fires.
> (Vera Brodsky Lawrence, *Music for Patriots,
> Politicians, and Presidents* [New York: The
> Macmillan Company, 1975], p. 53.)

28. Kramer, "Muskets in the Pulpit," p. 244.

29. Moses Coit Tyler, *The Literary History of the
American Revolution: 1776-1783*, Vol. II (New York: Frederick
Ungar Publishing Company, 1957), p. 162.

30. Lowell, *The Complete Works*, pp. 361-362.

31. Barrett, *Concord Fight*, p. 30.   John Greenleaf
Whittier echoes a similar feeling:

> Their death-shot shook the feudal tower,
> And shattered slavery's chain as well:
> On the sky's dome, as on a bell,
> Its echoes struck the World's great hour.
> (E. G. Porter, *Souvenir of Lexington*
> [Boston: James R. Osgood and Co., 1875],
> p. 1.)

32. Benson J. Lossing, *Seventeen and Seventy-Six*
(Detroit: Singing Tree Press, 1970), p. 152. (First
published in 1847.)

33. *Ceremonies at the Dedication of the Soldiers'
Monument in Concord, Mass.* (Concord: Benjamin Tolman,
1867), p. 19.

The Monument was to be an example to all of the courage of
the soldiers. At the dedication Emerson gave an address,
saying in part:

> 'Tis certain that a plain stone like this,
> standing on such memories, having no

> reference to utilities, but only to the
> grand instincts of the civil and moral
> man...becomes a sentiment, a poet, a
> passenger, an altar where the noble
> youth shall in all time come to make
> his sweet vows. (Ibid., p. 31.)

34. Ibid., p. 66. Several poems offered at the Dedication also stressed the theme of the fertile and nourishing blood of the Minutemen, necessary for the birth of liberty.

35. Ibid., p. 11.

36. Jonas Clarke, "The Fate of Blood-Thirsty Oppressors, and God's Tender Care of His Distressed People," a sermon preached at Lexington, 19 April 1776, p. 28.

37. Davidson, *Propaganda and the Revolution*, p. 189.

38. E. F. Worcester, *Concord and Lexington* (Boston: The Worcester Press, 1909), p. 62.

On July 7, 1774, Isaiah Thomas began using the picture of a rattlesnake attacking a griffon as the masthead of the *Massachusetts Spy*. "The snake is in pieces designated G, SC, NC, V, M, P, NJ, NY, NE, and above the piece is the motto 'Join or Die.'" (Donald H. Creswell, comp., *The American Revolution in Drawings and Prints*, with a foreword by Sinclair H. Hutchins [Washington: Library of Congress, 1975], p. 266.)

39. Prescott and Nelson, *Prose and Poetry*, p. 86.

40. Bartlett, *Concord Fight*, p. 23.

41. Merle Curti, "Dime Novels and the American Tradition," *Yale Review* 26 (1937): 775.

42. Irma B. Jaffe, *John Trumbull, Patriot-Artist of the American Revolution* (Boston: New York Graphic Society, 1975), p. 94. This, of course, is not a purely American trait. The bronze sculpture by Auguste Rodin, *The Burghers of Calais* (1886), is a powerful example of self-sacrifice. (See *War and Peace, Man Through His Art*, Vol. I [Greenwich, Connecticut: New York Graphic Society, 1964], pp. 57-60.)

43. For comprehensive background on these plays, see Norman Philbrick, ed., *Trumpets Sounding: Propaganda Plays of the American Revolution* (New York: Benjamin Blom, Inc., 1972).

44. Ibid., p. 230.

45. Ibid., p. 246.

46. Ibid.

47. Ibid., p. 130.

48. Ibid., p. 87.

49. Ibid., p. 105. Arthur Schlesinger points out in "Patriotism Names the Baby," *New England Quarterly* 14 (December, 1940), that Joseph Warren became a popular name. This shows another way that Americans remember their heroes. In the Puritan period, those "who embarked for North America were like the rest of their brethren. If we forget the sur- names, the passenger lists suggest the crossing of the Red Sea rather than the Atlantic." In the Revolutionary period and after, there was a shift to martial heroes because "military chieftains seemed most fitting to symbolize the intensified struggle for colonial rights." (pp. 612 and 615.)

50. During the Centennial Celebration of Concord Fight, a Rev. Reynolds explained that the Minutemen had waited to fire until the British shot:

>   In all human history there is no more
>   noble instance of the subordination of
>   passion to duty than the silence, until
>   the lawful order came, of those four
>   hundred muskets at North Bridge.
>   (*Proceedings at the Centennial*, p. 55.)

51. All three stanzas from Prescott and Nelson, *Prose and Poetry*, pp. 235-236.

52. Edward Everett, *An Address*, Delivered at Lexington, 19 April 1835 (Charlestown: William W. Wheildon, 1835), p. 8.

According to Porter, the American soldier was motivated by pure patriotism. After the massacre at Lexington, the Minutemen courageously stood up to the British at Concord.

>   Hirelings would never have done it;
>   timid, cautious men would not have
>   favored it; But these heroes were
>   made of sterner stuff; and they had
>   the honor of being the first in arms
>   to show the world what Americans

>meant when they spoke of liberty and
>inalienable rights.
>(*Souvenir of Lexington*, p. 10.)

53. Frank Luther Mott, "The Newspaper Coverage of
Lexington and Concord," *New England Quarterly* 17 (December,
1944): 500.

54. Kramer, "Muskets in the Pulpit," p. 38.

55. Philip Freneau, *Poems Relating to the American
Revolution* (New York: W. S. Widdleton, 1865), p. 114.
Hicken's *American Fighting Man* also stresses this, pp. 38-
40.

56. Emerson, *Historical Discourse*, p. 40. John
Kirkland's Phi Beta Kappa Address in Boston in 1798 revealed the longing for the presence of the primal heroes:

>We have learned to love our country,
>because we are near it, and in it...
>because the sweat of our Fathers'
>brows has subdued its soil; their
>blood watered its fields, and their
>revered dust sleeps in its bosom;
>because it embraces our Fathers and
>Mothers.
>(Merle Curti, *The Roots of American
>Loyalty* [New York: Columbia University
>Press, 1946], p. 52.)

57. The Minuteman tradition obviously spread beyond
the realm of warfare. The pattern was suggested by a
speech at the Centennial Celebration:

>Wherever party spirit shall strain
>the ancient guaranties of Freedom;
>or bigotry and ignorance shall lay
>their fatal hands upon education;
>or the arrogance of cast shall
>strike at equal rights; or corrup-
>tion shall poison the very springs
>of national life,--there minute-men
>of liberty, are your Lexington
>Green and Concord Bridge; and as
>you love your country and your kind,
>and would have your children rise up
>and call you blessed, spare not the
>enemy.
>(p. 118.)

58. Richard Maxwell Brown, "Violence and the American Revolution," in Stephen G. Kurtz and James H. Hutson, eds., *Essays on the American Revolution* (Chapel Hill: University of North Carolina Press, and New York: W. W. Norton and Company, 1973), p. 113.

59. Harold S. Schultz, *Nationalism and Sectionalism in South Carolina: 1852-1860* (Durham: Duke University Press, 1950), p. 226.

60. For details on the popularity of the war in dime novels, see Edward J. Leithead, "The Revolutionary War in Dime Novels," *American Book Collector* 18 (April-May, 1969): 14-21.

61. Ibid., p. 18.

62. Curti, "Dime Novels," p. 771.

63. Ernest Peixoto, *A Revolutionary Pilgrimage* (New York: Charles Scribner's Sons, 1917), p. viii.

64. Townsend Scudder, *Concord: American Town* (Boston: Little, Brown and Company, 1947), p. 323.

65. Harry Jones, Jr., *The Minutemen* (Garden City, New York: Doubleday and Company, 1968), p. 38.

66. Ibid., p. 284. Unlike the attitude of the modern Minutemen, John Shy notes that there has been a shift away from using the Revolution as a model for social action. "That current revolutionaries, unlike previous American dissidents, no longer identify with the American Revolution may be one of the most important changes in our contemporary intellectual history." (Shy, *People Numerous and Armed*, p. 116.)

67. Shy, *People Numerous and Armed*, p. 239. Shy suggests that the "inner rhythm" of our wars stretches past the nineteenth century into the world wars.

68. Emerson, *Historical Discourse*, p. 36.

69. Cedric Larson, "Patriotism in Carmine: One Hundred and Sixty-Two Years of Fourth of July Orations," *Quarterly Journal of Speech* 26 (February, 1940): 15.

70. Tuveson, *Redeemer Nation*, p. 196.

71. Gail Hamilton, "A Call to My Country-Women," *Atlantic Monthly* 11 (March, 1863): 348.

72. Tuveson discusses this apocalyptic view of history
in his chapter "The Ennobling War." Martial music of the
period reflected apocalyptic feeling. Songs like "John
Brown's Body," "The Battle Hymn of the Republic," and "We
Are Coming Father Abraham," illustrate this. (See Lawrence,
Music for Patriots, pp. 341-437.)

To show the need for apocalyptic action, artists and writers
created a brutal image of the enemy. It was a war of
"Civilization against Barbarism, Light against Darkness,
Right against Wrong." (W. Fletcher Thompson, *The Image of
War: The Pictorial Reporting of the American Civil War*
[New York: Thomas Yoseloff, 1959], p. 91.)

Artists used themes of the brutal treatment of prisoners,
atrocities in battle, and the barbarism of the Southern
guerillas to make their point. Thomas Nast in *Harper's
Weekly* portrayed the sins of the Southern warrior after
Second Bull Run:

> In a scene that reminded his readers
> of a Halloween specter dance, he showed
> the enemy ghouls with their camp followers
> stripping the Union corpses. Expressions
> of fiendish cruelty and stupidity twisted
> their faces. Then for contrast, Nast
> showed the anguish of several northern
> women who had come to the field to look
> for the bodies of their sons and husbands.
> (Thompson, p. 94.)

Southerners likewise portrayed Northern soldiers as demonic.
The editor of the *Atlanta Intelligencer* wrote:

> We are determined not only to achieve
> our independence at whatever cost but
> we will teach these Northern Goths and
> Vandals a lesson before this war is
> over which they will never forget....
> We will show them how superior is the
> valor of free men fighting on their
> own soil, for their altars and fire-
> sides, their wives, their children,
> and their dearest rights, to the hire-
> ling skills of treacherous and perfid-
> ious invaders.
> (Bell Irwin Wiley, *Embattled Confederates*,
> illustrated by Hirst D. Milhollen [New
> York: Harper and Row, 1964], p. 200.)

73. Tuveson, *Redeemer Nation*, p. 193.

74.   "Soldiers Memorial Service," *Century Illustrated Monthly Magazine* 38 (May, 1889): 156.

75.   Bell Irwin Wiley, *The Common Soldier in the Civil War*, Book One, *Billy Yank* (New York: Grossett and Dunlap, 1952), p. 360.

76.   Robert A. Lively, *Fiction Fights the Civil War* (Chapel Hill: The University of North Carolina Press, 1957), p. 44.   For an excellent account of the religion of the Lost Cause, see Charles Reagan Wilson, *Baptized in Blood: The Religion of the Lost Cause, 1865-1920* (Athens: The University of Georgia Press, 1980).

77.   Lively, *Fiction Fights the War*, p. 44.

78.   George Edward Vickers, *Gettysburg: A Poem* (Washington: n.p., 1890), p. 17.

79.   Elbridge Streeter Brooks, *The Story of the American Soldier in War and Peace* (Boston: D. Lothrop Company, 1889), p. 265.

80.   John H. Wallace, Jr., *The Blue and the Gray* (Montgomery, Alabama: Brown Printing Company, 1909), p. 6. In his recent novel of the Civil War, Michael Shaara has Colonel Chamberlain declare that an "American fights for mankind, for freedom; for the people, not the land." (Michael Shaara, *The Killer Angels* [New York: David McKay Company, Inc., 1974], p. 30.)

81.   Horace Wilbert Bolton, *Our Fallen Heroes* (Chicago: H. W. Bolton, 1892), p. 183.

82.   Bruce Catton captures the chaotic qualities of total war, saying:

> Ultimately, it is nothing less than the
> road to horror.   It obliterates the
> moralities and restraints which the race
> has so carefully built up through many
> generations....It can--and does--put an
> entire nation at the mercy of its most
> destructive instincts.   What you can do
> to your enemy comes, at last, to be
> limited not by any reluctance to inflict
> pain, misery, and death, and not by any
> feelings that there are limits to the
> things which a civilized people may do,
> but solely by your technical capacity to
> do harm.   Without suffering any pangs of

conscience, the group becomes prepared
to do things which no single member of
the group would for a moment contemplate.
(Quoted in Wayne Charles Miller, *An
Armed America: Its Face in Fiction*
[New York: New York University Press,
1970], p. 56.)

83.   Robert Penn Warren, *The Legacy of the Civil War:
Meditations on the Centennial* (New York: Random House,
1961), p. 46.   R. M. Weaver notes that Americans were
"pioneers" in total warfare.   "It is well-known that German
generals have been careful students of the American Civil
War."   (R. M. Weaver, "Southern Chivalry and Total War,"
Sewanee Review 53 [April, 1945]: 277.)

84.   Thompson, *Image of War*, p. 24.   Thompson believes
the traditional images remained powerfully entrenched, but
"In every war since 1865, more realistic images eventually
prevailed because War itself proved to be the artists' best
ally." (p. 186.)

85.   Wiley, *Billy Yank*, p. 66.

86.   Miller, *Armed America*, p. 50.

87.   Warren, *Legacy of War*, p. 48.   George Fredrickson
says that the Civil War made the concept of revolution or
rebellion "anathema to many Northerners, [and]...widened
the gulf that separated nineteenth century Americans from
their revolutionary heritage." (*The Inner Civil War*, p. 187.)

88.   Fredrickson, *Inner War*, p. 91.

89.   Ibid., p. 95.

90.   Daniel Aaron, *The Unwritten War. American Writers
and the Civil War* (New York: Alfred A. Knopf, 1973), p. 141.

91.   Fredrickson, *Inner War*, p. 88.

92.   Stuart C. Woodruff, *The Short Stories of Ambrose
Bierce: A Study in Polarity* (n.p.:   The University of
Pittsburgh Press, 1964), p. 67.

93.   Aaron, *Unwritten War*, p. 336.

94.   Fredrickson, *Inner War*, p. 167.

95.   The parameters of "work" are stretched here to include warfare.   Perhaps this is one of the early occurrences

of this formulation, which appears with regularity
in the world wars and after. The merging of war and work
further weakens the structure of warfare as a separate
experience and blends war with activity in everyday life.

96. John Clark Ridpath, "The Citizen Soldier; His
Part in War and Peace," delivered before the Veterans of
the Grand Army of the Republic at Amo, Indiana, 30 May
1890, p. 56. Noting the heroism of the Confederate soldier,
Wallace believes it emerged from the same source as the
Boys in Blue:

> They left their log-cabins on the
> mountains and their humble huts in
> the piney wods [sic], they crimsoned
> the battle fields with their blood
> and established for history a standard
> of invincible courage that will never
> be obliterated.
> (*The Blue and the Gray*, p. 8.)

97. Ridpath, "Citizen Soldier in War and Peace,"
p. 55.

98. Ibid., p. 22.

99. Oliver Wendell Holmes stated in his Memorial Day
Address of 1884:

> The generation that carried on the
> war has been set apart by its ex-
> perience. Through our great good
> fortune, in our youth our hearts
> were touched with fire. It was
> given to us to learn at the outset
> that life is a profound and passionate
> thing.
> (Quoted in Fredrickson, *Inner War*,
> p. 219.)

100. Quoted in Aaron, *Unwritten War*, p. 188.

101. Bell Irwin Wiley, *The Common Soldier in the Civil
War*, Book One, *Johnny Reb* (New York: Grossett and Dunlap,
1943), p. 29.

102. Ibid., p. 72.

103. Bruce Catton, *Prefaces to History* (New York:
Doubleday and Company, 1970), p. 2. Memory of veterans
became selective. As the *Century Magazine* puts it, "All is

forgotten except the fact that he once answered the call
of duty." (p. 157.)

104. Fredrickson, *Inner War*, p. 83.

105. In 1862 Cyrus Augustus Bartol delivered a sermon
in West Church in Boston entitled "The Remission by Blood."
His text was Heb. 9:22, "Without shedding of blood there
is no remission." He declared suffering necessary for a
purging of the disease in America. Politics, rhetoric,
philanthropy all failed. "Room was left only for the stern
meditation of war--the remission by blood." (Published in
Boston: Walker, Wise and Company, 1862, p. 6.)

106. John Hopkins Morison, "Dying for Our Country; A
Sermon on the Death of Capt. J. Sewall Reed and Rev. Thomas
Starr King," preached in the First Congregational Church in
Milton, 13 March 1864 (Boston: John Wilson and Son, 1864),
p. 14.

107. Tuveson, *Redeemer Nation*, p. 204. In "The Color
Sergeant," a mother asks if her son died thinking of his
country.

> Tell his comrades these words of his mother!
> All over the wide land to-day,
> The Rachels, who weep with each other,
> Together in agony pray.
> They know, in their great tribulation,
> By the blood of their children outpoured,
> We shall smite down the Foes of the Nation,
> In the terrible day of the Lord.
> (F. O. C. Darley, *A Selection of War Lyrics*
> [New York: James G. Gregory, 1864], p. 11.)

108. John Davidson, *Oration Delivered Before the
Legislature of New Jersey upon "Our Sleeping Heroes"*
22 February 1866 (Trenton, N.J.: Printed at the *State
Gazette Office*, 1866), p. 26.

Wallace Evans Davies, in his discussion of veterans groups,
reported the popular view that "the soldiers, having saved
the nation, had somehow forever after acquired a lien upon
it...'Who but the Soldier and his family should eat the
bread from the Soil his own blood has enriched.'" (Wallace
Evans Davies, *Patriotism on Parade: The Story of the
Veterans and Hereditary Organizations in America, 1783-1900*
[Cambridge, Mass.: n.p., 1955], p. 23.)

109. Gail Hamilton, "Call to My Country-Women,"
p. 349. She continues by suggesting that women exhibit
their own "martial soul":

> Father, husband, child,--I do not say,
> Give them up to toil, exposure, suffer-
> ing, death, without a murmur;--that
> implies reluctance. I rather say,
> Urge them to the offering; fill them
> with sacred fury; fire them with irre-
> sistible desire; strengthen them to
> heroic will. (p. 346.)

110. LaSalle Pickett, *The Bugles of Gettysburg*
(Chicago: F. G. Browne and Company, 1913), p. 15.

111. Cornelia J. M. Jordan, *Echoes From the Cannon*,
ed. by Theresa Jordan Ambler (Buffalo, N.Y.: Charles Wells
Moulton, 1899), p. 127.

112. William Barrows, *Honor to the Brave. A Discourse
delivered in The Old South Church, Reading, Mass., August 23,
1863, on the return of Company D, fiftieth Reg., Mass. Vols,
by the Rev. William Barrows* (Boston: John M. Whittemore and
Company, 1863), p. 17.

113. Edward Bellamy, "An Echo of Antietam," in *The
Blindman's World and Other Stories*, The American Short Story
Series, Vol. 4 (New York: Garrett Press, 1968), pp. 42-43.

114. Mircea Eliade, *Myth and Reality*, trans. by
Willard R. Trask (New York: Harper and Row, 1963), p. 81.

115. Milton Badger, *Welcome to the Returned Soldiers.
An Address delivered at Madison, Conn., July 4th, 1865 by
Rev. Milton Badger, D.D.* (New Haven: Tuttle, Morehouse and
Taylor, Printers, 1865), p. 12. In a similar vein, and also
with a further twist of Catherine Albanese's title, E. G.
Porter, referring to the Civil War Monument at Lexington,
said, "The Sons Defended what the Fathers won." (*Souvenir
of Lexington*, p. 15.)

116. Brooks, *American Soldier*, p. 239.

117. Fredrickson, *Inner War*, p. 37.

118. Ibid., p. 62.

119. Wiley, *Billy Yank*, p. 29.

120. Brooks, *American Soldier in War and Peace*, p. 311.

121.   Davidson, "Our Sleeping Heroes," p. 14.

122.   Stephen Vincent Benét, *John Brown's Body*, with an introduction and notes by Jack L. Capps and C. Robert Kemble (New York: Holt, Rinehart and Winston, Inc., 1968), p. 188.

Songs of the Confederacy also used the memory of '76 to frame the conflict.   In "The Bonnie Blue Flag," one verse says:

>   Then here's to our Confed'racy,
>   Strong are we and brave,
>   Like patriots of old we'll fight
>   Our heritage to save.

In "Seventy-Six and Sixty-One" a verse declares:

>   There's many a grave in all the land,
>   And many a crucifix,
>   Which tells how that heroic band
>   Stood firm in seventy-six--
>   Ye heroes of the deathless past,
>   Your glorious race is run,
>   But from your dust springs freemen's trust,
>   And blows for sixty-one.
>   (Both from H. M. Wharton, *War Songs and
>   Poems of the Southern Confederacy 1861-
>   1865* [Philadelphia: n.p., 1904], pp. 24
>   and 287-288.)

123.   *Ceremonies at the Dedication of the Soldier's Monument in Concord, Mass.*   (Concord: Benjamin Tolman, 1867), p. 8.

124.   Badger, *Welcome Returned Soldiers*, p. 10.

125.   Fredrickson, *Inner War*, p. 82.

126.   Davidson, *Our Sleeping Heroes*, p. 26.   A fine musical example of this new birth is a jubilee song written for the Fourth of July celebration of 1876:

>   Fling forth the nation's banner
>   In its glory on the air!
>   'Tis the ancient flag of freedom,
>   Not a star is missing there:
>   Our triumph and redemption,
>   For the people are all free;
>   And the jubilee hath sounded--
>   Universal Liberty.

Chorus:
    Shout! The good time has come,
    Our Nation now is free;
    Echo the chorus wide,
    Proclaim the Jubilee!

    The Dove of Peace is brooding
    O'er the desolated earth,
    And the flowers again are springing
    In our freedom's second birth.
    Ring out the bells of glory,
    Call our noble veterans home;
    From the fields of war and carnage,
    Greet the heroes as they come.
    (Lawrence, *Music for Patriots*, p. 432.)

127. Bartol, "Remission by Blood," p. 19. What arose instead was much closer to Melville's prophecy of an imperial United States at odds with the Edenic hopes of the eighteenth century founders.

128. Warren, *Legacy of War*, p. 92.

129. Millis, *Arms and Men*, p. 70.

130. J. Frank Hanly, *The Battle of Gettysburg* (Cincinnati: Jennings and Graham, 1912), p. 16.

131. Ibid., pp. 29-30.

132. George J. Gross, *The Battlefield of Gettysburg* (Philadelphia: Collins Printer, 705 Jayne Street, 1866), p. 24.

133. Benét, *John Brown's Body*, p. 298.

134. Vickers, *Gettysburg*, p. 2.

135. Nicholas A. Meligakes, *The Spirit of Gettysburg* (Gettysburg, Pa.: Bookmart, 1950), p. 189. Both sides showered their warriors at Gettysburg with accolades for honor, courage, and the sacrifice of their lives. Captain James T. Long recalls Bret Harte's poem which shows the spirit of '76, present in the figure of an old man living in Gettysburg: John Burns. Burns asked if he could fight with the Union soldiers. The troops made fun of him.

    While Burns, unmindful of jeer and scott,
    Stood there picking the Rebels off--
    With his long brown rifle and bell-crown hat
    And the swallow-tails they were laughing at.

'Twas but a moment: for that respect
Which clothes all courage their voices checked;
And something the wildest could understand
Spake in the old man's strong right hand,
And his corded throat, and the lurking frown
Of his eyebrows under his old bell-crown;
Until, as they gazed, there crept an awe
Through the ranks, in whispers, and some men saw,
In the antique vestments and long white hair,
The Past of the Nation in battle there.
. . . .
Thus raged the battle. You know the rest:
How the rebels, beaten and backward pressed,
Broke at the final charge and ran;
At which John Burns, a practical man,
Shouldered his rifle, unbent his brows,
And then went back to his bees and cows.
(Captain James T. Long, *The 16th Decisive
Battle of the World. Gettysburg* [n.p.:
Gettysburg Compiler Print, 1911], p. 93.)

136. George Ripley Stewart, *Pickett's Charge* (Boston:
Houghton Mifflin Company, 1959), p. ix.

137. Henry Sweeter Burrage, *Gettysburg and Lincoln;
The Battle, the Cemetery, and the National Park* (New York:
G. P. Putnam's Sons, 1906), p. 83.

138. James W. Eaton, "Pickett's Charge at Gettysburg,"
address at annual meeting of the Military Order of the Loyal
Legion of the United States, 1 November 1962, pp. 14-15.

139. Meligakes, *Spirit of Gettysburg*, p. 114.

140. Hanly, *Battle of Gettysburg*, p. 85. In Michael
Shaara's novel, rebirth is expressed this way:

The true rain came in a monster wind...
drowning the fires, flooding the red
creeks, washing the rocks and the grass
and the white bones of the dead,
cleansing the earth and soaking it
thick and rich with water and wet again
with clean cold rainwater, driving the
blood deep into the earth, to grow
again with the roots toward Heaven.

It rained all that night. The next
day was Saturday, the Fourth of July.
(Shaara, *Killer Angels*, p. 365.)

141. Burrage, *Gettysburg and Lincoln*, p. 177.

142. Bolton, *Our Fallen Heroes*, p. 43. This sort of artifact has been largely ignored in America by historians of religion. As E. M. Fleming says, an artifact is

> made at a particular time and place, in
> response to a specific need, to perform
> a socially meaningful function, expressing
> values through design, ornament, symbol,
> and style which were a part of a definite
> cultural tradition.
> ("Early American Decorative Arts as Social
> Documents," *Mississippi Valley Historical
> Review* 45 [September, 1958]: 227.)

143. Stewart, *Pickett's Charge*, p. 290.

144. Aaron suggests that the encampments where re-unions were held "seemed the culmination of some predestined chronicle, another example of good mysteriously evolving from evil." (*Unwritten War*, p. 207.)

145. Jack McLaughlin, *Gettysburg: The Long Encampment* (New York: Appleton-Century, 1963), p. 232.

146. *The Union Sergeant or, The Battle of Gettysburg* (Springfield, Mass.: George W. Sergeant, Publisher, 1873), p. 2.

147. Paul Philippoteaux, *Cyclorama of the Battle of Gettysburg* (n.p.: Harper and Brothers, 1868), p. 14. The pages of this pamphlet are not numbered.

148. Paul C. Spehr, *The Civil War in Motion Pictures* (Washington: Library of Congress, 1961), p. 7.

149. William A. Frassanito, *Gettysburg, A Journey in Time* (New York: Charles Scribner's Sons, 1975), front flap.

150. Ibid., p. 59.

151. Eaton, "Pickett's Charge," p. 9.

152. Catton, *Prefaces to History*, p. 73.

153. Warren, *Legacy of War*, p. 4.

154. Gerald F. Linderman, *The Mirror of War: American Society and the Spanish-American War* (Ann Arbor: The University of Michigan Press, 1974), p. 93.

155.   Thomas C. Leonard, *Above the Battle: War-Making in America From Appomattox to Versailles* (New York: Oxford University Press, 1978), p. 24.

156.   Millis, *Arms and Men*, p. 157.

157.   Leonard, *Above the Battle*, p. 98.   The naval expert was a new hero because of his expertise in dealing with war technology.

158.   Ibid., p. 81.   See his section "The Illusive Arsenal," pp. 75-110.

159.   Frederick Cople Jaher, *Doubters and Dissenters: Cataclysmic Thought in America, 1885-1918* (New York: The Free Press of Glencoe, Ill., 1964), p. 79.

160.   Linderman, *Mirror of War*, p. 58.

161.   Quoted in Linderman, p. 59.   The Frontpiece of *Harper's Pictorial History of the War with Spain*, with an introduction by Maj. Gen. Nelson A. Miles (New York: Harper and Brothers, 1899), shows the feminine figure of Liberty holding a flag and sword, flanked by a rough rider and a sailor.   In one sense, soldiers were only agents of the guiding destiny which called America to conquest in the name of humanity.

162.   Both statements from *Harper's Pictorial History*, p. vii.

163.   Linderman's section on "The Image of Enemy and Ally," pp. 114-147, offers an excellent discussion of the demonization of the enemy.   American perceptions of the Cubans are fascinating.   They were seen, depending on where one's sympathies lay, as oppressed whites or oppressed blacks.   To Protestants, they appeared to be rising up against Catholic oppression.   To Catholics, they were suffering under Spanish tyranny as Ireland suffered under English tyranny.   In any case, after Americans landed in Cuba, the heroic image of the Cuban "freedom fighters" disappeared.   Expressions of contempt were common, for what kind of ideals could ragged dirty men be fighting for? Also, see Drinnon, *Facing West*, pp. 255-351.

164.   Richard Hofstadter, "Cuba, the Philippines, and Manifest Destiny," *The Paranoid Style in American Politics and Other Essays* (New York: Harper and Row, 1965), p. 181.

165.   Jaher, *Doubters and Dissenters*, p. 87.

166. Walter Hines Page, "The War with Spain and After," *Atlantic Monthly* 81 (June, 1898): 726.

167. Jaher, *Doubters and Dissenters*, p. 85. Edward Bellamy's *Looking Backward* reflected an appreciation of wartime patriotism, and the motives which inspired the soldier were looked on with favor as motivation in civilian society of 2000. Leonard's *Above the Battle* cites other various political analogues to war, pp. 114-115.

168. Linderman, *The Mirror of War*, p. 29.

169. For Roosevelt, the Rough Riders were like Minutemen. They were instinctive warriors. American character made them that way. Sports and war were closely related: football was a kind of "miniature Civil War." Fredrickson suggests:

> With Roosevelt, the "strenuous life" ideal
> had come full circle. Beginning with
> Parkman's glorification of physical strife
> as drawing out the masculine fighting qual-
> ities, it had been transmuted by young men
> who were tired of war into the ideal of
> "useful citizenship" in time of peace; in
> the eighties and early nineties, it had
> regained its emphasis on physical courage--
> to be demonstrated, however, in the West or
> on the playing field rather than on the
> battlefield. In the Age of Imperialism we
> are back to an essentially military ideal.
> (*Inner Civil War*, p. 225.)

170. Linderman, *The Mirror of War*, p. 77.

171. *War Addresses of Woodrow Wilson*, with an intro- duction and notes by Arthur Ray Leonard (Boston: Ginn and Company, 1918), p. 34.

172. Albert Eugene Gallatin, *Art and the Great War* (New York: E. P. Dutton and Company, 1919), p. 43.

173. Leonard, *Above the Battle*, p. 149.

174. I. F. Clarke describes the numerous war fantasies that appeared in the years before the war and noted their symbolic power:

> For the first time in the history of
> international politics, as a direct

result of universal literacy and mass
journalism, the writing of popular
fiction had begun to have a recognizable
effect on the relations between countries,
since these tales of the war-to-come
encouraged British and Germans to see
themselves as inevitable enemies.
(I. F. Clarke, *Voices Prophesying War,
1763-1984* [London: Oxford University
Press, 1966], p. 143.)

175. Jack Spears, "World War I on the Screen," *Films
in Review* 17 (May, 1966): 276.

176. Ibid., p. 276.

177. Among the greatest pro-war films before our entrance were Cecil B. DeMille's *Joan the Woman* and *The Little
American*. In the first, heroic battle scenes were the
backdrop for the story of a peasant girl leading the French
against the enemy. Spears notes that it was used to "pro-
mote the idea that Anglo-Saxons had a moral obligation to
come to France's aid because of their having burned Joan at
the stake." ("World War I on the Screen," p. 282.) In *The
Little American* Mary Pickford, one of the most popular
American actresses, played a girl captured by the Germans
while working on war relief and held as a spy. There was
great outrage among American men when the Prussian colonel
threatened her with rape.

Newsreels also shifted to a preparedness stance. Scenes of
battle on the western front became common, and in January,
1917, surprisingly enough, an official German war film
opened at the Strand Theater in New York.

178. The plots varied somewhat. Moffett has America
emerging victorious only because of the technical genius of
Thomas Edison, while Walker presents a far gloomier picture.
His book ends with the Germans firmly in control of eastern
America and asking for billions of dollars in indemnity before they leave. The Chief of Staff advises the President
to pay, and to make sure that America has learned her lesson,
and never will be caught unprepared again! Both novels portray the German army and navy as calm professionals, while
America is totally helpless because she is unprepared and has
only the considerable courage that is uniquely American to
defend her. In both novels the Panama Canal is blown up,
trapping our navy in the Pacific, an interesting note perhaps
lurking in the fears surrounding the recent treaty discussions.

179.   George T. Blakey, *Historians on the Homefront* (Lexington: The University of Kentucky Press, 1970), p. 47.

180.   Ray H. Abrams, *Preachers Present Arms* (Scottsdale, Pa.:   Herald Press, 1969), p. 116.

181.   Quoted in *Current Opinion* 63 (July, 1917): 6.

182.   They were, of course, fighting God's war.   Arthur Empey wrote the most popular narrative of the war in 1917, declaring that the war is God's war.

> If it wasn't, America would not have un-
> sheathed the sword, because America has
> fought and shall fight only on the side
> of right.   She could not do otherwise
> and be American.
> (Arthur Guy Empey, *"Over the Top"* [New
> York: G.P. Putnam's Sons, 1917], p. 61.)

183.   Abrams, *Preachers Present Arms*, p. 57.   His chapter "The Holy War," pp. 49-76, is revealing of the attitude of the clergy toward war and the warrior as crusade and crusader.

184.   Charles V. Genthe, *American War Narratives, 1917-1918; A Study and Bibliography* (New York: David Lewis, 1969), p. 37.

185.   George J. Hecht, comp. and ed., *The War in Cartoons*, with a new introduction for the Garland edition by Charles Chatfield (New York: Life Publishing, Inc., 1971), p. 64.

186.   Ibid., p. 9.   Gallatin, Hecht and Baynes all have representative cartoons and posters from the period.   See Ken Baynes, *War* (Boston, Mass.:   Boston Book and Art Publisher, 1970), and *War as Viewed by Life* (New York: Life Publishing Company, 1914).

187.   Stanley Cooperman, *World War I and the American Novel* (Baltimore: The Johns Hopkins Press, 1967), p. 50.

188.   I. F. Clarke points out the power of romantic images for British troops.   One of the persistent myths at the front was the tale of the "Angel of Mons," a group of heavenly warriors fighting with the British.

> The ultimate irony is that in their moment
> of greatest anxiety, and at the start of

> the first great technological war in
> history, the people of a highly in-
> dustrialized world power should find
> comfort and hope in a legend of angels
> who fought upon the clouds.
> (*Voices Prophesying War*, p. 106.)

189.   The romantic image of an infantry charge with
fixed bayonets was so strong that it governed military
tactics and consequently dictated mass slaughter when confronted by machine guns and other weapons of modern war.

190.   Leonard, *Above the Battle*, p. 152.

191.   One of the individual heroes of the war was of
this type, a romantic figure conjuring up images of classical
American riflemen.   Sergeant York was a

> transplanted colonist of the eighteenth
> century; he is the backwoodsman of the
> days of Andrew Jackson....It has been
> said of the residents of the Cumberland
> Mountains that they are the purest Anglo-
> Saxons to be found to-day and not even
> England can produce so clear a strain.
> (Samuel Kinkade Cowan, *Sergeant York and
> His People* [New York: Grossett and
> Dunlap, 1922], p. 77.)

York combined the skill of the riflemen (picking off not
only German machine gunners, but a line of charging Germans
starting with the one furthest away) with the virtues of a
warrior who hated war; he was an elder in his church.   He
truly was seen as a sinless warrior.   The necessity of killing had been forced upon him, yet he was true to his mission,
and the country looked upon him as a hero.   He continued sinless ways by founding the York Foundation with the money that
poured in to him.   This foundation was set up to help educate
mountain children.

192.   Genthe, *War Narratives*, p. 56.   The spirit of
other wars was also present.   In a "Win the War" parade in
1918, a mother carried a sign proclaiming:

> I was born in 1863
> The spirit of war surrounded me
> Now the spirit of war has come again
> And I have a son with--
> The Fighting Men!
> (Mark Sullivan, *Our Times, The United States
> 1900-1925*, Vol. V: *Over Here: 1914-1918* [New
> York: Charles Scribner's Sons, 1933], p. 465.)

193. Cooperman, *War and the Novel*, p. 33.

194. Stephen Crane, *The Red Badge of Courage*, edited by Sculley Bradley et al. (New York: W. W. Norton and Company, Inc., 1962), p. 109.

195. Cooperman, *War and the Novel*, p. 47.

196. Winifred Kirkland, "The New Death," *The Atlantic Monthly* 121 (May, 1918): 580.

197. Timothy Lyons, "Hollywood and World War I," *Journal of Popular Film* 1 (Winter, 1972): 19.

198. Barbara Jones and Bill Howell, *Popular Arts of the First World War* (New York: McGraw-Hill Book Company, 1972), p. 23.

199. Genthe, *War Narratives*, p. 72. Others, particularly post-war writers, spoke not of the rebirth of warriors through battle, but of their "death."

200. Floyd Gibbons, *"And They Thought We Wouldn't Fight"* (New York: George H. Doran Company, 1918), p. 338.

201. William Conningsby Dawson, *The Glory of the Trenches* (London: John Lane, 1918), p. 57.

202. Both statements in Abrams, *Preachers Present Arms*, p. 60.

203. *Current Opinion* 63 (July, 1917): 6.

204. Gibbons, *"Thought We Wouldn't Fight"*, pp. 220-221.

205. Genthe, *War Narratives*, p. 35.

206. Dawson, *Glory of the Trenches*, pp. 50-51.

207. Abrams, *Preachers Present Arms*, p. 160. He cites from the *Advocate of Peace*.

208. *Current Opinion* 63 (October, 1917): 267.

209. Gallatin, *Art and War*, p. 22. The historical precedents of war and heroic images of warriors no longer fit, and artists were forced to search for new categories.

210. *The Artist and War in the Twentieth Century*, introduction by T. G. Rosenthal, BBC Radio Series (London:

British Broadcasting Corporation, 1967), p. 2.

211.   Robert Haven Schauffler and A. P. Sanford, eds., *Armistice Day* (New York: Dodd, Mead and Company, 1928), p. 138.

212.   Jones and Howell, *Popular Arts of the War*, p. 119.

213.   Ibid., p. 11.   Contrast this clean view of war with a book that went through six printings showing the agony of war,   Frederick A. Barber's *The Horror of It: Camera Records of War's Gruesome Glories* (New York: Association Press, 1932).   The book's intent was to refute romantic ideas about war by showing the "gruesome reality."

214.   Aichinger, *American Soldier in Fiction*, p. 10.

215.   Kenneth Lynn, "Violence in American Folklore," in *Visions of America*, with an introduction by Robert H. Walker, Contributions in American Studies No. 6 (Westport, Conn.:   Greenwood Press, Inc., 1973), p. 201.

216.   Cooperman, *War and the Novel*, p. 75.

217.   Ibid., p. 8.

218.   Theodore P. Greene, *America's Heroes: The Changing Models of Success in American Magazines* (New York: Oxford University Press, 1970), p. 310.

219.   Leonard, *Above the Battle*, p. 175.

220.   Jones and Howell, *Popular Arts of the War*, p. 74.

221.   Leonard, *Above the Battle*, p. 165.

222.   Sullivan, *Our Times*, Vol. V, p. 26.

223.   Jones and Howell,*Popular Arts of the War*, p. 33.

224.   Wecter, *Hero in America*, p. 410.

225.   Genthe, *War Narratives*, p. 47.   The nostalgia for this kind of war is still seen in the group called The World War One Aero Historians, and also in the popular figure of Snoopy fighting the Red Baron.

226.   Jack Spears, "World War I on the Screen," *Films in Review* 17 (June-July, 1966): 350.

227. *New York Times*, 10 November 1921, p. 1.

228. Both statements from the *New York Times*, 12 November 1921, p. 2.

229. Not only the soldier returned home, but also the fertile ground upon which he made his regenerative sacrifice. The Unknown Soldier was buried in soil brought from American battlefields in France.

CHAPTER THREE

1. Paul Fussell, *The Great War and Modern Memory* (London: Oxford University Press, 1975), p. 321.

2. William E. Leuchtenberg, "The New Deal and the Analogue of War," in John Braeman, Robert H. Bremmer, and Everett Walters, eds., *Change and Continuity in Twentieth-Century America* (n.p.: Ohio State Press, 1964), p. 105.

3. Ibid., p. 111.

4. Ibid., p. 116. Waldemar Kaempffert notes that industry used war as a model in many ways, in

> organization, discipline, standardi-
> zation, the co-ordination of transport
> and supply, the separation of line and
> staff, the division of labor (cavalry,
> infantry, artillery)....Such is the
> influence of the military that "soda
> jerkers," nurses, trainmen, waiters,
> elevator boys, theater ushers, and
> street sweepers are uniformed.
> (Waldemar Kaempffert, "War and Technology,"
> *The American Journal of Sociology* 46
> [January, 1946]: 443.)

5. Abrams, *Preachers Present Arms*, pp. 267-268.

6. Fear about the rise of the Nazis may be seen in many ways. In 1937 H. G. Wells wrote *The Croquet Player*, a story about an evil spot in England traced back to the bones of prehistoric men buried there. The spot is disturbed by

diggers and the evil spirits return, infecting the people
with cruelty. Thus could Wells express his fear of war and
of the nature of man, " the same fearing, snarling, fighting
beast he was a hundred thousand years ago. " (Charles C.
Walcutt, "Fear Motifs in the Literature Between the Wars,"
South Atlantic Quarterly XLVI [1947]: 229.)

Lillian Hellman's *Watch on the Rhine* and Robert E. Sherwood's
There Shall Be No Night express in dramatic form the necessity of resisting the Nazis and many of the American plays
of the late thirties and forties looked to America as the
savior of the world, tending to vilify the enemy, and "to
imply that any means useful in insuring their defeat are
morally acceptable." (Jane F. Bonin, *Major Themes in Prize-
Winning American Drama*, with a preface by Paul T. Nolan
[Metuchen, New Jersey: The Scarecrow Press, 1975], p. 83.)

     7. Quoted in Henry Steele Commager, "What are the
Fundamental Issues of the War?" in *America Organizes to Win
the War* (New York: Harcourt, Brace and Company, 1942): 1.

     8. William A. Bacher, ed., *The Treasury Star Parade:
27 Radio Plays*, with an introduction by Henry Morgenthau, Jr.
(New York: Farrar and Rinehart, 1942), p. 379.

     9. Charles Albert Plumley, *Our Emancipation Proclom-
ation* [sic] Address by the Honorable Charles A. Plumley,
United States Representative at Large from Vermont, delivered
over the Red Network of the National Broadcasting Company,
February 12, at 6:30 p.m., EWT (Washington, D.C.: National
Broadcasting Company, 1942), p. 4.

     10. Stewart Alsop, "Wanted: A Faith to Fight For,"
Atlantic (May, 1941): 597.

     11. Richard Polenberg, ed., *America at War: The Home
Front, 1941-1945* (Englewood Cliffs, N.J.: Prentice-Hall,
Inc., 1968), p. 3.

     12. John Blum, *V Was For Victory*, p. 339.

     13. Edward M. Kirby and Jack W. Harris, *Star-Spangled
Radio*, with a foreword by David Sarnoff (Chicago: Ziff-
Davis Publishing Company, 1948), p. 183. For the full text,
see Debs Myers, Jonathan Kilbourn and Richard Harrity, eds.
and sels., *Yank--The GI Story of the War* (New York: Duell,
Sloan and Pearle, 1947), p. 90.

     14. Kirby, *Star-Spangled Radio*, p. 181

15.   Geoffrey Perrett, *Days of Sadness, Years of Triumph: The American People 1939-1945* (New York: Coward, McCann and Geoghegan, Inc., 1973), p. 276.

16.   The war and warriors reached into many areas of American life.   Perrett cited the attitudes in schools: "Spelling lessons mixed military terms with everyday words; English classes offered propaganda analysis; arithmetic problems used airplanes where once they used apples." (Perrett, *Days of Sadness*, p. 368.)

Richard R. Lingeman notes that the heroes of comic books "Batman and Robin, Flashman, Plastic Man, Captain America, Captain Marvel, the Green Lantern, the Spirit, et al., defeated a variety of biliously yellow-skinned Japs and fat Germans."   (Richard R. Lingeman, *Don't You Know There's a War On?   The American Home Front, 1941-1945* [New York: G. P. Putnam's Sons, 1970], p. 307.)

Perhaps the most heroic image of the warrior which has found its way into American life is Joseph Rosenthal's Pulitzer Prize-winning photograph of the flag-raising on Iwo Jima taken in February, 1945.   The picture "was assured the widest distribution in history and certain immortality." ("Marines on Iwo Jima," *Newsweek* [April 16, 1945]: 82.) The picture has been used in over three million war posters, on a three-cent stamp, in over fifteen thousand paintings, and on cards of different kinds.

17.   John Blum, "The G.I. in the Culture of the Second World War," *Ventures* 8 (1969): 52.

18.   S. L. A. Marshall, "How Is the Army Organized to Fight the War?" *America Organizes*, p. 100.

19.   Stewart Holbrook, *None More Courageous: American War Heroes of Today* (New York: The Macmillan Company, 1944), p. 90.

20.   Winston Churchill, "Today's Battles: Men Not Machines Win Wars," *Collier's* 104 (October 7, 1939): 63.

21.   Ernie Pyle, *Here is Your War* (New York: Henry Holt and Company, 1943), p. 178.

22.   Robert Sherrod, *Tarawa: The Story of a Battle* (New York: Duell, Sloan and Pearce, 1944), p. 149.

23.   John Hersey, "Experience by Battle," *Life* (December 27, 1943): pp. 73 and 75.

24. Ernie Pyle, *Brave Men* (New York: Henry Holt and Company, 1943), p. 275.

25. Blum, "The G.I. in the Culture of War," p. 56.

26. Blum, *V Was For Victory*, p. 70.

27. Both from Editors of Yank, *The Best From Yank: The Army Weekly* (New York: E. P. Dutton and Company, 1945), p. 24.

28. Myers, *Yank--The GI Story*, p. 64.

29. Bill Mauldin, "How GI Joe Was Born," *Life* (March 27, 1944): 14.

30. Particularly W. L. White, *They Were Expendable* (New York: Harcourt Brace and Company, 1942); Richard Tregaskis, *Guadalcanal Diary* (New York: Popular Library Edition, 1943); John Hersey, *Into the Valley* (New York: A. A. Knopf, 1943); and Ira Wolfert, *Battle for the Solomons* (Boston: Houghton Mifflin Company, 1943).

31. Harold Hawks' movie about the World War I hero, *Sgt. York*, helped people visualize the necessity of war. Louis Jacobs writes, "By showing what happened to an average American who though he read his Bible and was a pacifist, yet became a war hero, the film subtly and astutely rallied popular feeling for participation in the war." (Louis Jacobs, "World War II and the American Film," *Cinema Journal* 7 [Winter, 1967-1968]: 10.)

After 1945, the warrior was often a professional on the screen, idealistic yet realistic, cognizant of his task. Such warriors were played by John Wayne in *They Were Expendable* and *Back to Bataan*, Dana Andrews in *A Walk in the Sun*, and Robert Mitchum in *The Story of GI Joe*. John Wayne was the epitome of the professional warrior in later movies, such as *The Wings of Eagles*, *Operation Pacific*, *Sands of Iwo Jima*, and *Flying Leathernecks*. These screen warriors exhibit "undying devotion to duty and an unqualified subscription to a disciplined, unemotional approach to warfare." (Russell Earl Shain, "An Analysis of Motion Pictures About War Released by the American Film Industry, 1939-70," [Ph.D. dissertation, University of Illinois at Urbana-Champaign, 1972], p. 188.)

32. Myers, *Yank--The GI Story*, p. 11.

33. H. S. Canby, "Hero For America: Aerial Warfare
Producing This New Hero Type," *Saturday Review of Literature*
25 (May 23, 1942): 10.

34. Mara Nacht Mayor, "The Heroic Image During World
War II," (Yale Miscellaneous Manuscripts, Yale University
Library, May, 1963), p. 9.

35. Lingeman writes, "War unleashed and mobilized the
powerful energy of American production; it gave workingmen
jobs and made them part of a knightly quest whose goal was
the killing of the hydra-headed fascist monster." (Lingeman, *Don't You Know There's a War On?*, p. 133.)

36. *Life* (April 4, 1942): 44. In the March 2, 1942,
issue, *Life* portrayed six ways to invade the U.S. There are
scenes of Japanese and Germans bombing America, and the Japanese are shown tying American prisoners with a special
pain-producing knot. Another invasion fantasy was on radio,
entitled "Chicago, Germany." A voice declared, "Achtung!
....Attention! At five three today, October eighth, 1944,
the army of occupation entered the city limits of Chicago!
The war is definitely over!" (Bacher, *The Treasury Star
Parade*, p. 315.)

Likewise, Madison Avenue effectively demonstrated the realities of the war to the public. In one ad for American
Locomotive, the reader "is given a final glimpse beyond the
converging barrels of Japanese rifles at the Rising Sun
fluttering over the Capitol dome." The ad suggests that
many overseas have been "up against it," and so will we be
if the Japs win. (Frank W. Fox, *Madison Avenue Goes to War:
The Strange Military Career of American Advertising: 1941-
45*, Charles E. Merrill Monograph Series in the Humanities
and Social Sciences [Provo, Utah: Brigham Young University
Press, 1975], p. 58.)

37. Shain, "Motion Pictures About War," p. 147.

38. For example, the act of buying war bonds or giv-
ing blood was a sacrifice of war. Posters constantly asked,
"'Can You Look Him in the Eye?, Lend a Hand...He Gave One,
What Did You Do Today...For Freedom?'" (Fox, *Madison Avenue
Goes to War*, p. 65.)

39. Marie Bonaparte, *Myths of War*, trans. by John
Rodker (London: Imago Publishing Company, n.d.), p. 19.

40. Pyle, *Brave Men*, p. 12.

41. Capt. Richard H. Chase, "It Makes Christians,"
Life (October 4, 2943): 62.

42. Pyle, *Here is Your War*, p. 742. Many war reporters
recorded the contempt that soldiers felt for civilians at
home who had no idea of what war was about. Battle experience was a unique experience, and set warriors apart. A
good example of how combat and training for war can be a
stimulus of conversion is Robert Aldrich's movie *The Dirty
Dozen*, portraying a band of criminals who become a crack combat unit and end as sacrificial heroes.

43. Bacher, *The Treasury Star Parade*, pp. 15-16.

44. Ibid., p. 20.

45. Kirby, *Star-Spangled Radio*, p. 31.

46. Arthur Upham Pope, "How Can Individuals Keep a
Healthy Morale in Wartime," *America Organizes*, p. 251.

47. Lingeman, *Don't You Know There's a War On?*, p. 197.

48. Shain, "Motion Pictures About War," p. 67.

49. Lingeman, *Don't You Know There's a War On?*, p. 200.
Bastogne, the "Gettysburg" of World War II, was another heroic
stand, but with a happy ending. *The Saturday Evening Post*
reported that General McAuliffe and the 101st Airborne "fought
with storybook courage and they never lost their sense of
humor." The movie *Battleground* appeared in 1949 and was dedicated to "the battered bastards of Bastogne." (Ivan Butler,
The War Film [South Brunswick: A. S. Barnes and Company,
1974], p. 83.)

50. Documentary films such as *Marines on Tarawa*, *The
Battle of Midway*, *Report From the Aleutians*, and *Fighting
Lady* brought the war home in another "authentic" fashion.
Often the reality of the war became the fiction of the movies.
In June, 1943, *Time* reported:

> The war began to look like a movie; brave
> Americans dashing across the blue Mediter-
> ranean and up golden Sicilian beaches to
> plant the Stars and Stripes among a grateful
> populace.

Other kinds of fiction presented the war. Radio's adventure
programs focused on wartime themes. The documentary "This
is War," consisting of thirteen half-hour shows, was sold to

seven hundred stations. Dramas and even variety shows had
martial themes. In addition, *Publisher's Weekly* counted over
two hundred seventy war novels from 1939-1945.

51. Sherrod, *Tarawa*, p. 113.

52. Ibid., p. 102.

53. There are a number of good illustrations reproduced
in Fox, *Madison Avenue Goes to War*.

54. Ibid., p. 71.

55. Ibid., p. 61.

56. Ibid., p. 63. War as an exciting event was often
linked again with sports in the public mind. Bill Stern, an
NBC commentator, used football language to describe basic
training:

> Let's watch one of these teams in action
> right now. Just out in front of us an
> infantry squad of twelve men is practicing
> an advance against an imaginary enemy. It
> seems pretty simple, doesn't it? Just a
> line of twelve men moving forward and win-
> ning ground...but in football, did you ever
> hear of the whole team carrying the ball at
> once?....No...someone has to take care of
> the interference and blocking. And that's
> exactly what happens here. Each squad of
> twelve men has two men who do nothing but
> block out would-be enemy tacklers. Only
> here, the enemy tacklers are anti-tank guns,
> machine gun nests, and pill-boxes--and if
> they slap a tackle on an advancing infantry-
> man, the chances are he'll stay down for good.
> (Kirby, *Star-Spangled Radio*, p. 45.)

Another interesting symbolic link between sports and war in
this period is the 1938 Louis-Schmeling fight. One reporter
wrote:

> Every American fighter who meets the Germans
> will have a double task on his hands....Sub-
> duing the enemy in the ring as well as sup-
> pressing the growing spirit of the Teuton
> fighters.

Louis's victory was a victory for the American way of life. After the war began, Louis was introduced to soldiers as "the first American to k.o. a Nazi." (Anthony O. Edmonds, "The Second Louis-Schmeling Fight--Sport, Symbol, and Culture," *Journal of Popular Culture* IV [1973]: 45 and 49.)

Sport was seen as one preparatory exercise for war, as well as "play" warfare itself. The athletic background of many World War II leaders was seen as crucial to their heroic make-up.

57. Fox, *Madison Avenue Goes to War*, p. 61.

58. Columbia Broadcasting System, *From Pearl Harbor into Tokyo: The Story as Told by War Correspondents on the Air* (New York: Columbia Broadcasting System, 1945), p. 296.

59. Perrett, *Days of Sadness*, p. 418.

60. Fox, *Madison Avenue Goes to War*, p. 87.

61. George W. Gray, "Science and the Warrior," *Infantry Journal* 54 (June, 1944): 51.

62. Hersey, "Experience by Battle," p. 48.

63. Fox, *Madison Avenue Goes to War*, p. 72.

64. Ernie Pyle, *Last Chapter* (New York: Henry Holt and Company, 1946), p. 5. The Germans were generally seen as attacking Western civilization, as illustrated by Thomas Hart Benton's poster "Again" (1943). The Germans here persecute Jesus on the cross. For a fine collection of propaganda posters from many countries, see Anthony Rhodes, *Propaganda: The Art of Persuasion: World War II* (New York: Chelsea House, 1976).

65. Bacher, *Treasury Star Parade*, p. 359.

66. Richard Polenberg, *War and Society: The United States, 1941-1945* (Philadelphia: J. B. Lippincott Company, 1972), p. 135.

67. *Time* (March 19, 1945): 32.

68. Myers, *Yank--The GI Story*, p. 148.

69. *Time* (March 19, 1945): 106. The idea of quantity of dead as indicative of the success of the mission is to be found in our Indian wars, in our conflict in the Philippines, and in the much noted body-count in Vietnam.

70. Holbrook, *None More Courageous*, p. 93.

71. Nicholas J. Spykman, Professor of International Relations at Yale, noted in 1942 that war was now total war. "The struggle is waged continuously....Total war is permanent war." (Charles C. Alexander, *Nationalism in American Thought 1930-1945*, The Rand McNally series on the History of American Thought and Culture [Chicago: Rand McNally and Company, 1969], p. 196.)

Even terms of surrender were expressed in total terms. Unconditional surrender was an unlimited aim. The loss of structure and ritual order in this kind of warfare is recognized by Ihab Hassan, who notes that violence in modern fiction is spatial rather than temporal. "Force in the contemporary world...is unmediated by ritual and ceremony; it is stark as nothing human or perhaps divine can be." (Ihab Hassan, "The Novel of Outrage: A Minority Voice in Postwar American Fiction," *American Scholar* 34 [1966]: 242.)

Likewise, Frederick Hoffman has suggested five stages of dehumanization in modern violence. The assailant is seen as person, as ideological instrument, as mob, as machine, and as landscape. There is, finally, a complete withdrawal of the "humanly familiar." (See Frederick J. Hoffman, *The Mortal No: Death and the Modern Imagination* [Princeton, New Jersey: Princeton University Press, 1964].)

72. As noted, the idea of the body count is a good example of this. Gil Elliot suggests, "The taking of human life loses its meaning, the significance of scale is deprived of any value, and human beings are marginalized in the record of human affairs." (Gil Elliot, *Twentieth Century Book of the Dead* [London: Allen Lane, The Penguin Press, 1972], p. 2.)

73. In Aichinger, *The American Soldier in Fiction*, p. 35.

74. Aichinger detects the feelings of ambivalence toward the professional warrior: dislike of his use of arbitrary authority and admiration for his competence as a leader:

> Novelists grappled with the problem of the general officer whose apparent fascism was disturbingly counterbalanced by those qualities of competence and aplomb that draw an instinctive response from the American mind.
> (Ibid., p. 54.)

75. Joseph J. Waldmeir, *American Novels of the Second World War*, Studies in American Literature, Volume XX (The Hague: Mouton, 1969), p. 122.

76. Myers, *Yank--The GI Story*, p. 163.

77. John Lardner, "D-Day, Iwo Jima," *The New Yorker* (March 17, 1945): 68-69.

78. Archibald MacLeish, "The Image of Victory," *Atlantic* 170 (July, 1942): 1-16.

79. Waldmeir, *American Novels of the Second World War*, p. 31.

80. For example, Waldmeir writes:

> War is evil, but this war, because it is necessary, is good; this war is necessary in order to defeat fascism which is con-summately evil primarily because it is pragmatically based on the belief that the necessary is the good; the war can only be waged successfully by responsible indi-viduals, but only through the medium of the armed services which by their very nature militate against individualism. Finally, the novelists see the services to be them-selves basically fascistic, which results in the ultimate paradox--evil must be used in behalf of good even though its use in-sures the continuance of evil.
> (Ibid., p. 143.)

81. John Keegan, *The Face of Battle* (New York: n.p., 1976), p. 322.

82. Fox, *Madison Avenue Goes to War*, p. 2. James Agee commented on war newsreels, "We have no business seeing this sort of experience except through our presence and partici-pation." (Raymond Fielding, *The American Newsreel, 1911-1967* [Norman, Oklahoma: Oklahoma University Press, 1972], p. 293.)

83. Katherine Kuh, "War and the Visual Arts," *Antioch Review* 6 (September, 1946): 400.

84. Ibid., p. 404.

85. E. P. Richardson, *Painting in America* (New York: Thomas Y. Crowell, 1956), p. 409.

86. See Wittner, *Rebels Against War*, "The Good News of Damnation," pp. 125-150.

87. Michael J. Yavenditti, "John Hersey and the American Conscience: The Reception of Hiroshima," *Pacific Historical Review* XLIII (1974): 25.

88. Ibid., p. 47. In 1947, MGM produced a full length movie, *The Beginning of the End.* It portrayed President Truman agonizing over his decision and implied that leaflets would warn of the attack. Americans could thus read Hersey with a clear conscience, for the decision portrayed was made in a thoughtful and morally sensitive way.

89. Robert Jay Lifton, *Death in Life: Survivors of Hiroshima* (New York: Random House, 1967), p. 14. Lifton finds that after Hiroshima words like chivalry, etc., cannot have the glorious meaning they once had in war. We share now only in "species annihilation."

Leslie Fiedler suggests:

> The notions of glory, honor, and courage
> lose all meaning when in the West men,
> still nominally Christian, come to believe
> that the worst thing of all is to die--
> when, for the first time in a thousand
> years, it is possible to admit that no
> cause is worth dying for.
> (Aichinger, *The American Soldier in
> Fiction*, p. 65.)

90. Lifton, *Death in Life*, p. 404. He goes on to say that the psychological sense of center disappeared, people's identities were destroyed. There was, in the total contamination of the bomb, a "limitlessness in time and space," and the inversion of the natural order of life, "the unnatural order of death-dominated life."

91. Clarke, *Voices Prophesying War*, p. 198.

92. Kingsley Widmer, "American Apocalypse: Notes on the Bomb and the Failure of Imagination," in Warren French, ed., *The Forties: Fiction, Poetry, Drama* (Deland, Florida: Everett Edward, Inc., 1969): 148.

A sense of impending apocalypse is also found in much of the protest music of the sixties; for example, Dylan's "Hard Rain's A-Gonna Fall" and "Talkin' World War Three Blues," P. F. Sloan's "Eve of Destruction," and Tom Lehrer's "So Long Mom (I'm off to drop the bomb)."

93. Quoted in J. William Fulbright, *The Crippled Giant* (New York: Random House, 1972), p. 9.

94. Carl Solberg, *Riding High: America in the Cold War* (New York: Mason and Lipscomb, 1973), p. 40.

That the symbolic power of these images was dominant is noted by George F. Kennan:

> The purest expression of the phenomenon
> ...seems to me to have been rendered
> not in its physical reality but in its
> power as a dream, or a nightmare....Its
> deepest reality lies strangely enough
> in its manifestation as a dream.
> (Les K. Adler and Thomas G. Paterson,
> "Red Fascism: The Merger of Nazi Germany
> and Soviet Russia in the American Image
> of Totalitarianism, 1930s-1950s," *American
> Historical Review* LXXV [1970]: 1063-1064.)

The Red Scare did produce semi-factual war fantasy literature and imagined warlike situations. The government published a pamphlet entitled "Survival Under Atomic Attack," while four million joined the sky watchers to look for such an attack. Institutions everywhere had regular air-raid drills, and one was remiss by not marking Conelrad stations on radios.

95. In Richard J. Barnet, *Roots of War* (Baltimore: Penguin Books, 1973), p. 19.

96. Peter C. Rollins, "Victory at Sea: Cold War Epic," *Journal of Popular Culture* 6 (1973): 468.

97. Ibid, p. 478. The nostalgia for the "dangerous beauty" of the war and the drama of decisive warfare in our history is expressed by John F. Dulles' desire, "'What we need to do...is to recapture the kind of crusading spirit of the early days of the Republic.'" (Carl Solberg, *Riding High*, p. 224.)

98. Clarke, *Voices Prophesying War*, p. 203.

99. George Grella, "James Bond: Culture Hero," *New Republic* (May 30, 1964): 17.

100. Solberg, *Riding High*, p. 466.

101. Daniel J. Leab, "Cold War Comics," *Columbia Journalism Review* III (Winter, 1965): 43. Country music also was militantly anti-Communist in the fifties. In Roy Acuff's "Advice to Joe," he sings:

> You will see the lightning flashing,
> hear atomic thunders roll,
> When Moscow lies in ashes,
> God have mercy on your soul,
> Here's a question, Mister Stalin,
> and it's you who must decide,
> When atom bombs start falling,
> do you have a place to hide?
> (Jens Lund, "Country Music Goes to War:
> Songs for the Red-Blooded American,"
> *Popular Music and Society* 1 [Summer, 1972]:
> 213.)

As in World War II and Vietnam, country music never wavered in support of America's wars.

102. For obvious reasons, both the concept of the fertility of warfare and the possibility of a warrior's re-generative sacrifice was changed by the advent of nuclear weapons. Hans Morgenthau wrote that we could no longer talk about freeing West Berlin as we once talked about freeing the colonies. War is no longer an extension of past wars, but a "qualitative transformation of the meaning of our existence." (Hans J. Morgenthau, "Death in the Nuclear Age," in Nathan A. Scott, Jr., ed., *The Modern Vision of Death* [Richmond: John Knox Press, 1967]: 76.)

103. Aichinger, *The American Soldier in Fiction*, p. 68.

104. Morton H. Halperin, "The Limiting Process in the Korean War," *Political Science Quarterly* LXVIII (March, 1963): 16.

105. Ibid., p. 25.

106. In his famous speech at West Point in 1962, MacArthur emphasized his longing for the real, significant world of battle: the meaning of life for the warrior.

> The shadows are lengthening for me....I
> listen vainly for the witching melody of
> faint bugles blowing reveille, of far
> drums beating the long roll. In my
> dreams I hear again the crash of guns,
> the rattle of musketry, the strange,
> mournful mutter of the battlefield.
> (Douglas MacArthur, *Duty, Honor, Country*
> [New York: Rolton House Publishers,
> Inc., 1962], pp. 30-31.)

107. Russell E. Shain, "Hollywood's Cold War," *Journal of Popular Film* 4 (1974): 345.

108. Shain, "Motion Pictures About War," p. 173.

109. Morgenthau, "Death in the Nuclear Age," p. 77.

110. For good background, see Bernard Fall, *Street Without Joy: From the Indochina War to the War in Viet-Nam* (Harrisburg, Pa.: The Stackpole Company, 1961); and *The Two Vietnams: A Political and Military Analysis*, 2nd rev. ed. (New York: Praeger, 1967); Marvin E. Gettleman, ed., *Viet-Nam: History, Documents and Opinions on a Major World Crisis* (New York: Fawcett World Library, 1965); David Halberstam, *The Best and the Brightest* (Greenwich, Conn.: Fawcett Publications, Inc., 1972); George C. Herring, *America's Longest War: The United States and Vietnam, 1950-1975* (New York: John Wiley and Sons, 1979); Roger Hilsman, *To Move a Nation: The Politics of Foreign Policy in the Administration of John F. Kennedy* (Garden City, New York: Doubleday and Company, 1967); Townsend Hoopes, *The Limits of Intervention* (New York: David McKay Company, Inc., 1969); George McTurnan Kahin and John W. Lewis, *The United States in Vietnam*, rev. ed. (New York: Dell Publishing Company, 1969); Marvin Kalb and Elie Abel, *Roots of Involvement: The U.S. in Asia, 1784-1971* (New York: W. W. Norton and Company, 1971); *The Pentagon Papers* (New York: Quadrangle Books, 1971); and for excellent bibliographic information, see Milton Leitenberg and Richard D. Burns, comps., *The Vietnam Conflict* (Santa Barbara: Clio Press, 1973); and Peter Braestrup, "Vietnam as History," *The Wilson Quarterly* (Spring, 1978): 178-187.

111. In 1954, Eisenhower characterized the struggle for Indochina as crucial because of the domino principle. "You have a row of dominos set up, you knock over the first one, and what will happen to the last one is the certainty that it will go over very quickly." Thus, if Indochina fell, the rest of Asia, including Japan, would not be far behind. (Solberg, *Riding High*, p. 231.)

The mythic certainty of this principle was illustrated well by a conversation reportedly between Merle Haggard and a friend:

> "Well, one thing's for sure," said Fuzzy,
> a veteran of the Korean War who fervently
> believes in "Okie" and "Fighting Side."
> "If we don't hurry up and stop 'em over
> there, pretty soon we're gonna be fighting
> 'em in Bakersfield. Right there at the
> Kern Canyon, by God."
> "Fighting who?" said Haggard, straight-faced.
> "The damn Communists, that's who."

"They interested in Bakersfield?"
"Aw, you know what I mean, Merle."
"Ain't no rice there."
Fuzz's sap was rising. "Naw, it's that
'domino theory.' If we don't stop 'em in
Vietnam, they'll take the rest of Asia.
Then they'll take Australia, Hawaii, and
the whole world."
"Where'd you read that at?" said Haggard.
"I didn't have to read it. By God, I know."
(In Robert Jewett, *The Captain America
Complex: The Dilemma of Zealous Nationalism*
[Philadelphia: The Westminster Press, 1973],
p. 134.)

Further, Richard Barnet writes:

At what can only be described as a
religious level, the real enemies are
chaos and disorder, which threaten to
undermine one's power. Despite his
devotion to the rhetoric of "freedom,"
the national security manager puts his
trust in hierarchy. Because the world
is dangerous, because man's nature is
essentially evil, structures must be
maintained within which people will
know and keep their place. The most
threatening political development of
the postwar world is a revolution,
because the essence of revolution is a
redefinition of place.
(Barnet, *Roots of War*, p. 74.)

112. Peter Stromberg, "A Long War's Writing: American
Novels About the Fighting in Vietnam While Americans Fought,"
(Ph.D. dissertation, Cornell University, 1974), p. 2.

113. John Mueller, "Trends in Popular Support for the
Wars in Korea and Vietnam," *American Political Science
Review* LXV (1971): 350.

114. *The Vietnam Hearings*, with an introduction by
J. William Fulbright (New York: Random House, 1966), p. 33.
The absence of ritual structure both in the war and in the
perceptions of the war invaded many accounts by both participants and observers. It led to a phenomenon we have
noticed before, a nostalgia for war in its classic form.
For example, in the movie *Three Days of the Condor*, CIA
officer Higgins asks his boss what he misses most about the
First and Second World Wars...the excitement perhaps? "No,"
said his boss, "the clarity." War novels also noted the

absence of structure. In John Sack's *M*, after a village
is burned, Sack writes, "finally he could do something with
a clear bearing on America's war effort, clear in a physical
sense if hazy around the edges in the sense of grand
strategy." (Clinton R. Sanders, "The Portrayal of War and
the Fighting Man in Novels of the Vietnam War," *Journal of
Popular Culture* 3 [1969]: 559.)

115. Lifton, *Home From the War*, p. 40.

116. Charles J. Levy, "ARVN as Faggots: Inverted
Warfare in Vietnam," *Transaction* 8 (October, 1971): 20.

117. Phillip Caputo, *A Rumor of War* (New York:
Ballantine Books, 1977), pp. 272-273.

118. Stromberg, "A Long War's Writing," p. 246.

119. Ibid., p. 248.

120. Loudon Wainwright, "In Search of a Vietnam Hero:
H. D. Meyerkurd's Death," *Life* (May 28, 1965): 24. Meyerkurd
is portrayed here as the classic American warrior, the kind
Maxwell Taylor spoke of in his 1963 West Point commencement
address. "One sensed the influence of the American Soldier
in his role as teacher of the armies of freedom." (Halberstam, *The Best and the Brightest*, p. 583.)

121. Editors of *Army Times*, *American Heroes of the
Asian Wars* (New York: Dodd, Mead and Company, 1968), p. 109.

122. Tim O'Brien, *If I Die in a Combat Zone, Box Me
Up and Ship Me Home* (New York: Dell, 1969), p. 168.

123. "Remembrance of Things Past," *Newsweek* (May 5,
1975): 21.

124. *Vietnam Hearings*, p. 192.

125. The nature of such policies as the B-52 raids,
free-fire zones, search and destroy missions and defoliation
denied the possibility of careful distinction between civilians and combatants. Jonathan Schell says:

> When we go into a village...we classify
> all the people into different categories.
> But these categories do not depend on
> something we perceive about them; they
> depend on what we do to them. If we kill
> them, they are Vietcong. If we capture
> them and tie them up, they are Vietcong
> suspects. If we grab them and move them

to a camp, they are hostile civilians.
Having done this to many people who were
in fact innocent, the definitions we have
imposed become real. The men who have
been tied up or tortured actually become
our enemies and shoot real bullets at us,
but still we are facing the shadow of our
own actions.
(Erwin Knoll and Judith Nies McFadden,
eds., *War Crimes and the American Conscience*
[New York: Holt, Rinehart and Winston,
1970], p. 111.)

126. Lucian K. Truscott, "Body Count: The Degrading
Illusion," *Nation* 211 (November 16, 1970): 487.

127. Philip Slater, "Kill Anything that Moves," in
Pursuit of Loneliness, rev. ed. (Boston: Beacon Press,
1976), p. 44.

128. Jensen, *Myth and Cult*, p. 170.

129. Sanders, "The Portrayal of War and the Fighting
Man," p. 560.

130. Caputo, *A Rumor of War*, p. 121.

131. Ibid., p. 153. He also notes the absence of
heroic style in the deaths of this war. "Certainly I had
no illusions that my death, if it came, would be a sacrifice. It would merely be a death, and not a good one either.
A good death involved a certain amount of choice, ritual,
and style. There were no good deaths in the war." (p. 247.)

132. C. D. B. Bryan, *Friendly Fire* (New York: G. P.
Putnam's Sons, 1976), p. 60.

133. Lifton, *Home From the War*, p. 56. Herbert Carter,
a GI who gave himself a foot injury to get out of "fighting"
at My Lai, said, "The people didn't know what they were dying
for and the guys didn't know why they were shooting them."
(Seymour Hersh, "My Lai 4: A Report on the Massacre and Its
Aftermath," *Harper's* 240 [May, 1970]: 84.

The sacrality of the military concept of mission was stated
well by Douglas MacArthur in conferring the death sentence
on General Yamashita, a Japanese officer convicted of responsibility in civilian deaths in World War II:

> The soldier, be he friend or foe, is
> charged with the protection of the weak
> and unarmed. It is the very essence and
> reason for his being. When he violates
> this sacred trust, he not only profanes
> his entire cult but threatens the very
> fabric of international society. The
> traditions of fighting men are long and
> honorable. They are based upon the noblest
> of human faiths--sacrifice. This officer
> ...has failed this irrevocable standard;
> has failed his duty to his troops, to his
> country, to mankind; has failed utterly
> his soldier faith.
> ("Massacre Trial: A Shift in the War,"
> *U.S. News and World Report* [December 15,
> 1969]: 25.)

134. Halberstam also informs us that in 1938, General
Joe Stilwell was puzzled at Japanese atrocities in China.
He concluded in part that the Japanese soldiers saw their
mission as a crusade to liberate the Chinese, and when their
efforts are not appreciated, "'It is a shocking rejection of
his idealism,' and the Japanese soldier raged against 'the
people who he believes have denied him his chivalry.'"
(Halberstam, *The Best and the Brightest*, p. 471.)

135. Larry J. Winn, "My Lai: Birth and Death of a
Rhetorical Symbol," (Ph.D. dissertation, University of
Virginia, 1974), p. 29.

136. Ibid., pp. 78-79.

137. Wayne Greenhaw, *The Making of a Hero: The Story
of Lieut. William Calley, Jr.* (Louisville, Kentucky: Touchstone Publishing Company, 1971), p. 210.

138. Winn, "My Lai," p. 96.

139. Greenhaw, *Making of a Hero*, p. 191.

140. Winn, "My Lai," pp. 63-64. As many accounts did,
this one accepted mistakenly that there was gunfire from the
village.

141. Lifton has written:

> All Americans are survivors of the Vietnam
> holocaust, and are faced with the task of
> recognizing and bringing significance to
> their death immersion. In this man-made--
> essentially American-made--holocaust, the

secular equivalent to divine punishment
may be found in the shocking emergence of
the sins of our national past, long hidden
under a cloak of unadulterated virtue to
the point of threatening the entire American historical experiment.
(Lifton, *Home From the War*, p. 505.)

The search dealt with, among other things, America as
aggressor (against the Indians). The parallels between the
Vietnam war and the American Indian wars have been seen by
many observers. Frances Fitzgerald writes:

In Vietnam American officers liked to call
the area outside of gun control "Indian
country." It was a joke...no more than a
figure of speech, but it put the Vietnam
war into a definite historical and mythological perspective: the Americans were
once again embarked upon a heroic and (for
themselves) almost painless conquest of an
inferior race. To the American settlers
the defeat of the Indians had seemed not
just a nationalist victory, but an achievement made in the name of humanity--the
triumph of light over darkness, of good
over evil, and of civilization over brutish
nature. Quite unconsciously, the American
officers and officials used a similar
language to describe their war against the
NLF....The Viet Cong did not live in places,
they "infested areas"; to "clean them out"
the American forces went on "sweep and
clear" operations....Westmoreland spoke of
the NLF as "termites."
(Frances Fitzgerald, *Fire in the Lake* [New
York: Random House, 1973], pp. 491-492.
Also see the excellent chapters on this
theme in Drinnon, *Facing West*.)

142. Daniel Berrigan, *The Trial of the Catonsville
Nine* (Boston: Beacon Press, 1970), p. 59.

143. Michael Novak, "The Battle Hymn of Lt. Calley...
and the Republic," *Commonweal* (April 30, 1971): 186.

144. "Only the Vietcong has committed atrocities in
Vietnam." (Vice-President Humphrey, May 13, 1965.) "We
should be proud of our country because the Americal Division
rules of engagement are based on Judeo-Christian [sic]

traditions and are moral, unlike those of the enemy."
(Chief Chaplain Shaw, November 29, 1969.) (Both statements
are taken from Albert Kahn, *The Unholy Hymnal* [New York:
Simon and Schuster, 1971], pp. 56 and 64.)

145. *Newsweek* (December 15, 1969): 35.

146. Winn, "My Lai," p. 16. For examples of American
resistance to the event, see Edward M. Opton, Jr., and
Robert Duckles, "It Didn't Happen and Besides, They Deserved
It," in Richard Falk, Gabriel Kolko, and Robert Jay Lifton,
eds., *Crimes of War* (New York: Random House, 1971), pp.
441-444.

147. In the midst of this symbolic dislocation, Hugh
Sidey reported that President Nixon was forced to reach for
identity "with some common things in American life which
are wholesome and durable and have not been tainted by the
Vietnam war." Thus, he reached to sports for solace and
attended the Arkansas-Texas football game. (*Life* [Dec-
ember 12, 1969]: 4.) However, the world of sports was not
immune. Joseph Ellis and Robert Moore report that the
terrible academy (especially West Point) football teams
of the late sixties and early seventies (losing in 1973 to
California 45-0, and to Alabama 66-0) had a serious effect
on cadet morale. One writer decided there were parallels
between football strategy at the Academy and military
strategy in Vietnam:

> We seem to be getting tied in awful lot
> of wars lately....But I guess that's
> easy to understand when our football
> teams at West Point are only trying to
> keep the score respectable.
> (Quoted in Ellis and Moore, *School for
> Soldiers*, p. 202.)

Even *Sports Illustrated* did not escape the shadow of Vietnam
and the memory of atrocities. The June 9, 1975, issue
featured a story on the Steelers' running back and Vietnam
veteran entitled "Rocky Bleier's War," pp. 76-80+.

Michael Arlen reported that people could not even get the
"picture" of Vietnam from daily journalism. See Michael J.
Arlen, *Living Room War* (New York: Viking Press, 1969).
Lifton suggests that television reporting removed people
from the "proper impact of war." Gloria Emerson underlines
one of the dangers of "tv war." She reports a woman's
statement:

> They looked alike....The Second World War
> was very impressive to a child; it was
> also a kind of entertainment, and they
> painted Vietnam in the same style. It
> took some of the teeth out of it. It put
> Vietnam under the same moral umbrella as
> World War II.
> (Gloria Emerson, *Winners and Losers:
> Battles, Retreats, Gains, Losses and
> Ruins From a Long War* [New York: Random
> House, 1976], p. 11.)

Edward Epstein suggests that television coverage of the war
did as much in the early years to support the war as it did
in the later years to criticize it. See Edward J. Epstein,
"Vietnam: What Happened vs. What We Saw," *TV Guide* 21
(September 19, 1973): 6-10, and (October 13, 1973): 49-54.

148. Mark Baker, *NAM* (New York: William Morrow and
Company, Inc., 1981), p. 85.

149. Reviews of Vietnam war movies illustrate the
diversity of perception of the war in America. The best
full-length study of these films is Julian Smith, *Looking
Away: Hollywood and Vietnam* (New York: Charles Scribner's
Sons, 1975). Also helpful are Lance Morrow, "Vietnam Comes
Home," *Time* (April 23, 1979): 22-28; J. Pym, "Bullet in the
Head: Vietnam Remembered," *Sight and Sound* 48 (Spring,
1979): 82-84+; Lawrence Suid, "Hollywood and Vietnam," *Film
Comment* 15 (September, 1979): 20-25; P. McInerney, "Apoca-
lypse Then: Hollywood Looks Back at Vietnam," *Film
Quarterly* 33 (Winter, 1979/80): 21-32; Jerome Klinkowitz,
The American 1960s: Imaginative Acts in a Decade of Change
(Ames: The Iowa State University Press, 1980).

150. Lund, "Country Music Goes to War," p. 218. Rich
Leib in "Country Music--A Sign of Our Time?" (unpublished
paper, University of California, Santa Barbara, 1978) lists
a number of pro-war songs performed by country artists in
the mid-late sixties.

151. Leib, "Country Music," p. 13.

152. Francine du Plessix Gray, "Slum Landlords in
Eden," *Saturday Review of the Society* (December, 1972): 77.

153. Emerson, *Winners and Losers*, p. 115.

154. Bryan, *Friendly Fire*, pp. 55-57.

155. "How Should Americans Feel?" *Time* (April 14,
1975): 27.

156. Baker, *NAM*, p. 290.

157. Jay A. Jeffrey, "After Vietnam: I. In Pursuit of Scapegoats," *Harper's* (July, 1978): 18.

158. Caputo, *A Rumor of War*, p. 213. Peter Osnos has studied a town of twenty thousand which lost nine men in Vietnam. Neither the mayor nor the clergy could remember them; their names appeared on no statues. He concludes that the war had "little direct influence on individual lives, at least that people could identify. On the other hand, the war apparently did have a substantial effect on people's attitudes." (Peter Osnos, "The War and Riverdale," in Anthony Lake, ed., *The Legacy of Vietnam. The War, American Society, and the Future of American Foreign Policy* [New York: New York University Press, 1976], p. 67.)

Recently, of course, the Vietnam memorial has been approved for construction in Washington. Controversy has surrounded the design, the color, the inscriptions. For brief comment on these issues, see J. Martin, "Plaque for Vietnam: Question of Plaque Near Tomb of Unknown Soldier," *Nation* 226 (April 8, 1978): 389-390; "Needless Obstacle," *New Republic* (May 31, 1980): 7-8; "Honored at Last," *Time* July 14, 1980): 23; "Stop that Monument," *National Review* (September 18, 1981): 1064; W. Von Eckardt, "Storm Over a Vietnam Memorial," *Time* (November 9, 1981): 103; N. B. Hannah, "Open Book Memorial," *National Review* (December 11, 1981): 1476; A. Gabor, "Vietnam Memorial Meets Snag That May Prevent Groundbreaking," *Architectural Record* 170 (February, 1982): 28; and Hugh Sidey, "Tribute to Sacrifice," *Time* (February 22, 1982): 19.

159. "The Impact of Vietnam: Part I," *The Center Magazine* (July/August, 1979): 29.

160. Peter Marin, "Coming to Terms with Vietnam," *Harper's* 261 (December, 1980): 50.

In addition to the numerous novels and autobiographies written by veterans during the war years, recent interest in the veterans and the significance of their message may be seen in Chuck Noell and Gary Wood, *We Are All POW's* (Philadelphia: Fortress Press, 1975); Arthur Egendorf, "Vietnam Veteran Rap Groups and Themes of Post-War Life," *Journal of Social Issues* 31 (1975): 111-124; Robert Jay Lifton, "The Post-War War," *Journal of Social Issues* 31 (1975): 181-195; Lawrence M. Baskir and William A. Strauss, *Chance and Circumstance: The Draft, the War and the*

Vietnam Generation (New York: Vintage Books, 1978); Al
Santoli, *Everything We Had. An Oral History of the Vietnam
War by Thirty-Three American Soldiers Who Fought It* (New
York: Random House, 1981); Jerome Klinkowitz and John
Somer, eds., *Writing Under Fire: Stories of the Vietnam
War* (New York: Dell, 1978); Tracy Kidder, "Soldiers of
Misfortune," *Atlantic* (March, 1978): 41-52+; "The Impact
of Vietnam: Part I," *The Center Magazine* (July/August,
1979): 15-36; "The Impact of Vietnam: Part II," *The Center
Magazine* (September/October, 1979): 31-52; "Five Years
Later," *U.S. News and World Report* (April 28, 1980): 30-33;
A. D. Horne, ed., *The Wounded Generation: America After
Vietnam* (Englewood Cliffs, N.J.: Prentice-Hall, Inc.,
1981); "Vietnam: Will There Be a Collective Healing?"
The Center Magazine (July/August, 1981): 14-28; Lance
Morrow, "The Forgotten Warriors," *Time* (July 13, 1981):
18-25; Peter Marin, "Living in Mortal Pain," *Psychology
Today* (November, 1981): 68-80; R. Witherspoon, "Black
Vietnam Vets: No Peace Yet," *Essence* 12 (December, 1981):
76-77; "What Vietnam Did to Us," *Newsweek* (December 14,
1981): 46-97; J. Seligmann, "A Good Year for Vietnam Vets,"
Newsweek May 17, 1982): 16.

161. Walter Capps, *The Unfinished War: Vietnam and
the American Conscience* (Boston: Beacon Press, 1981), p. 16.

Revision of America's role in the war is already underway.
Popular interpretations include Guenter Lewy's belief that
America committed no war crimes in Vietnam, William Westmoreland's belief that we lot the war because of poor
support back home (prejudiced, of course, by a liberal
media), and suggestions by Peter Berger and Norman
Podhoretz that in light of the tragic fate of many in
Vietnam and Cambodia, American ideals and tactics were not
as bad as we thought. For these and divergent interpreta-
tions, see Peter Berger, "Indochina and the American Con-
science," *Commentary* 69 (February, 1980): 29-39; David P.
Chandler, "Post Mortes on the Wars in Indo-China: A Review
Article," *The Journal of Asian Studies* XL, No. 1 (November,
1980): 77-86; Noam Chomsky et al., "Vietnam and Cambodia,"
Dissent 25 (4) (1978): 386-391; William L. Griffen and
John Marciano, *Teaching the Vietnam War* (Montclair, New
Jersey: Allanheld Osmun, 1979); Irving Howe and Michael
Walzer, "Were We Wrong About Vietnam?" *New Republic* 181
(August 18, 1979): 15-18; Henry Kissinger, *White House
Years* (Boston: Little, Brown, 1979), and *Years of Up-
heaval* (Boston: Little, Brown, 1981); Walter Lafeber,
"The Last War, the Next War, and the New Revisionists,"
Democracy 1 (January, 1981): 93-103; Guenter Lewy, *America
in Vietnam* (New York: Oxford University Press, 1978);

Norman Podhoretz, *Why We Were in Vietnam* (New York: Simon and Schuster, 1982); William C. Westmoreland, *A Soldier Reports* (Garden City: Doubleday, 1976).

    162. Robert Jay Lifton, *The Broken Connection: On Death and the Continuity of Life* (New York: Simon and Schuster, 1979), p. 369.

    163. Capps, *The Unfinished War*, p. 133.

    164. Quoted in Capps, *The Unfinished War*, p. 129.

SELECTED BIBLIOGRAPHY

PREFACE

BOOKS

Benedict, Ruth. *The Chrysanthemum and the Sword*. Boston: Houghton Mifflin Company, 1964.

Bramson, Leo and Goethals, George W. *War: Studies from Psychology, Sociology, Anthropology*. New York: Basic Books, 1964.

Campbell, Joseph. *The Hero With a Thousand Faces*. 2nd ed. Bollingen Series XVII. Princeton: Princeton University Press, 1968.

Cohn, Norman. *The Pursuit of the Millennium*. 2nd ed. New York: Harper and Row, 1961.

Divale, William T., Comp. *Warfare in Primitive Societies: A Selected Bibliography*. Los Angeles: California State College, Los Angeles, 1971.

Dumézil, George. *The Destiny of the Warrior*. Translated by Alf Hiltebeitel. Chicago: The University of Chicago Press, 1969.

Eliade, Mircea. *The Myth of the Eternal Return: Or Cosmos and History*. Bollingen Series XLVI. Translated by Willard R. Trask. n.p.: Princeton University Press, 1954.

_____. *Rites and Symbols of Initiation*. Translated by Willard R. Trask. New York: Harper and Row, 1958.

_____. *Myth and Reality*. Translated by Willard R. Trask. New York: Harper and Row, 1963.

_____. *Cultural Fashions and History of Religions*. Wesleyan University Center for Advanced Studies, 1967.

_____. *Histoire des Croyances et des Idées Religieuses*
     Paris: Payot, 1976.

Fussell, Paul. *The Great War and Modern Memory*. New York:
     Oxford University Press, 1975.

Gray, J. Glenn. *The Warriors: Reflections on Men in
     Battle*. New York: Harper and Row, 1967.

Huizinga, Johann. *Homo Ludens*. Boston: Beacon Press,
     1955.

Jaeger, Werner W. *Paideia: The Ideals of Greek Culture*.
     3 vols. New York: Oxford University Press, 1945.

Jensen, Adolf E. *Myth and Cult Among Primitive Peoples*.
     Translated by Marianna Tax Choldin and Wolfgang
     Weissleder. Chicago: University of Chicago Press,
     1963.

Larson, Gerald James, ed. *Myth in Indo-European Antiquity*.
     Berkeley: University of California Press, 1974.

Littleton, C. Scott. *The New Comparative Mythology*.
     Berkeley: University of California Press, 1973.

Nitobe, Inazō. *Bushido: The Soul of Japan*. Rutland,
     Vermont: Charles E. Tuttle Company, 1969.

Pedersen, Johannes. *Israel, Its Life and Culture*. 2 vols.
     London: Geoffrey Cumberlege, Oxford University Press,
     1925 and 1940.

Schulte Nordholte, H. G. *The Political System of the Atoni
     of Timor*. The Hague: Martinus Nijhoff, 1971.

Seward, Jack. *Hara-Kiri: Japanese Ritual Suicide*.
     Rutland, Vermont: Charles E. Tuttle Company, 1969.

Soustelle, Jacques. *The Daily Life of the Aztecs*.
     Middlesex, England: Penguin Books Ltd., 1964.

Tuveson, Ernest Lee. *Redeemer Nation: The Idea of America's
     Millennial Role*. Chicago: University of Chicago
     Press, 1968.

Van Baal, Jan. *Dema: Description and Analysis of Marind-
     Anim Culture*. The Hague: Martinus Nijhoff, 1966.

Varley, H. Paul. *Samurai*. New York: Dell Publishing
     Company, 1970.

Vernant, Jean-Pierre. *Problemes de la Guerre dans la Gréce Ancienne.* Civilisations et Societies 11. Paris-La Haye: Mouton and Company, 1968.

Wach, Joachim. *Types of Religious Experience: Christian and Non-Christian.* London: Routledge and Kegan Paul, Ltd., 1951.

Wright, Quincy. *A Study of War.* Chicago: University of Chicago Press, 1942.

ARTICLES

Andreas, Carol R. "War Toys and the Peace Movement." *Journal of Social Issues* 25 (January, 1969): 83-99.

Chagnon, Napoleon. "Yanomamō Social Organization and Warfare." In *War*, pp. 109-159. Edited by Morton Fried, Marvin Harris, and Robert Murphy. Garden City, New York: The Natural History Press, 1967.

Ellis, F. H. "Patterns of Aggression and the War Cult in Southwestern Pueblos." *Southwestern Journal of Anthropology* 7 (1951): 177-201.

Fathauer, G. H. "The Structure and Causation of Mohave Warfare." *Southwestern Journal of Anthropology* 10 (1954): 97-118.

Harner, M. "Jivaro Souls." *American Anthropologist* 64 (1962): 258-272.

Kennedy, John G. "Ritual and Intergroup Murder: Comments on War, Primitive and Modern." In *War and the Human Race*, pp. 40-61. Edited by Maurice Walsh. Amsterdam: Elsevier Publishing Company, 1971.

Littleton, C. Scott. "Some Possible Indo-European Themes in the Iliad." In *Myth and Law Among the Indo-Europeans*, pp. 229-246. Edited by Jaan Puhvel. Berkeley: University of California Press, 1970.

Rodman, Barbee-Sue. "War and Aesthetic Sensibility: An Essay in Cultural History." *Soundings* 51 (Fall, 1968): 308-326.

Chapter One

BOOKS

Albanese, Catherine L. *Sons of the Fathers. The Civil Religion of the American Revolution.* Philadelphia: Temple University Press, 1976.

Allen, Robert Sharon. *Lucky Forward.* New York: The Vanguard Press, Inc., 1947.

Ambrose, Stephen E. *Crazy Horse and Custer.* Garden City, New York: Doubleday and Company, 1975.

Army Times, eds. *Warrior: The Story of Gen. George S. Patton.* New York: G. P. Putnam's Sons, 1967.

Ayer, Frederick, Jr. *Before the Colors Fade: Portrait of a Soldier.* Foreword by Omar N. Bradley. Dunwoody, Georgia: Norman S. Berg, 1971.

Blumenson, Martin. *The Patton Papers, 1885-1940.* Boston: Houghton Mifflin Company, 1972.

_____. *The Patton Papers, 1940-1945.* Boston: Houghton Mifflin Company, 1972.

Bryan, William Alfred. *George Washington in American Literature, 1775-1865.* Westport, Connecticut: Greenwood Press, 1970.

Bush, Clive. *The Dream of Reason: American Consciousness and Cultural Achievement from Independence to the Civil War.* Great Britain: Edward Arnold, 1977.

Codman, Charles. *Drive.* Boston: Little, Brown and Company, 1957.

Cunliffe, Marcus. *Soldiers and Civilians. The Martial Spirit in America, 1775-1865.* Boston: Little, Brown and Company, 1968.

_____. *George Washington: Man and Monument.* Boston: Little, Brown and Company, 1958.

Custer, George A. *My Life on the Plains.* Norman: University of Oklahoma Press, 1962.

Custer, Elizabeth B. *"Boots and Saddles," Or, Life in
    Dakota with General Custer.* With an introduction by
    Jane R. Stewart. Norman: University of Oklahoma
    Press, 1961.

Donnelle, A. J. *Cyclorama of Custer's Last Battle or the
    Battle of the Little Big Horn.* New York: Argonaut
    Press, 1966.

Ellis, Joseph and Moore, Robert. *School for Soldiers.
    West Point and the Profession of Arms.* New York:
    Oxford University Press, 1974.

Elson, Ruth Miller. *Guardians of Tradition: American
    Schoolbooks of the Nineteenth Century.* Lincoln:
    University of Nebraska Press, 1964.

Essame, H. *Patton. A Study in Command.* New York: Charles
    Scribner's Sons, 1974.

Farago, Ladislas. *Ordeal and Triumph.* New York: Ivan
    Obolensky, Inc., 1964.

Frost, Lawrence. *The Custer Album.* Seattle: n.p., 1964.

Goebel, Dorothy Burne and Goebel, Julius, Jr. *Generals in
    the White House.* Freeport, New York: Books for
    Libraries Press, 1971.

Graham, W. A. *The Custer Myth: A Source Book of Custeriana.*
    Harrisburg, Pa.: The Stackpole Company, 1953.

Harvey, Frederick L. *History of the Washington Monument
    and the National Monument Society.* Washington, D.C.:
    Norman T. Elliot Printing Company, 1902.

Headley, J. T. *Washington and His Generals.* 2 vols. New
    York: Baker and Scribner, 1850.

Luce, Edward and Luce, Evelyn S. *Custer Battlefield
    National Monument.* Historical Handbook Series No. 1.
    Washington, D.C.: National Park Service, 1957.

Luce, Edward S. *Keogh, Comanche and Custer.* Ashland,
    Oregon: Lewis Osborne, 1974.

Monaghan, Jay. *Custer: The Life of General George Arm-
    strong Custer.* Boston: Little, Brown and Company,
    1959.

Patton, George Smith. *War as I Knew It.* Boston: Houghton
    Mifflin Company, 1947.

Rosenburg, Bruce. *Custer and the Epic of Defeat.* Uni-
    versity Park: The Pennsylvania State University
    Press, 1974.

Russell, Don. *Custer's Last.* Fort Worth, Texas: Amon
    Carter Museum of Western Art, 1968.

Schauffer, Robert Haven, ed. *Washington's Birthday.*   New
    York: Moffat, Yard and Company, 1913.

Shaffer, Arthur H. *The Politics of History: Writing the
    History of the American Revolution 1783-1815.*
    Chicago: Precedent Publishing, 1975.

Slotkin, Richard. *Regeneration Through Violence: The
    Mythology of the American Frontier 1600-1860.*   Middle-
    town, Connecticut: Wesleyan University Press, 1973.

Steckmesser, Kent. *The Western Hero in History and Legend.*
    Norman: University of Oklahoma Press, 1965.

Taylor, Joshua. *America as Art.* Washington: Smithsonian
    Institution Press, 1976.

Whittaker, Frederick, ed. *A Complete Life of General
    George A. Custer.* New York: Sheldon and Co., 1876.

ARTICLES

Bryan, W. A.   "George Washington, Symbolic Guardian of
    the Republic." *William and Mary Quarterly,* 3rd
    Series, VII (January, 1950): 53-63.

Curti, Merle.   "Dime Novels and the American Tradition."
    Yale Review 26 (1937): 761-778.

Dippie, Brian W.   "Bards of the Little Big Horn." *Western
    American Literature* 1 (Fall, 1966): 175-195.

Kelly, J. R.   "The Battle of the Little Big Horn.   Requiem
    for the Men in the Shadows." 1957. Wyles Collection,
    University of California, Santa Barbara.

McAuliffe, Eugene. "The Seventh United States Cavalry:
    Too Long Neglected." March 1, 1957. Wyles Collection,
    University of California, Santa Barbara.

McGrane, Reginald C. "George Washington: An Anglo American
    Hero." *Virginia Magazine of History and Biography*
    LXIII (January, 1955): 3-14.

Mullett, Charles F. "The Classical Influences on the
    American Revolution." *The Classical Journal* 35
    (November, 1939): 92-104.

Nettels, C. P. "The Washington Theme in American History."
    Proceedings of the Massachusetts Historical Society
    LXVIII (1952): 171-198.

Pearce, Roy Harvey. "The Significance of the Captivity
    Narrative." *American Literature* 19 (March, 1949):
    1-20.

Taft, Robert. "The Pictorial Record of the Old West--
    Custer's Last Stand." *Kansas Historical Quarterly*
    XIV (November, 1946): 361-390.

CHAPTER TWO

BOOKS

Aaron, Daniel. *The Unwritten War. American Writers and
    the Civil War*. New York: Alfred A. Knopf, 1973.

Abrams, Ray H. *Preachers Present Arms*. Scottdale, Pa.:
    Herald Press, 1969.

Aichinger, Peter. *The American Soldier in Fiction. 1880-
    1963*. Ames: Iowa State University Press, 1975.

Ambrose, Stephen E. *Duty, Honor, Country. A History of
    West Point*. Baltimore: The Johns Hopkins Press,
    1966.

Bacher, William A., ed. *The Treasury Star Parade*. With
    an introduction by Henry Morgenthau, Jr. New York:
    Farrar and Rinehart, Inc., 1942.

Bartlett, Samuel Ripley. *Concord Fight: A Poem*. Boston:
A. Williams and Company, 1860.

Baynes, Ken. *War*. Boston, Mass.: Boston Book and Art
Publisher, 1970.

Bellamy, Edward. *The Blindman's World and Other Stories*.
The American Short Story Series, Vol. 4. New York:
Garrett Press, 1968.

Benét, Stephen Vincent. *John Brown's Body*. Introduction
and notes by Jack C. Capps and C. Robert Kemble.
New York: Holt, Rinehart and Winston, Inc., 1968.

Bolton, Horace Wilbert. *Our Fallen Heroes*. Chicago:
H. W. Bolton, 1892.

Brooks, Elbridge Streeter. *The Story of the American
Soldier in War and Peace*. Boston: D. Lothrop
Company, 1889.

Burrage, Henry S. *Gettysburg and Lincoln: The Battle,
the Cemetery, and the National Park*. New York:
G. P. Putnam's Sons, 1906.

Catton, Bruce. *Prefaces to History*. Garden City, New
York: Doubleday and Company, 1970.

Clarke, I. F. *Voices Prophesying War, 1763-1984*. London:
Oxford University Press, 1966.

Cobb, Irvin. *The Glory of the Coming*. New York: Goerge
H. Doran Company, 1918.

Columbia Broadcasting System. *From Pearl Harbor into Tokyo:
The Story as Told by War Correspondents on the Air*.
New York: Columbia Broadcasting System, 1945.

*Ceremonies at the Dedication of the Soldiers Monument in
Concord, Mass.* Concord: Benjamin Tolman, 1867.

Cooperman, Stanley. *World War I and the American Novel*.
Baltimore: The Johns Hopkins Press, 1967.

Cowan, Samuel Kinkade. *Sergeant York and His People*.
New York: Grossett and Dunlap, 1922.

Cresswell, Donald H., comp. *The American Revolution in
Drawings and Prints*. Foreword by Sinclair H.
Hutchings. Washington: Library of Congress, 1975.

Davidson, Philip. *Propaganda and the American Revolution.*
1763-1783. Chapel Hill: The University of North
Carolina Press, 1941.

Empey, Arthur Guy. *"Over the Top."* New York: G. P.
Putnam's Sons, 1917.

Frassanito, William A. *Gettysburg: A Journey in Time.*
New York: Charles Scribner's Sons, 1975.

Fredrickson, George M. *The Inner Civil War.* New York:
Harper and Row, 1965.

French, Allen. *The Day of Concord and Lexington.* Boston:
Little Brown and Company, 1925.

Freneau, Philip. *Poems Relating to the American Revol-*
ution. New York: W. S. Widdleton, 1865.

Gallatin, Albert Eugene. *Art and the Great War.* New
York: E. P. Dutton and Company, 1919.

Genthe, Charles V. *American War Narratives, 1917-1918:*
A Study and Bibliography. New York: David Lewis,
1969.

Gibbons, Floyd. *"And They Thought We Wouldn't Fight."*
New York: George H. Doran Company, 1918.

Gross, George J. *The Battlefield of Gettysburg.* Philadelphia: Collins, Printer, 705 Jayne Street, 1866.

Gross, Robert A. *The Minutemen and Their World.* New
York: Hill and Wang, 1976.

Haller, William. *The Rise of Puritanism.* Philadelphia:
University of Pennsylvania Press, 1972.

Hanly, J. Frank. *The Battle of Gettysburg.* Cincinnati:
Jennings and Graham, 1912.

Harper's Pictorial History of the War with Spain. Introduction by Maj. Gen. Nelson A. Miles. New York:
Harper and Brothers Publishers, 1899.

Hinkel, John V. *Arlington: Monument to Heroes.* Englewood Cliffs, N.J.: Prentice-Hall, Inc., 1970.

Jones, Barbara and Howell, Bill. *Popular Arts of the First*
World War. New York: McGraw-Hill Book Company, 1972.

Lawrence, Vera Brodsky. *Music for Patriots, Politicians, and Presidents*. New York: Macmillan and Company, 1975.

Leonard, Thomas C. *Above the Battle*. New York: Oxford University Press, 1978.

Lindermann, Gerald F. *The Mirror of War: American Society and the Spanish-American War*. Ann Arbor: The University of Michigan Press, 1974.

Lively, Robert A. *Fiction Fights the Civil War*. Chapel Hill: The University of North Carolina Press, 1957.

Logan, John A. *The Volunteer Soldier of America*. Chicago: R. S. Pearce and Company, 1887.

McLaughlin, Jack. *Gettysburg: The Long Encampment*. New York: Appleton-Century, 1963.

Meligakes, Nicholas A. *The Spirit of Gettysburg*. Gettysburg, Pa.: Bookmart, 1950.

Miller, Wayne Charles. *An Armed America, Its Face in Fiction*. New York: N.Y.U. Press, 1970.

Millis, Walter. *The Martial Spirit*. Cambridge, Mass.: The Riverside Press, 1931.

————. *Arms and Men*. New York: Mentor Books, 1956.

Moffett, Cleveland. *The Conquest of America*. New York: George H. Doran Company, 1916.

O'Neill, Edward H. *A History of American Biography 1800-1935*. Philadelphia: The University of Pennsylvania Press, 1935.

Philbrick, Norman, ed. *Trumpets Sounding; Propaganda Plays of the American Revolution*. New York: Benjamin Blom, Inc., 1972.

Pickett, LaSalle. *The Bugles of Gettysburg*. Chicago: F. G. Browne and Company, 1913.

Prescott, Frederick C. and Nelson, John H., eds. *Prose and Poetry of the Revolution*. Port Washington, New York: Kennikat Press, Inc., 1969.

Proceedings at the Centennial Celebration of Concord Fight, April 19, 1875. Concord, Mass.: Published by the town, 1876.

Royster, Charles. *A Revolutionary People at War*. Chapel
    Hill: University of North Carolina Press, 1979.

Russell, Francis, and editors of *American Heritage* Maga-
    zine. *Lexington, Concord and Bunker Hill*. New York:
    American Heritage Publishing Company, Inc., 1963.

Shy, John. *A People Numerous and Armed*. New York: Oxford
    University Press, 1976.

Spehr, Paul C., comp. *The Civil War in Motion Pictures*.
    Washington: Library of Congress, 1961.

Stewart, George Ripley. *Pickett's Charge*. Boston: Hough-
    ton Mifflin Company, 1959.

The Artist and War in the Twentieth Century. With an
    introduction by T. G. Rosenthal. BBC Radio Series.
    London: British Broadcasting Corporation, 1967.

Thompson, W. Fletcher. *The Image of War*: *The Pictorial
    Reporting of the American Civil War*. New York:
    Thomas Yoseloff, 1959.

Tyler, Moses Coit. *The Literary History of the American
    Revolution, 1763-1776*. Vol. I. New York: Fredrick
    Ungar Publishing Company, 1957.

United States National Gallery of Art. *American Battle
    Painting 1776-1918*. Washington: The U.S. Government
    Printing Office, 1947.

Vanderslice, John M. *Gettysburg. A History of the Gettys-
    burg Battlefield Memorial Association*. Philadelphia:
    Memorial Association, 1897.

Vickers, George Edward. *Gettysburg, A Poem*. Washington:
    n.p., 1890.

Walker, John B. *America Fallen! The Sequel to the Euro-
    pean War*. New York: Dodd, Mead and Company, 1915.

Wallace, John H., Jr. *The Blue and the Grey*. Montgomery,
    Alabama: Brown Printing Company, 1909.

Warren, Robert Penn. *The Legacy of the Civil War*: *Medita-
    tions on the Centennial*. New York: Random House, 1961.

Wiley, Bell Irwin. *The Common Soldier in the Civil War*.
    Book One: *The Life of Billy Yank*. New York: Grossett

and Dunlap, 1952. Book Two: *The Life of Johnny Reb*.
New York: Grossett and Dunlap, 1943.

_____. *They Who Fought Here*. New York: The Macmillan
Company, 1959.

ARTICLES

Adams, Zabdiel. "The Evil Designs of men made subservient
     by God to the Public Good; particularly illustrated in
     the rise, progress and conclusion of the American war."
     A *Sermon* preached at Lexington on the Nineteenth of
     April, 1783. Boston: Printed by Benjamin Edes and
     Sons, in Cornhill. Early American Imprints, 17807.

Badger, Milton. *Welcome to the Returned Soldiers. An
     Address Delivered at Madison, Conn., July 4th, 1865
     by Rev. Milton Badger, D.D.* New Haven: Tuttle,
     Morehouse and Taylor, Printers, 1865.

Barrows, William. *Honor to the Brave. A Discourse Deliv-
     ered in The Old South Church, Reading, Mass., August
     23, 1863, on the return of Company D, fiftieth reg.,
     Mass. Vols. by the Rev. William Barrows*. Boston:
     John M. Whittemore and Company, 1863.

Bartol, Cyrus Augustus. *The Remission by Blood, A Tribute
     to Our Soldiers and the Sword. Delivered in The West
     Church*. Boston: Walker, Wise, and Company, 1862.

Behlmer, Rudy. "World War I Aviation Films." *Films in
     Review* 18 (August-September, 1967): 413-433.

Buffington, Arthur H. "The Puritan View of War." *Publi-
     cations of the Colonial Society of Massachusetts*
     XXVIII (April, 1931): 67-86.

Clarke, Jonas. "The Fate of Blood-thirsty Oppressors, and
     God's tender care of his distressed people." A sermon
     preached at Lexington, April 19, 1776. Boston:
     Printed by Powars and Willis. [sic] Early American
     Imprints, 14679.

Craighead, Alexander. "Military Art in America, 1750-1914."
     Military Collector and Historian 15-17 (1963-1965):
     15: 35-40, 73-79; 16: 10-13, 42-45; 17: 42-48,
     76-80.

Selected Bibliography   253

Davidson, John. *Oration Delivered Before the Legislation
     of N.J. upon "Our Sleeping Heroes," February 22nd,
     1866, by John Davidson Esq., of Elizabeth, N.J.*
     Trendon, N.J.: Printed at the *State Gazette Office*,
     1866.

Eaton, James W. "Pickett's Charge at Gettysburg." Address
     at Annual Meeting of the Military Order of the Loyal
     Legion of the United States, Nov. 1, 1962. Indian-
     apolis, Indiana: n.p., Wyles Collection, University
     of California, Santa Barbara.

Emerson, Ralph Waldo. *A Historical Discourse Delivered
     Before the Citizens of Concord, 12 Sept. 1835, on the
     Centennial Anniversary of the Incorporation of the
     Town.* Boston: W. B. Clarke, 1935.

Everett, Edward. *An Oration Delivered on the Battlefield
     of Gettysburg (November 19, 1863) at the Consecration
     of the Cemetery.* New York: Baker and Godwin, 1863.

_____. *An Address, Delivered at Lexington, on the 19th
     of April, 1835.* Charlestown: William W. Wheildon,
     1835.

Goodrich, Lloyd. "The Painting of American History."
     American Quarterly 3 (1951): 283-294.

Hamilton, Gail. "A Call to My Country-Women." *Atlantic
     Monthly*, March, 1863, pp. 345-349.

Handlin, Oscar. "The Civil War as Symbol and as Actuality."
     The Massachusetts Review II (Autumn, 1961): 133-143.

Higginbotham, Don. "American Historians and the Military
     History of the American Revolution." *American
     Historical Review* LXX (1964): 18-34.

Hillyer, George. "Battle of Gettysburg. Address before
     the Walton County Georgia Confederate Veterans,
     Aug. 2nd, 1904." Wyles Collection, University of
     California, Santa Barbara.

Hofstadter, Richard. "Cuba, The Philippines, and Manifest
     Destiny." In *The Paranoid Style in American Politics
     and Other Essays*, pp. 145-187. New York: Harper and
     Row, 1965.

Kirstein, L. "American Battle Art: 1588-1944." *Magazine
     of Art* 37 (March-May, 1944): 104-109; 146-151; 184-189.

Kramer, Leonard J. "Muskets in the Pulpit: 1776-1783."
    Presbyterian Historical Society Journal 31-32
    (December, 1953, and March, 1954): 31: 229-244;
    32: 37-51.

Kuh, Katherine. "War and the Visual Arts." *Antioch
    Review* 6 (September, 1946): 398-409.

Leithead, Edward J. "The Revolutionary War in Dime
    Novels." *American Book Collector* 19 (April-May):
    14-21.

Morison, John Hopkins. *Dying for our country: A sermon
    on the death of Captain J. Sewall Reed and Rev.
    Thomas Starr King; preached in The First Congrega-
    tional Church in Milton, March 13, 1864.* Boston:
    Printed by John Wilson and Son, 1864.

Mott, Frank Luther. "The Newspaper Coverage of Lexington
    and Concord." *New England Quarterly* XVII (December,
    1944): 489-503.

Persons, Stow. "The Cyclical Theory of History in
    Eighteenth Century America." *American Quarterly*
    6 (1954): 147-163.

Ridpath, John Clark. "The Citizen Soldier; his part in
    war and peace." Delivered before the Veterans of
    the Grand Army of the Republic at Amo, Indiana,
    May 30, 1890. Wyles Collection, University of
    California, Santa Barbara.

Soderbergh, Peter A. "Aux Armes! The Rise of the Holly-
    wood War Film." *South Atlantic Quarterly* 65
    (Autumn, 1966): 509-522.

Whitehill, Walter Muir. *Amos Doolittle, 1754-1832. In
    Freedom's Cause, A Portfolio of Revolutionary War
    Engravings by Amos Doolittle.* Chicago: R. R.
    Donnelley and Sons, Lakeside Press, 1974.

Chapter Three

BOOKS

Aldridge, John W. *The Devil in the Fire: 1951-1971*.
New York: Harper's Magazine Press Book, 1972.

America Organizes to Win the War. New York: Harcourt,
Brace and Company, 1942.

Arlen, Michael. *Living Room War*. New York: Viking
Press, 1967.

Army Times, eds. *American Heroes of the Asian Wars*. New
York: Dodd, Mead and Company, 1968.

Baker, Mark. *NAM*. New York: William Morrow and Company,
Inc., 1981.

Barnet, Richard J. *Roots of War*. Baltimore: Penguin
Books, 1973.

Berrigan, Daniel. *The Trial of the Catonsville Nine*.
Boston: Beacon Press, 1970.

Blum, John Morton. *V Was For Victory. Politics and
American Culture During World War II*. New York:
Harcourt Brace Jovanovich, 1976.

Bryan, C. D. B. *Friendly Fire*. New York: G. P. Putnam's
Sons, 1976.

Capps, Walter. *The Unfinished War: Vietnam and the
American Conscience*. Boston: Beacon Press, 1982.

Caputo, Philip. *A Rumor of War*. New York: Ballantine
Books, 1977.

Emerson, Gloria. *Winners and Losers: Battles, Retreats,
Gains, Losses and Ruins from a Long War*. New York:
Random House, 1976.

Falk, Richard A.; Kolko, Gabriel; and Lifton, Robert J.,
eds. *Crimes of War*. New York: Random House, 1971.

Fitzgerald, Francis. *Fire in the Lake*. New York: Random
House, 1973.

Fox, Frank W. *Madison Avenue Goes to War: The Strange Military Career of American Advertising: 1941-1945.* Charles E. Merrill Monograph Series in the Humanities and Social Sciences. Provo, Utah: Brigham Young University Press, 1975.

French, Warren, ed. *The Forties: Fiction, Poetry, Drama.* Deland, Florida: Everett/Edwards, Inc., 1969.

Greenhaw, Wayne. *The Making of a Hero: The Story of Lieut. William Calley, Jr.* Louisville, Kentucky: Touchstone Publishing Company, 1971.

Halberstam, David. *The Best and the Brightest.* Greenwich, Connecticut: Fawcett Publications, Inc., 1972.

Haldeman, Joe. *War Year.* New York: Holt, Rinehart and Winston, 1972.

Harvey, Frank. *Air-War Vietnam.* New York: Bantam Books, 1967.

Herr, Michael. *Dispatches.* New York: Alfred A. Knopf, 1977.

Horne, A. D. *The Wounded Generation: America After Vietnam.* Englewood Cliffs, N.J.: Prentice-Hall, Inc., 1981.

Howe, Susanne. *Novels of Empire.* New York: Columbia University Press, 1949.

Kahin, George McTurnan and Lewis, John W. *The United States in Vietnam.* Rev. Ed. New York: Dell Publishing Company, 1969.

Kalb, Marvin and Abel, Elie. *Roots of Involvement. The U.S. in Asia 1784-1971.* New York: W. W. Norton and Company, 1971.

Kirby, Edward M. and Harris, Jack W. *Star-Spangled Radio.* Foreword by David Sarnoff. Chicago: Ziff-Davis Publishing Company, 1948.

Klinkowitz, Jerome and Somer, John, eds. *Writing Under Fire: Stories of the Vietnam War.* New York: Dell, 1978.

Knoll, Erwin and McFadden, Judith Nies, eds. *War Crimes and the American Conscience.* New York: Holt, Rinehart and Winston, 1970.

Kovic, Ron. *Born on the Fourth of July*. New York: Pocket
    Books, 1977.

Lake, Anthony, ed. *The Vietnam Legacy: The War, American
    Society and the Future of American Foreign Policy*.
    New York: New York University Press, 1976.

Leitenburg, Milton and Burns, Richard D., comps. *The
    Vietnam Conflict*. Santa Barbara: Clio Press, 1973.

Lifton, Robert J. *Home From the War*: *Vietnam Veterans--
    Neither Victims nor Executioners*. New York: Simon
    and Schuster, 1973.

_____. *Death in Life: Survivors of Hiroshima*. New York:
    Random House, 1967.

Lingeman, Richard R. *Don't You Know There's a War On?
    The American Home Front, 1941-1945*. New York: G. P.
    Putnam's Sons, 1970.

Mauldin, Bill. *Up Front*. New York: Henry Holt and
    Company, 1945.

Myers, Debs; Kilbourn, Jonathan; and Harrity, Richard.,
    sels. and eds. *Yank--The GI Story of the War*. New
    York: Duell, Sloan and Pearce, 1947.

O'Brien, Tim. *If I Die in a Combat Zone*. n.p.: Dela-
    corte Press, 1973.

_____. *Going After Cacciato*. New York: Delacorte
    Press/Seymour Lawrence, 1978.

Perrett, Geoffrey. *Days of Sadness, Years of Triumph: The
    American People 1939-1945*. New York: Coward, McCann
    and Geoghegan, Inc., 1973.

Polenberg, Richard, ed. *America at War: The Home Front,
    1941-1945*. Englewood Cliffs, N.J.: Prentice-Hall,
    Inc., 1968.

_____. *War and Society: The United States, 1941-1945*.
    Philadelphia: J. B. Lippincott Company, 1972.

Polner, Murray. *No Victory Parades: The Return of the
    Vietnam Veteran*. New York: Holt, Rinehart and
    Winston, 1971.

Pyle, Ernie. *Brave Men*. New York: Henry Holt and Com-
    pany, 1943.

_____. *Here Is Your War*. New York: Henry Holt and
     Company, 1943.

_____. *Last Chapter*. New York: Henry Holt and Company,
     1946.

Rabe, David. *The Basic Training of Pavlo Hummel and Sticks
     and Bones: Two Plays by David Rabe*. New York: Viking
     Press, 1973.

Reischauer, Edwin O. *Beyond Vietnam: The United States
     and Asia*. New York: Alfred A. Knopf, 1968.

Rhodes, Anthony. *Propaganda: The Art of Persuasion: World
     War II*. Edited by Victor Margolin. New York: Chelsea
     House Publishers, 1976.

Sack, John and Calley, William Laws. *Lieutenant Calley:
     His Own Story*. New York: The Viking Press, 1971.

Santoli, Al. *Everything We Had. An Oral History of the
     Vietnam War by Thirty-Three American Soldiers Who
     Fought It*. New York: Random House, 1981.

Shain, Russell Earl. "An Analysis of Motion Pictures About
     War Released by the American Film Industry, 1939-1970."
     Ph.D. dissertation, University of Illinois at Urbana-
     Champaign, 1972.

Sherrod, Robert. *Tarawa: The Story of a Battle*. New
     York: Duell, Sloan and Pearce, 1944.

Smith, Julian. *Looking Away: Hollywood and Vietnam*. New
     York: Mason and Lipscomb, 1973.

Stromberg, Peter L. "A Long War's Writing: American Novels
     About the Fighting in Vietnam While Americans Fought."
     Ph.D. dissertation, Cornell University, 1974.

The Vietnam Hearings. With an introduction by J. William
     Fulbright. New York: Random House, 1966.

Vietnam Veterans Against the War. *The Winter Soldier
     Investigation: An Inquiry into American War Crimes*.
     n.p.: Beacon Press, 1972.

Waldmeir, Joseph J. *American Novels of the Second World
     War*. Studies in American Literature. Vol. XX. The
     Hague: Mouton, 1969.

Winn, Larry J. "My Lai: Birth and Death of a Rhetorical Symbol." Ph.D. dissertation, University of Virginia, 1974.

Winner, Carol Ann. "A Study of American Dramatic Productions Dealing with the War in Vietnam." Ph.D. dissertation, University of Denver, 1975.

Yank, eds. *The Best From Yank: The Army Weekly*. New York: E. P. Dutton and Company, 1945.

ARTICLES

Adler, Les K. and Paterson, Thomas G. "Red Fascism: The Merger of Nazi Germany and Soviet Russia in the American Image of Totalitarianism." *American Historical Review* LXXV (1970): 1046-1064.

Ahlstrom, Sydney E. "National Trauma and Changing Religious Values." *Daedalus* 107 (Winter, 1978): 13-29.

Alsop, Stewart. "Wanted: A Faith to Fight For." *Atlantic*, May, 1941, pp. 594-597.

Baldwin, Hanson W. "The Saga of Wake." *Virginia Quarterly* 18 (Summer, 1942): 321-335.

Bergen, Bernard and Rosenberg, Stanley. "Culture as Violence." *Humanitas* 12 (May, 1976): 195-205.

Blum, John M. "The GI in the Culture of the Second World War." *Ventures* 8 (1968): 51-56.

Branfman, Fred. "Indochina: The Illusion of Withdrawal." *Harper's*, May, 1973, pp. 65-76.

Burgum, Edwin Berry. "Art in Wartime: The Revival of the Heroic Tradition." *Science and Society* 6 (1942): 331-351.

Cooperman, Stanley. "American War Novels: Yesterday, Today, and Tomorrow." *Yale Review* 61 (June, 1972): 517-529.

Eisenhart, Wayne R. "You Can't Hack It Little Girl: A Discussion of the Covert Psychological Agenda of

Modern Combat Training." *Journal of Social Issues* 31 (1975): 13-23.

Gertsch, W. Darrell. "The Strategic Air Offensive and the Mutation of American Values." *Rocky Mountain Social Science Journal* 11 (1974): 37-50.

Goldberg, Art. "Vietnam Vets: The Anti-War Army." *Ramparts Magazine*, July, 1971, pp. 10-17.

Hersey, John. "Experience by Battle." *Life*, December 27, 1943, pp. 48-84.

_____. "Hiroshima." *New Yorker*, August 31, 1946, pp. 15-60.

Hersh, Seymour. "The Decline and Near Fall of the U.S. Army." *Saturday Review of the Society*, December, 1971, pp. 58-65.

Jacobs, Louis. "World War II and the American Film." *Cinema Journal* 7 (Winter, 1967-1968): 1-21.

Leab, Daniel J. "Cold War Comics." *Columbia Journalism Review* III (Winter, 1965): 42-47.

Leib, Rich. "Country Music. A Sign of Our Time?" 1978 (typewritten).

Leuchtenberg, William E. "The New Deal and the Analogue of War." In *Change and Continuity in Twentieth Century America*, pp. 81-144. Edited by Robert H. Bremmer and Everett Walters. n.p.: Ohio State University Press, 1964.

Levy, Charles J. "ARVN as Faggots: Inverted Warfare in Vietnam." *Transaction* 8 (October, 1971): 18-27.

Lifton, Robert J. "The Postwar War." *Journal of Social Issues* 31 (1975): 181-195.

Lund, Jens. "Country Music Goes to War: Songs for the Red-Blooded American." *Popular Music and Society* 1 (Summer, 1972): 210-230.

Lyons, Timothy. "Hollywood and World War I." *Journal of Popular Film* 1 (Winter, 1972): 15-30.

Marin, Peter. "Coming to Terms with Vietnam." *Harper's*, December, 1980, pp. 41-56.

"Massacre at My Lai." *Life*, December 5, 1969, pp. 36-45.

Mayer, Mara Nacht. "The Heroic Image During World War II." Yale Miscellaneous Manuscripts, Yale University Library. 1963.

McConnell, Frank D. "Vietnam and 'Vietnam': A Note on the Pathology of Language." *Soundings* 52 (Summer, 1968): 195-207.

Mueller, John E. "Trends in Popular Support for the Wars in Korea and Vietnam." *American Political Science Review* LXV (1971): 358-375.

Pilisuk, Mark. "The Legacy of the Vietnam Veteran." *Journal of Social Issues* 31 (1975): 3-12.

Rollins, Peter C. "Victory at Sea: Cold War Epic." *Journal of Popular Culture* 6 (1973): 463-481.

Sanders, Clinton R. "The Portrayal of War and the Fighting Man in Novels of the Vietnam War." *Journal of Popular Culture* 3 (1969): 553-564.

Wolfe, Gary K. "Dr. Strangelove, Red Alert, and Patterns of Paranoia in the 1950s." *Journal of Popular Film* (1976): 57-67.

Yavenditti, Michael J. "John Hersey and the American Conscience: The Reception of Hiroshima." *Pacific Historical Review* XLIII (1974): 24-49.

INDEX

STUDIES IN AMERICAN RELIGION

Edward Linenthal is a professor of religion at the University of Wisconsin at Oshkosh.

FOR A COMPLETE LIST OF TITLES AND PRICES
PLEASE WRITE:
The Edwin Mellen Press
P.O. Box 450
Lewiston, New York   14092